Processing 2: Creative Coding Hotshot

Learn Processing with exciting and engaging projects to make your computer talk, see, hear, express emotions, and even design physical objects

Nikolaus Gradwohl

[PACKT] open source
PUBLISHING
community experience distilled

BIRMINGHAM - MUMBAI

Processing 2: Creative Coding Hotshot

First published: May 2013

Production Reference: 1130513

Published by Packt Publishing Ltd.
Livery Place
35 Livery Street
Birmingham B3 2PB, UK.

ISBN 978-1-78216-672-6

www.packtpub.com

Cover Image by Nikolaus Gradwohl (nikki@local-guru.net)

Credits

Author
Nikolaus Gradwohl

Reviewers
Mag. Erwin Gradwohl
Kasper Kamperman
Tim Pulver
R.A. Robertson

Acquisition Editor
Kartikey Pandey

Lead Technical Editor
Joel Noronha

Technical Editors
Veronica Fernandes
Ishita Malhi
Hardik B. Soni

Project Coordinator
Hardik Patel

Proofreader
Paul Hindle

Indexer
Tejal R. Soni

Graphics
Ronak Dhruv

Production Coordinator
Prachali Bhiwandkar

Cover Work
Prachali Bhiwandkar

About the Author

Nikolaus Gradwohl was born in 1976 in Vienna, Austria, and always wanted to become an inventor like Gyro Gearloose. When he got his first Atari, he decide that becoming a computer programmer was the closest he could get to that dream. He has since made a living writing programs for nearly anything that can be programmed, ranging from an 8-bit microcontroller to mainframes. In his free time, he likes gaining knowledge on programming languages and operating systems.

Nikolaus has been using Processing since 2008, and has written countless sketches and some Processing libraries.

You can see some of his work on his blog at `http://www.local-guru.net/`.

This is a huge thank you for my wife, Mars, and my kids for all their support, patience, and love.

I want to thank Zita, "the Spacegirl", for her feedback on the first project and on my robots.

I would also like to give a big thank you for all the help, answers, reminders to deadlines, and feedback to Amber D'souza, Kartikey Pandey, Hardik Patel, and Joel Noronha from Packt Publishing.

About the Reviewers

Mag. Erwin Gradwohl is a retired consultant and former bank auditor, interested in programming, music, and videos.

Kasper Kamperman is a teacher and creative coder based in Enschede, Netherlands. He works on the Art and Technology program at the Saxion University of Applied Sciences, where he teaches subjects like Interaction Design and Programming and Physical Computing.

Besides his work as a teacher, Kasper designs and develops interactive installations. He has a fascination for light and currently uses Processing and Arduino to prototype and develop dynamic light objects.

You can check out his projects at `http://www.kasperkamperman.com`.

I would like to thank the Processing development team for creating this great open source programming language and environment. Also thanks to the writer of this book, Nikolaus Gradwohl, and the Packt Publishing team, it was a pleasure to review this book.

Tim Pulver is an interface design student from Potsdam, Germany. He studied software engineering while at University, giving him the knowledge to realize his creative ideas. He uses Processing as an artistic medium for building his own tools. One of his recent projects is a gigantic real-time data visualization software, which is used for visualizing global crop production. It has been specifically made to be viewed in a planetarium/full dome environment.

In another project, Tim wrote a program that translated an image of an eye based on its structure into unique jewelry, which was printed out using a 3D printer.

He likes the idea of sharing and free culture. In 2011, he founded the electronic music netlabel Yarn Audio, which supports sharing and remixing of the released music. All the cover artwork for this netlabel has been generated using Processing too.

I would like to thank my family for their support, Isi for motivating me to do what I do now, and Hanna and Paul for inspiring talks and chili con carne.

R.A. Robertson discovered Processing late in the summer of 2008, and with it, the joy of generative art. Along with some occasional forays into Quartz Composer, Ross found Processing to be an entrance into the world of procedural literacy as well as a path for understanding nature, society, and himself.

For most of his adult life, Ross has studied music and design (formally and otherwise), and spent many years as a professional Aikido instructor in Austin, Texas. In addition, he holds a Bachelor's degree in Cultural Anthropology from the University of Texas in Austin. Although superficially disparate, these streams converge with programming as multivalent languages whose grammar, syntax, vocabulary, and structure serve to inform and enhance one another. Ross' work is a continuing effort to unify these elements into a coherent way of design for the purpose of exploring beauty, the meanings of fitness, and the cultivation of a better human being capable of creating a better world for all.

Ross is the founder and host for Processing's Austin meet-up group, and owner of the nascent Still Moving Designs studio.

A lover of travel, Ross is pleased to call Austin his home base, where he resides with his lovely consort, companion, and friend, Dr. Catherine Parsoneault. Ross has three grown children—Ehren, Calen (and his delightful bride Taylor), and Raanan—who are unequivocally to him the most interesting and wonderful people on this planet. For Ross, the time spent in discourse and shared activity with these amazing people is better than Heaven's own manna.

www.PacktPub.com

Support files, eBooks, discount offers and more

You might want to visit www.PacktPub.com for support files and downloads related to your book.

Did you know that Packt offers eBook versions of every book published, with PDF and ePub files available? You can upgrade to the eBook version at www.PacktPub.com and as a print book customer, you are entitled to a discount on the eBook copy. Get in touch with us at service@packtpub.com for more details.

At www.PacktPub.com, you can also read a collection of free technical articles, sign up for a range of free newsletters and receive exclusive discounts and offers on Packt books and eBooks.

PACKTLIB™

http://PacktLib.PacktPub.com

Do you need instant solutions to your IT questions? PacktLib is Packt's online digital book library. Here, you can access, read and search across Packt's entire library of books.

Why Subscribe?

- Fully searchable across every book published by Packt
- Copy and paste, print and bookmark content
- On demand and accessible via web browser

Free Access for Packt account holders

If you have an account with Packt at www.PacktPub.com, you can use this to access PacktLib today and view nine entirely free books. Simply use your login credentials for immediate access.

Table of Contents

Preface

Processing is an open source programming language that was invented by Casey Reas and Benjamin Fry in 2001 for the Aesthetics and Computation group at the MIT Media Lab. The language is designed to serve as a sketchbook for visual design applications, media art, electronic arts, and teaching.

Processing 2: Creative Coding Hotshot will present you with nine exciting complete projects that will show you how to go beyond the basics and make your programs see, hear, and feel.

The projects show you how to make use of devices like a Kinect sensor board or an Arduino board in the Processing sketches.

What this book covers

Project 1, Romeo and Juliet, will help you learn how to make some cardboard robots that perform the famous balcony scene from Shakespeare's Romeo and Juliet. We will create some talking robots using a pair of cheap speakers and some cardboard boxes, and learn how to install and use a text-to-speech library in Processing.

Project 2, The Stick Figure Dance Company, will help you in creating a dance company that is controlled using Microsoft Kinect. The dancers will be controlled using the Kinect skeletal tracking. After we have managed to control one stick figure, we will make more and more stick figures show up until we have a whole dance company, dancing the same moves the player makes.

Project 3, The Disco Dance Floor, will teach us how to play music and create a sound-reactive dance floor, since there is no dancing without music. We will learn how to use the Processing-sound API to make an audio visualizer. Then we will turn the 2D visualizer into a 3D dancefloor and invite our stick figure dance company from the previous project to dance on it.

Project 4, Smilie-O-Mat, will help you in creating an application that allows the user to create a smiley that matches his or her current mood using a customized user interface. This smiley can then be posted to a social network to let your buddies know how you currently feel, because sometimes a picture tells more than 140 characters.

Project 5, The Smilie-O-Mat Controller, helps you generate a custom controller board using Arduino and use it to simplify the adjustment of the Smilie-O-Mat controller from our previous project. For the controller, we will use an Arduino board, learn how to set up a simple electronic circuit, and then how to interface it with a computer. Then we will use the input parameters generated by the controller to change the face of a smiley and post it to a social network.

Project 6, Fly to the Moon, explores the different modes Processing offers and teaches you how to export a sketch for the Web or run it as an Android app. We will create a small moon-lander-like game from scratch and learn how to adapt it to run on different hardware as well as use different input devices.

Project 7, The Neon Globe, wonders what world-domination plans would be without a spinning neon globe? Here, we will learn how to generate a rotating 3D sphere that we will turn into a spinning globe using image textures and some lighting. We will later highlight the continent borders and make them glow using a GLSL filter.

Project 8, Logfile Geo-visualizer, will help us learn how to visualize some data on the spinning globe we generated in the previous project. We will use a web server logfile as our input and learn how to parse it in Processing. Then, we will geocode the data and use the geocoordinates of the page requests to draw something on our globe.

Project 9, From Virtual to Real, will help us learn how to turn mathematics into physical objects. We will learn how to unleash the beauty of mathematical functions and use them to generate a printable object like a pen box or a flower vase. Then, we will learn how to export the object to a format that can be fed into a 3D printer.

What you need for this book

Project 2, The Stick Figure Dance Company, shows you how to use Kinect to create a stick figure that is controlled by the player's movements. To run this example, you will need a Kinect sensor board and a power adapter for it.

Project 5, The Smilie-O-Mat Controller, uses an Arduino board and some electronic components to create a customized hardware controller.

In *Project 6, Fly to the Moon*, we will create a game that runs on a PC, in a web browser, and on an Android device. If you want to see the game on a real device instead of an emulator, you need an Android mobile phone or tablet.

Project 9, From Virtual to Real, shows you how to create a 3D shape and turn it into a physical object using 3D printing or an online 3D printing service.

Who this book is for

If you are a programmer or a visual artist that already has some experience with the Processing environment or another language similar to Java and want to make programs that reach beyond a window on your screen, this book is for you.

Conventions

In this book, you will find several headings appearing frequently.

To give clear instructions of how to complete a procedure or task, we use:

Mission Briefing

This section explains what you will build, with a screenshot of the completed project.

Why Is It Awesome?

This section explains why the project is cool, unique, exciting, and interesting. It describes what advantage the project will give you.

Your Hotshot Objectives

This section explains the major tasks required to complete your project.

- Task 1
- Task 2
- Task 3
- Task 4, and so on

Mission Checklist

This section explains any pre-requisites for the project, such as resources or libraries that need to be downloaded, and so on.

Task 1

This section explains the task that you will perform.

Prepare for Lift Off

This section explains any preliminary work that you may need to do before beginning work on the task.

Engage Thrusters

This section lists the steps required in order to complete the task.

Objective Complete - Mini Debriefing

This section explains how the steps performed in the previous section allow us to complete the task. This section is mandatory.

Classified Intel

The extra information in this section is relevant to the task.

You will also find a number of styles of text that distinguish between different kinds of information. Here are some examples of these styles, and an explanation of their meaning.

Code words in text are shown as follows: "Now we add a `mousePressed()` method to our sketch, which gets called if someone clicks on our sketch window."

A block of code is set as follows:

```
void mousePressed() {
  tts.speak("Hello, I am a Computer");
}
```

When we wish to draw your attention to a particular part of a code block, the relevant lines or items are set in bold:

```
void setup() {
  String[] rawLines = loadStrings
  ( "romeo_and_juliet.txt" );

  ArrayList lines = new ArrayList();
  for ( int i=0; i<rawLines.length; i++) {
    if (!"".equals(rawLines[i])) {
      String[] tmp = rawLines[i].split("#");
      lines.add( new Line( tmp[0], tmp[1].trim() ));
    }
  }

}
```

New terms and **important words** are shown in bold. Words that you see on the screen, in menus or dialog boxes for example, appear in the text like this: "In the **Library Manager** dialog, enter `ttslib` in the search field to filter the list of libraries."

> Warnings or important notes appear in a box like this.

> Tips and tricks appear like this.

Reader feedback

Feedback from our readers is always welcome. Let us know what you think about this book—what you liked or may have disliked. Reader feedback is important for us to develop titles that you really get the most out of.

To send us general feedback, simply send an e-mail to `feedback@packtpub.com`, and mention the book title via the subject of your message.

If there is a topic that you have expertise in and you are interested in either writing or contributing to a book, see our author guide on `www.packtpub.com/authors`.

Customer support

Now that you are the proud owner of a Packt book, we have a number of things to help you to get the most from your purchase.

Downloading the example code

You can download the example code files for all Packt books you have purchased from your account at `http://www.packtpub.com`. If you purchased this book elsewhere, you can visit `http://www.packtpub.com/support` and register to have the files e-mailed directly to you.

Downloading the color images of this book

We also provide you a PDF file that has color images of the screenshots/diagrams used in this book. The color images will help you better understand the changes in the output. You can download this file from http://www.packtpub.com/sites/default/files/downloads/6726OS_Processing_2_Creative_Coding_Hotshot_Color_Graphics.pdf.

Errata

Although we have taken every care to ensure the accuracy of our content, mistakes do happen. If you find a mistake in one of our books—maybe a mistake in the text or the code—we would be grateful if you would report this to us. By doing so, you can save other readers from frustration and help us improve subsequent versions of this book. If you find any errata, please report them by visiting http://www.packtpub.com/submit-errata, selecting your book, clicking on the **errata submission form** link, and entering the details of your errata. Once your errata are verified, your submission will be accepted and the errata will be uploaded on our website, or added to any list of existing errata, under the Errata section of that title. Any existing errata can be viewed by selecting your title from http://www.packtpub.com/support.

Piracy

Piracy of copyrighted material on the Internet is an ongoing problem across all media. At Packt, we take the protection of our copyright and licenses very seriously. If you come across any illegal copies of our works, in any form, on the Internet, please provide us with the location address or website name immediately so that we can pursue a remedy.

Please contact us at copyright@packtpub.com with a link to the suspected pirated material.

We appreciate your help in protecting our authors, and our ability to bring you valuable content.

Questions

You can contact us at questions@packtpub.com if you are having a problem with any aspect of the book, and we will do our best to address it.

Project 1
Romeo and Juliet

Robots and performing arts share a long history. In fact, the word "Robot" was first coined in 1920 for a play by the Czech author *Karel Čapek* named "Rossum's Universal Robots". The play featured six robots, but since nobody was able to build a talking Robot at that time, humans had to play them. Times have changed a lot and we don't need humans to disguise themselves as robots anymore. For this project, we will do it the other way round and make some robots who play the humans. Unfortunately, "Rossum's Universal Robots" would require nine humans and six robots, so I chose a scene that's simpler to perform. We are going to build a pair of robots who play the humans in the famous balcony scene from *Romeo and Juliet*.

Mission Briefing

To create the Processing sketches for this project, we will need to install the Processing library ttslib. This library is a wrapper around the FreeTTS Java library that helps us to write a sketch that reads out text. We will learn how to change the voice parameters of the `kevin16` voice of the FreeTTS package to make our robot's voices distinguishable. We will also create a parser that is able to read the Shakespeare script and which generates text-line objects that allow our script to know which line is read by which robot.

A `Drama` thread will be used to control the text-to-speech objects, and the `draw()` method of our sketch will print the script on the screen while our robots perform it, just in case one of them forgets a line. Finally, we will use some cardboard boxes and a pair of cheap speakers to create the robots and their stage. The following figure shows how the robots work:

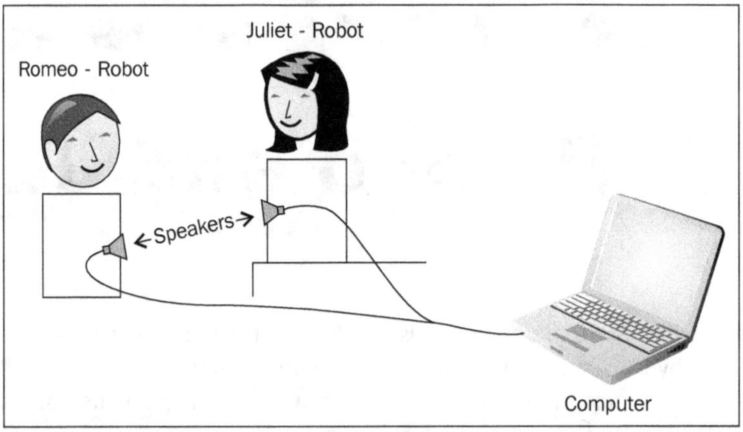

Why Is It Awesome?

Since the 18th century, inventors have tried to build talking machines (with varying success). Talking toys swamped the market in the 1980s and 90s. In every decent Sci-Fi novel, computers and robots are capable of speaking. So how could building talking robots not be awesome? And what could be more appropriate to put these speaking capabilities to test than performing a Shakespeare play? So as you see, building actor robots is officially awesome, just in case your non-geek family members should ask.

Your Hotshot Objectives

We will split this project into four tasks that will guide you through the generation of the robots from beginning to end. Here is a short overview of what we are going to do:

- Making Processing talk
- Reading Shakespeare
- Adding more actors
- Building robots

Making Processing talk

Since Processing has no speaking capabilities out of the box, our first task is adding an external library using the new Processing Library Manager. We will use the ttslib package, which is a wrapper library around the FreeTTS library.

We will also create a short, speaking Processing sketch to check the installation.

Engage Thrusters

1. Processing can be extended by contributed libraries. Most of these additional libraries can be installed by navigating to **Sketch** | **Import Library...** | **Add Library...**, as shown in the following screenshot:

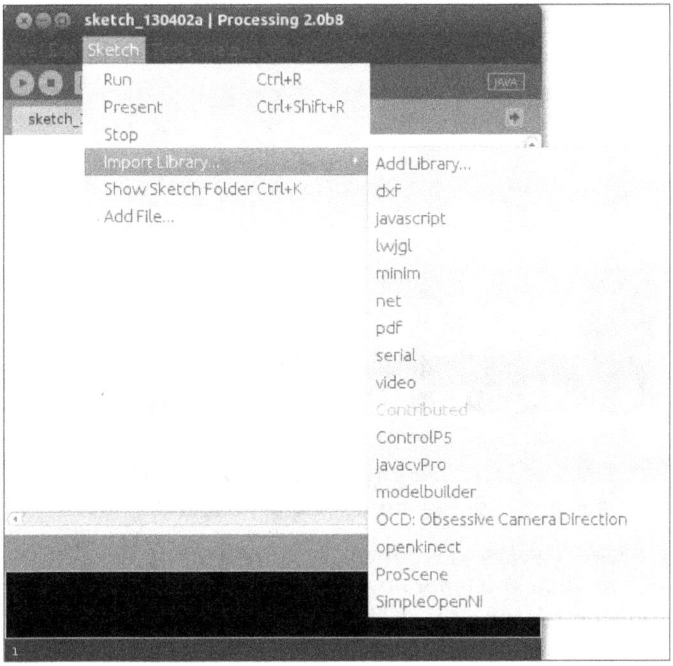

2. In the **Library Manager** dialog, enter `ttslib` in the search field to filter the list of libraries.

3. Click on the **ttslib** entry and then on the **Install** button, as shown in the following screenshot, to download and install the library:

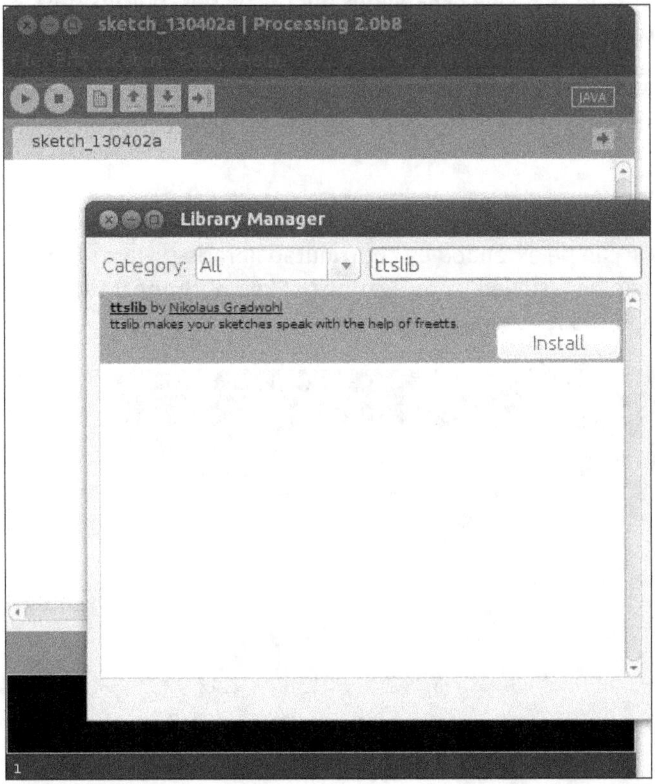

4. To use the new library, we need to import it to our sketch. We do this by clicking on the **Sketch** menu and choosing **Import Library...** and then **ttslib**.

5. We will now add the `setup()` and `draw()` methods to our sketch. We will leave the `draw()` method empty for now and instantiate a `TTS` object in the `setup()` method. Your sketch should look like the following code snippet:

```
import guru.ttslib.*;

TTS tts;
void setup() {
  tts = new TTS();
}

void draw() {
}
```

> **Downloading the example code**
>
> You can download the example code files for all Packt books you have purchased from your account at `http://www.packtpub.com`. If you purchased this book elsewhere, you can visit `http://www.packtpub.com/support` and register to have the files e-mailed directly to you.

6. Now we will add a `mousePressed()` method to our sketch, which will get called if someone clicks on our sketch window. In this method, we are calling the `speak()` method of the `TTS` object we created in the `setup()` method.

   ```
   void mousePressed() {
     tts.speak("Hello, I am a Computer");
   }
   ```

7. Click on the **Run** button to start the Processing sketch. A little gray window should appear.
8. Turn on your speakers or put on your headphones, and click on the gray window. If nothing went wrong, a friendly male computer voice named `kevin16` should greet you now.

Objective Complete - Mini Debriefing

In steps 1 to 3, we installed an additional library to Processing. The ttslib is a wrapper library around the FreeTTS text-to-speech engine.

Then we created a simple Processing sketch that imports the installed library and creates an instance of the `TTS` class. The `TTS` objects match the speakers we need in our sketches. In this case, we created only one speaker and added a `mousePressed()` method that calls the `speak()` method of our `tts` object.

Reading Shakespeare

In this part of the project, we are going to create a `Drama` thread and teach Processing how to read a Shakespeare script. This thread runs in the background and is controlling the performance. We focus on reading and executing the play in this task, and add the speakers in the next one.

Prepare for Lift Off

Our sketch needs to know which line of the script is read by which robot. So we need to convert the Shakespeare script into a more machine-readable format. For every line of text, we need to know which speaker should read the line. So we take the script and add the letter `J` and a separation character that is used nowhere else in the script, in front of every line our Juliet-Robot should speak, and we add `R` and the separation letter for every line our Romeo-Robot should speak. After all these steps, our text file looks something like the following:

```
R# Lady, by yonder blessed moon I vow,
R# That tips with silver all these fruit-tree tops --

J# O, swear not by the moon, the inconstant moon,
J# That monthly changes in her circled orb,
J# Lest that thy love prove likewise variable.

R# What shall I swear by?

J# Do not swear at all.
J# Or if thou wilt, swear by thy gracious self,
J# Which is the god of my idolatry,
J# And I'll believe thee.
```

I have already converted the script of the play into this format, and it can be downloaded from the book's support page at `http://www.packtpub.com/support`.

Engage Thrusters

Let's write our parser:

1. Let's start a new sketch by navigating to **File** | **New**.
2. Add a `setup()` and a `draw()` method.
3. Now add the prepared script to the Processing sketch by navigating to **Sketch** | **Add File** and selecting the file you just downloaded.
4. Add the following line to your `setup()` method:

   ```
   void setup() {
     String[] rawLines = loadStrings
     ( "romeo_and_juliet.txt" );
   }
   ```

5. If you renamed your text file, change the filename accordingly.
6. Create a new tab by clicking on the little arrow icon on the right and choosing **New Tab**.

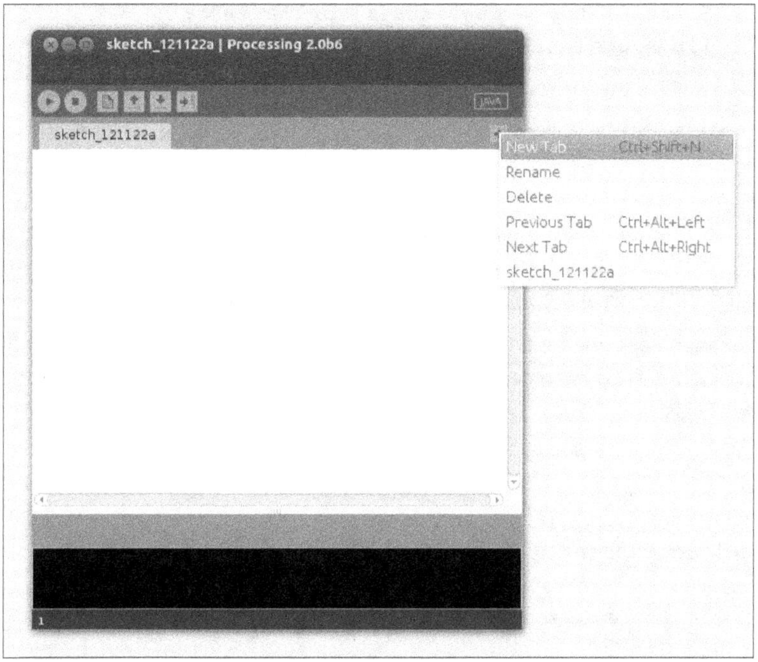

7. Name the class `Line`. This class will hold our text lines and the speaker.
8. Add the following code to the tab we just created:

```
public class Line {
  String speaker;
  String text;

  public Line( String speaker, String text ) {
    this.speaker = speaker;
    this.text = text;
  }
}
```

9. Switch back to our main tab and add the following highlighted lines of code to the `setup()` method:

```
void setup() {
  String[] rawLines = loadStrings
  ( "romeo_and_juliet.txt" );

  ArrayList lines = new ArrayList();
  for ( int i=0; i<rawLines.length; i++) {
    if (!"".equals(rawLines[i])) {
```

```
        String[] tmp = rawLines[i].split("#");
        lines.add( new Line( tmp[0], tmp[1].trim() ));
      }
    }

}
```

10. We have read our text lines and parsed them into the `lines` array list, but we still need a class that does something with our text lines. So create another tab by clicking on the arrow icon and choosing **New Tab** from the menu; name it `Drama`.

11. Our `Drama` class will be a thread that runs in the background and tells each of the speaker objects to read one line of text. Add the following lines of code to your `Drama` class:

```
public class Drama extends Thread {
  int current;
  ArrayList lines;
  boolean running;

  public Drama( ArrayList lines ) {
    this.lines = lines;
    current = 0;
    running = false;
  }

  public int getCurrent() {
    return current;
  }

  public Line getLine( int num ) {
    if ( num >=0 && num < lines.size()) {
      return (Line)lines.get( num );
    } else {
      return null;
    }
  }

  public boolean isRunning() {
    return running;
  }
}
```

12. Now we add a `run()` method that gets executed in the background if we start our thread. Since we have no speaker objects yet, we will print the lines on the console and include a little pause after each line.

```
public void run() {
  running = true;

  for ( int i =0; i < lines.size(); i++) {
    current = i;
    Line l = (Line)lines.get(i);
    System.out.println( l.text );
    delay( 1 );
  }
  running = false;
}
```

13. Switch back to the main sketch tab and add the highlighted code to the `setup()` method to create a `drama` thread object, and then feed it the parsed text-lines.

```
Drama drama;

void setup() {

  String[] rawLines = loadStrings
  ( "romeo_and_juliet.txt" );
  ArrayList lines = new ArrayList();
  for ( int i=0; i<rawLines.length; i++) {
    if (!"".equals(rawLines[i])) {
      String[] tmp = rawLines[i].split("#");
      lines.add( new Line( tmp[0], tmp[1].trim() ));
    }
  }

  drama = new Drama( lines );
}
```

14. So far our sketch parses the text lines and creates a `Drama` thread object. What we need next is a method to start it. So add a `mousePressed()` method to start the `drama` thread.

```
void mousePressed() {
  if ( !drama.isRunning()) {
    drama.start();
  }
}
```

15. Now add a little bit of text to the `draw()` method to tell the user what to do. Add the following code to the `draw()` method:

```
void draw() {
  background(255);
  textAlign(CENTER);
  fill(0);

  text( "Click here for Drama", width/2, height/2 );
}
```

16. Currently, our sketch window is way too small to contain the text, and we also want to use a bigger font. To change the window size, we simply add the following line to the `setup()` method:

```
void setup() {

  size( 800, 400 );

  String[] rawLines = loadStrings
  ( "romeo_and_juliet.txt" );
  ArrayList lines = new ArrayList();
  for ( int i=0; i<rawLines.length; i++) {
    if (!"".equals(rawLines[i])) {
      String[] tmp = rawLines[i].split("#");
      lines.add( new Line( tmp[0], tmp[1].trim() ));
    }
  }

  drama = new Drama( lines );
}
```

17. To change the used font, we need to tell Processing which font to use. The easiest way to find out the names of the fonts that are currently installed on the computer is to create a new sketch, type the following line, and run the sketch:

```
println(PFont.list());
```

18. Copy one of the font names you like and add the following line to the Romeo and Juliet sketch:

```
void setup() {

  size( 800, 400 );
  textFont( createFont( "Georgia", 24 ));

...
```

19. Replace the font name in the code lines with one of the fonts on your computer.

Objective Complete - Mini Debriefing

In this section, we wrote the code that parses a text file and generates a list of `Line` objects. These objects are then used by a `Drama` thread that runs in the background as soon as anyone clicks on the sketch window. Currently, the `Drama` thread prints out the text line on the console.

In steps 6 to 8, we created the `Line` class. This class is a very simple, so-called **Plain Old Java Object** (**POJO**) that holds our text lines, but it doesn't add any functionality.

The code that is controlling the performance of our play was created in steps 10 to 12. We created a thread that is able to run in the background, since in the next step we want to be able to use the `draw()` method and some `TTS` objects simultaneously.

The code block in step 12 defines a Boolean variable named `running`, which we used in the `mousePressed()` method to check if the sketch is already running or should be started.

Classified Intel

In step 17, we used the `list()` method of the `PFont` class to get a list of installed fonts. This is a very common pattern in Processing. You would use the same approach to get a list of installed midi-interfaces, web-cams, serial-ports, and so on.

Adding more actors

In this task, we will combine the things we did in the previous two tasks and add some `TTS` objects to our `Drama` thread. We will need two robot actors for this scene speaking with different voices, and since we want to build robots containing a speaker each, we need one of our `TTS` objects to speak on the left speaker and the other one on the right.

Unfortunately, FreeTTS only comes with one male voice, so we will have to increase the pitch of the voice for our Juliet-Robot.

Engage Thrusters

1. First, we open the sketch from the previous task and start by creating two `TTS` objects, one for each of our robot actors. Both use the default voice named `kevin16`, but we change the pitch for our Juliet-Robot.

   ```
   void setup() {
     size( 800, 400 );
     textFont( createFont( "Georgia", 24 ));
   ```

```
String[] rawLines = loadStrings
( "romeo_and_juliet.txt" );
ArrayList lines = new ArrayList();
for ( int i=0; i<rawLines.length; i++) {
  if (!"".equals(rawLines[i])) {
    String[] tmp = rawLines[i].split("#");
    lines.add( new Line( tmp[0], tmp[1].trim() ));
  }
}

TTS romeo = new TTS();
TTS juliet = new TTS();
juliet.setPitchShift( 2.4 );
drama = new Drama( lines, romeo, juliet );
}
```

2. Switch to the `Drama` thread and add two variables to our actors.

```
public class Drama extends Thread {
  TTS romeo;
  TTS juliet;

  int current;
  ArrayList lines;
  boolean running;
  …
```

3. We also need to extend the constructor of our `Drama` class to enable us to add the actors.

```
public Drama( ArrayList lines, TTS romeo, TTS juliet ) {
  this.lines = lines;
  this.romeo = romeo;
  this.juliet = juliet;
  current = 0;
  running = false;
}
```

4. In the `run()` method, we take the current line and choose the actor object depending on the actor variable we added to each line. We also don't need the `delay()` and the `println()` methods anymore.

```
public void run() {
  running = true;

  for ( int i =0; i < lines.size(); i++) {
    current = i;
    Line l = (Line)lines.get(i);
```

```
      if ( "J".equals( l.speaker )) {
        juliet.speak( l.text );
      }
      if ( "R".equals( l.speaker )) {
        romeo.speak( l.text );
      }
    }
    running = false;
  }
```

5. Since each of our robots gets his own speaker, we don't want to hear the text on both speakers. We want one robot to use the right one and the other robot, the left one. Fortunately, ttslib provides a `speakLeft()` and a `speakRight()` method, which do exactly what we need. So change the two `speak()` methods to look like the following:

```
...
if ( "J".equals( l.speaker )) {
    juliet.speakLeft( l.text );
}
if ( "R".equals( l.speaker )) {
  romeo.speakRight( l.text );
}
...
```

6. Currently, our `draw()` method is somewhat boring and also somewhat misleading if the `drama` thread is already running. So we will change it to display five lines of the currently read script. Add an `if` statement to the `draw()` method that checks the state of the `running` variable we added to our `Drama` thread earlier.

```
void draw() {
  background(255);
  textAlign(CENTER);
  fill(0);

  if ( !drama.isRunning() ) {
    text( "Click here for Drama", width/2, height/2 );
  } else {
  }
}
```

7. Now we add a `for` loop that displays the previous two lines, the line that's currently being read, and the next two lines of text in our sketch window. We will now change the text alignment so that it matches the speaker of our robot actors. The text will be aligned to the right if our robot uses `speakRight()`, and it will be aligned to the left if our robot uses `speakLeft()`.

```
void draw() {
  background(255);
  textAlign(CENTER);
  fill(0);

  if ( !drama.isRunning() ) {
    text( "Click here for Drama", width/2, height/2 );
  }
  else {
    int current = drama.getCurrent();
    for ( int i = -2; i < 3; i ++) {
      Line l = drama.getLine(i + current);
      if ( l != null) {
        if ( "J".equals( l.speaker )) {
          textAlign( LEFT );
          text( l.text, 10, height/2 + i * 30 );
        }
        else {
          textAlign( RIGHT );
          text( l.text, width - 10, height/2 + i * 30 );
        }
      }
    }
  }
}
```

8. To show the current line more prominently, we will change the color of the text. We set the color of the current line to black and all other lines to a lighter gray by adding a `fill()` statement to the `for` loop.

```
    for ( int i = -2; i < 3; i ++) {
      fill( abs(i) * 100 );
      Line l = drama.getLine(i + current);
      if ( l != null) {
        if ( "J".equals( l.speaker )) {
          textAlign( LEFT );
          text( l.text, 10, height/2 + i * 30 );
        }
```

```
        else {
          textAlign( RIGHT );
          text( l.text, width - 10, height/2 + i * 30 );
        }
      }
    }
```

9. Now run your code and click on the sketch window to start the `drama` thread.

Objective Complete - Mini Debriefing

In this task of our current mission, we added two `TTS` objects and changed the voice parameters to make them sound different in step 1. Then we extended our `Drama` thread and added `TTS` objects for the voices of our robot actors. In steps 4 and 5, we modified the `run` method to use the voices we just created instead of just printing the text lines.

In steps 6 to 9, we made changes to the `draw()` method and made it display five lines of text. The line that's currently spoken is black, and the two lines before and after it fade to a light gray.

The `fill()` method is used to change not only the fill color of an object, but also the text color. Because the index of our `for` loop runs from `-2` to `2`, we can simply take the absolute value and multiply it with 100 to get the gray level. The following is a screenshot of the running sketch:

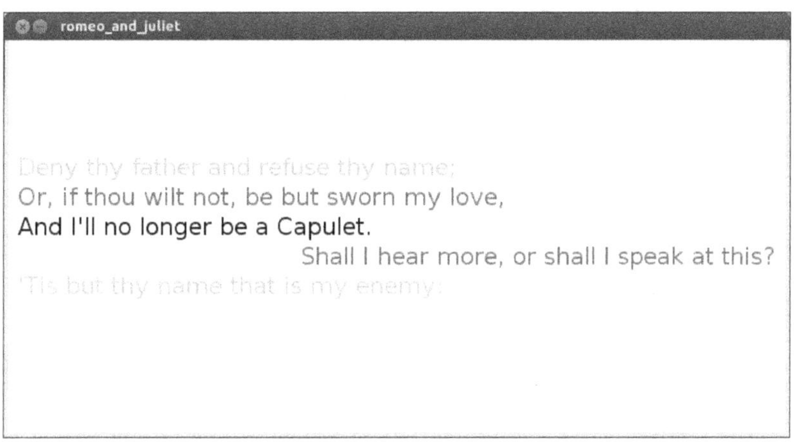

Classified Intel

FreeTTS and ttslib also allow you to use a binary TTS engine named MBROLA. Unfortunately, it's only distributed in binary form, and at the time of writing, it only works on Linux. So if you are using Linux and want to give it a try, you can make the following changes to our Romeo and Juliet sketch:

1. Open `http://tcts.fpms.ac.be/synthesis/mbrola.html` in your browser and click on **Download**. Download the MBROLA binary for your platform.
2. Download the `female_us1` voice from the MBROLA site.
3. Create a folder for the MBROLA binary and unzip the two packages you just downloaded. Make sure that the path to the MBROLA binary contains no blanks, since FreeTTS can't deal with it.
4. Rename the MBROLA binary to `mbrola`.
5. Now go back to your Romeo and Juliet sketch and add the following highlighted line to your `setup()` method:

```
void setup() {
  System.setProperty("mbrola.base", "/path/to/mbrola/");

  size( 800, 400 );
  textFont( createFont( "Georgia", 24 ));

  String[] rawLines = loadStrings
  ( "romeo_and_juliet.txt" );
  ArrayList lines = new ArrayList();
  for ( int i=0; i<rawLines.length; i++) {
    if (!"".equals(rawLines[i])) {
      String[] tmp = rawLines[i].split("#");
      lines.add( new Line( tmp[0], tmp[1].trim() ));
    }
  }

  drama = new Drama( lines );
  TTS romeo = new TTS();
  TTS juliet = new TTS();
  juliet.setPitchShift( 2.4 );
  drama = new Drama( lines, romeo, juliet );
}
```

6. Make the path of the system property point to the folder where your `mbrola` binary and the `us1` voice are located.
7. Now you can change the Juliet `TTS` object to the following:

```
TTS juliet = new TTS( "mbrola_us1" );
```

8. You will also need to change the pitch of the voice as `mbrola_us1` is already a female voice and we don't need to simulate it anymore.

MBROLA is a text-to-speech engine developed at the Faculte Polytechnique de Mons in Belgium. The author requires every publication that mentions their work to mention their book, *An Introduction To Text-To-Speech Synthesis, Thierry Dutoit, Kluwer Academic Publishers, Dordrecht, Hardbound, ISBN 1-4020-0369-2, April 1997, 312 pp.*

Building robots

Now we are ready for the final task of our *Romeo and Juliet* project. We will take some cardboard boxes, Styrofoam spheres, and a pair of cheap speakers or headphones and turn them into our robot-actors.

The robots described in this section are just my version. If you like, you can build them to be completely different and as complex or as simple as you want.

Prepare for Lift Off

To build our robots, we need some materials and tools, which should not be too hard to find. I used the following for my robot-actors:

- Two cardboard boxes for the bodies
- Two Styrofoam spheres for the heads
- A pair of cheap speakers or headphones
- Googly eyes
- Acrylic paint
- Marker pens
- Needles
- A hot glue gun

The following picture shows the main materials I used for my robots:

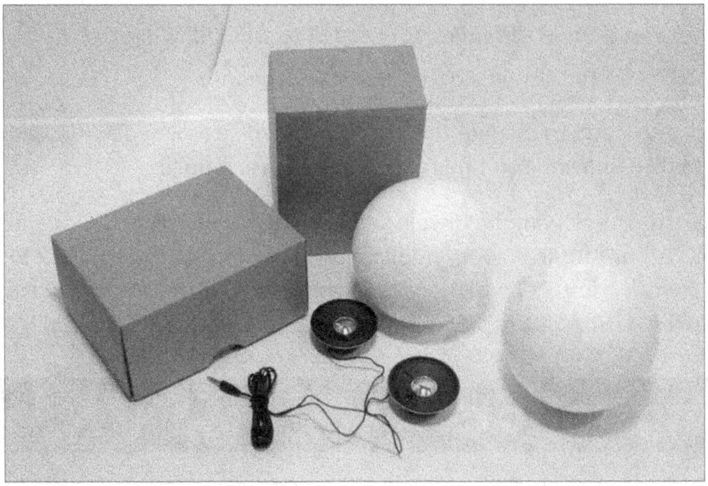

Engage Thrusters

Let's build some robots:

1. Disassemble your speakers and try to get rid of the body. We only need the speakers, but make sure you don't remove or destroy the cables.
2. Cut a hole into your cardboard boxes where the speakers should go. Make the holes a bit smaller than the speakers, as shown in the following picture, because we need to glue them to the box later:

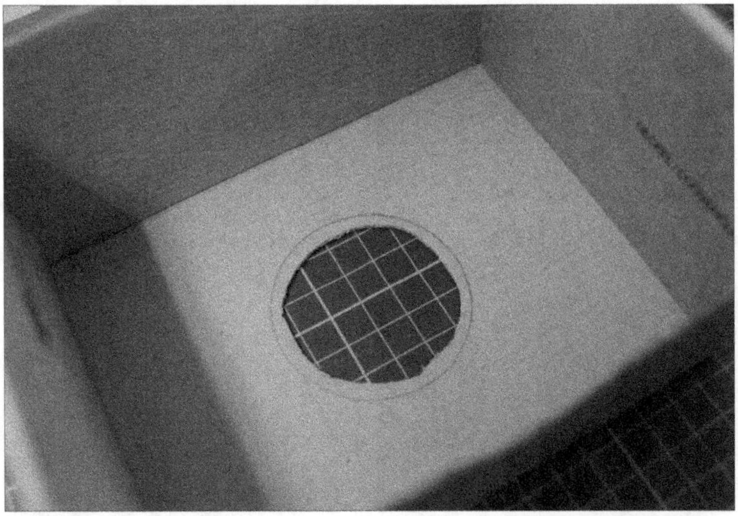

3. Paint your cardboard boxes. I made one white and the other green.
4. While the boxes are drying, paint some hair on the heads like in the following picture. I made Romeo-Robot's hair black and Juliet-Robot's hair brown.

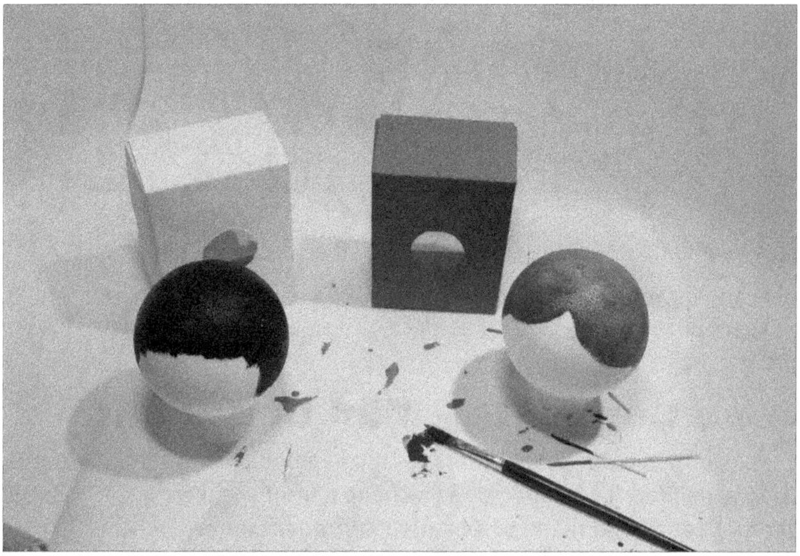

5. After the paint has dried, fix the speakers to the cardboard box using some hot glue, as shown in the following picture. Make sure you don't get any glue on the membrane of your speakers.

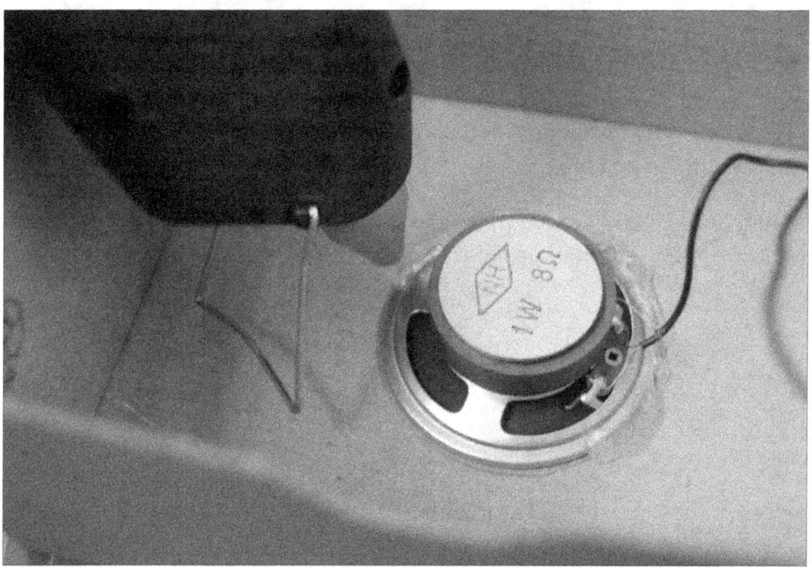

6. Now use some markers to draw a face for the robots. You can see the faces of my robots in the following picture:

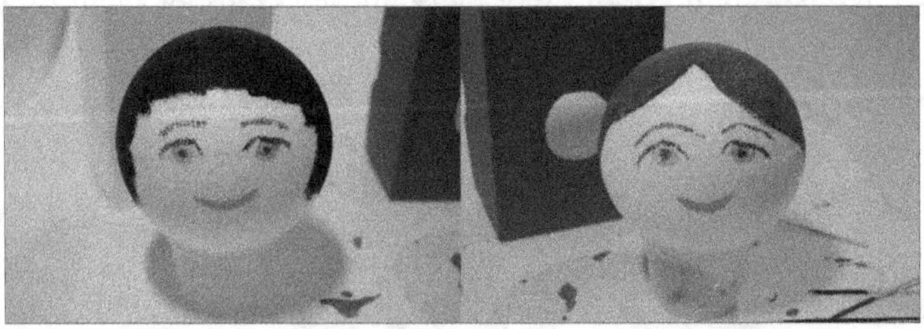

7. Use a needle to attach the heads to the bodies of the robots.
8. Now connect your robot-actors to your sound card and place Juliet on a balcony (for example an empty shoe-box) and make them act.

Objective Complete - Mini Debriefing

In this task, we completed our robot-actors by building bodies for them. We used some cardboard boxes, painted them, and added a cheap pair of speakers by gluing them into the boxes. Each robot got a head made of a painted Styrofoam sphere.

As I already said in the introduction to this task, there is no right or wrong way to build your robots. Build them as small or as big as you like. Add some hair, make them a nose, sew a dress for Juliet, draw Romeo a mustache, and so on.

Mission Accomplished

In this mission, we added speaking capabilities to Processing by installing the ttslib library. We learned how to simulate multiple speakers by changing the pitch of voice or installing an additional TTS engine on Linux.

We also defined a speak text format for the Shakespeare script to make parsing easier and created a `Drama` thread that manages our text lines and controls our robots.

We completed our robot-actors, and they are eagerly waiting to perform in front of an audience. So gather your friends and family and make your robots a stage. They will love it, trust me. Well, at least your robots will love it, as you can see in the following picture:

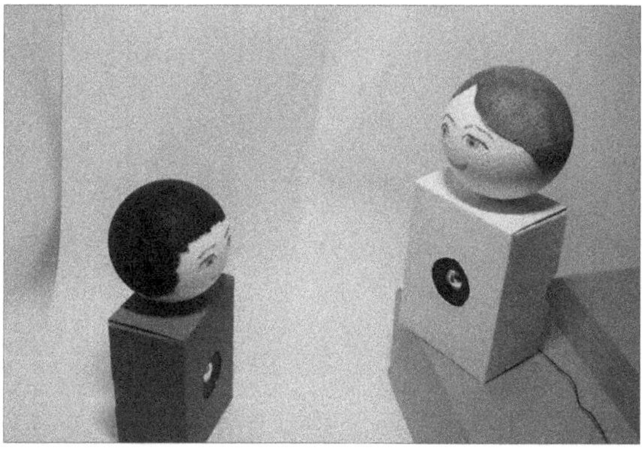

You Ready to go Gung HO? A Hotshot Challenge

Now that you have completed building your robot-actors, why don't you try to take them to the next level?

- Make them perform different plays. There are plenty of famous dialogs out there that could be performed by your robot-actors.
- Currently your robot-actors are stationary. Try to add some servo motors and make them move their heads using an Arduino.
- Connect some webcams to your computer and use Processing to record some videos of the performances from different angles.
- Make your robot-actors perform a play with a real actor.
- Make your robots read live input from the Web such as Twitter feeds or the news.
- Your robots don't have to look like humans; make them look like zombies, aliens, animals, and so on.

Project 2
The Stick Figure Dance Company

In *Project 1*, Romeo and Juliet we learned how to make Processing talk. In this project, we will learn how to make it see and dance. We will use Microsoft's Kinect to implement the seeing part and a dancing human to teach a group of stick figures how to dance. Unless you find someone else who is willing to lead your stick figures, you will have to get up and dance yourself.

Computer vision and 3D scanning have long been the domain of very specialized and expensive hardware and software. With the ever increasing computing power of CPUs and graphics cards, and new hardware controllers like Kinect, computer vision projects have invaded living rooms via various game controllers, and are accessible to everyday programmers like you and me.

Mission Briefing

In this project, we will learn how to connect Microsoft's Kinect to a computer and use depth imaging and user tracking from Processing. We will rush through the installation of the OpenNI framework in the first task, as this library is used by the Processing library **SimpleOpenNI**. We will then learn how to use the depth image feature of the Kinect infrared camera and the player tracking function in Processing.

Then, we will use the so-called skeleton tracker, not only to locate the user in front of the camera, but also the head, neck, and elbows. These 3D coordinates will allow us to control a stick figure.

In the final task of our current mission, we are going to add a group of additional dancers that will also be controlled by the 3D coordinates of the players' limbs.

You can see a screenshot of the final sketch here:

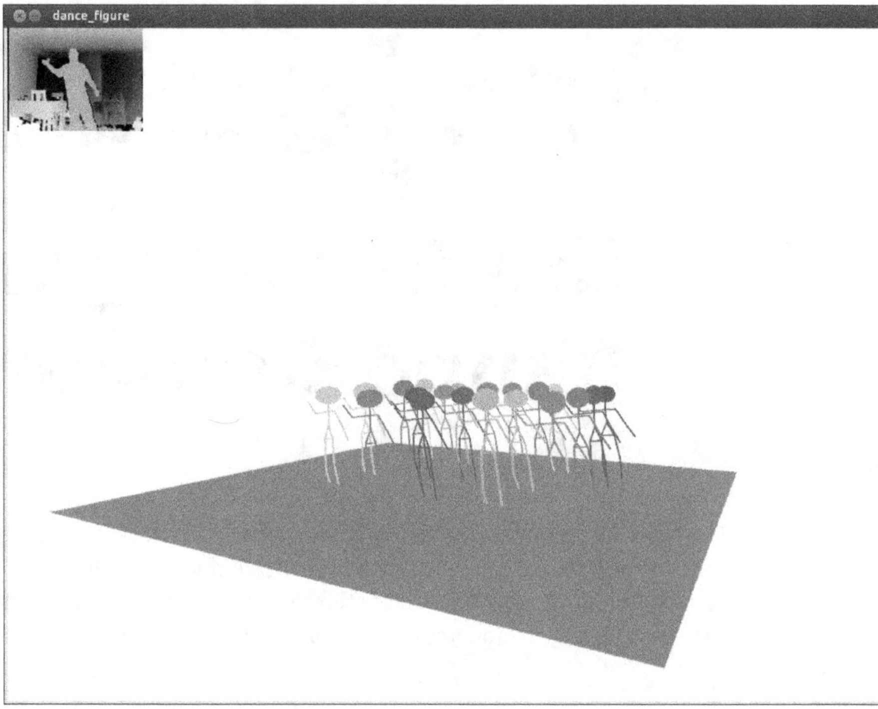

Why Is It Awesome?

Kinect enables a whole lot of new possibilities for interacting with a computer. It enables the player to control a computer by simply moving in front of the computer. How awesome is that? And as a nice side effect, it makes computer users move—something computer users usually don't shine at very much.

> **Disclaimer**
>
> The author is not responsible for injuries and accidents that arise if you place your limbs forcefully into places that are already occupied by other space-time aggregations. So please make sure you have enough free space around you while dancing.

Apart from tracking the positions of the user's body parts, Kinect also provides us with a depth map of the surrounding players and a bitmap that allows us to determine which pixels of the image belong to the player and which don't.

Your Objectives

This Hotshot project is split into the following four tasks:

- Connecting the Kinect
- Making Processing see
- Making a dancer
- Dance! Dance! Dance!

Mission Checklist

To complete this mission, you need a Kinect to connect to your computer. Kinect is connected to a USB port, but it needs more power than what a standard USB port can provide. Therefore, Kinect comes with a non-standard USB connector and a separate power connector. If you got your Kinect in a bundle with the Xbox 360, you will probably need to buy a USB power adapter for it; newer versions of the Xbox 360 provide a special port to connect the Kinect directly. You can get the adapters at an electronics store or online.

Since this project is about dancing, you will also need some music to dance to. The stick figures we are going to create are very tolerant when it comes to genres of music, so feel free to choose whatever music you like—Donna Summer, Zillertaler Schürzenjäger, Bobby Brown, Skrillex. If you like it, your stick figures will like it too.

Connecting the Kinect

In this first task, I will guide you through the installation of the OpenNI framework and a library from PrimeSense (the company that developed the Kinect for Microsoft). We will use OpenNI example programs to test our installation.

Engage Thrusters

1. At the time of writing, the most recent version of the OpenNI framework was 2.1 Beta, but the Processing framework that we are going to use for our next task requires Version 1.5.4 of the OpenNI framework. Open the site `http://www.openni.org/openni-sdk/openni-sdk-history-2/` in your browser, as shown in the following screenshot, and select the download package for your platform:

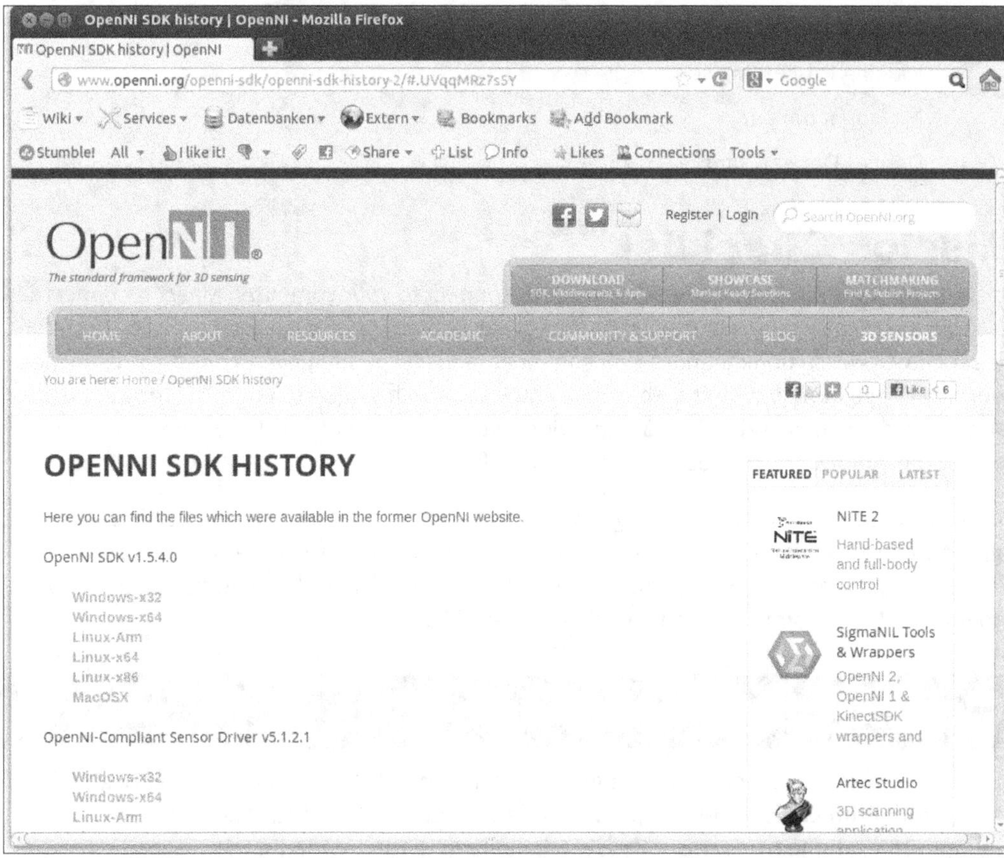

2. If you are running Linux or Mac OS X, open a Terminal window, go to the directory where you downloaded the file, and unpack it using the `tar` command; make sure to unpack it as root by running the `install.sh` script:

```
tar xvjf openni-bin-dev-linux-x86-v1.5.4.0.tar.bz2
cd OpenNI-Bin-Dev-Linux-x86-v1.5.4.0
sudo  ./install.sh
```

3. On Windows, just execute the MSI file you downloaded.
4. Repeat the above steps for the NiTE v1.5.2.21 file by downloading the package and installing it using the following commands:

```
tar xvjf nite-bin-linux-x86-v1.5.2.21.tar.bz2
cd NITE-Bin-Dev-Linux-x86-v1.5.2.21/
sudo ./install.sh
```

5. Now go to `https://github.com/avin2/SensorKinect/tree/unstable/Bin` and download the sensor package for Kinect. You do not need the sensor package you get from `http://openni.org`; this is for another sensor bar and won't work with Kinect.
6. Unpack the sensor package and install it on Linux or Mac OS X by running the following commands:

```
tar xvjf SensorKinect093-Bin-Linux-x86-v5.1.2.1.tar.bz2
cd Sensor-Bin-Linux-x86-v5.1.2.1/
sudo ./install.sh
```

7. On Windows, install the sensor package file by double-clicking on the MSI file.
8. Now connect your Kinect to the power adapter and then to an empty USB slot, and place it in front of your monitor. Make sure you have some free space in your room to stand in front of the sensor bar, as shown in this diagram:

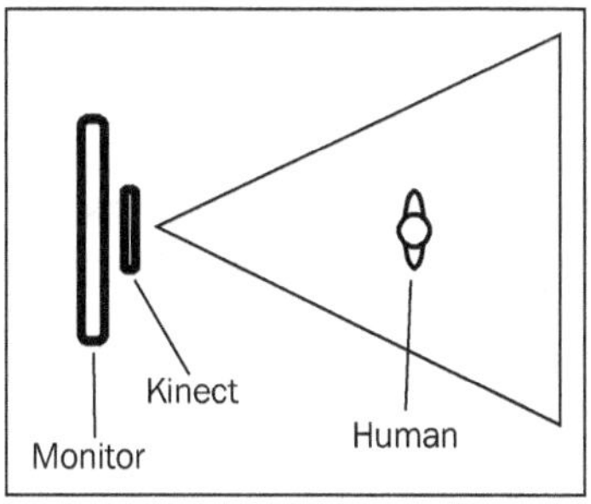

9. Go to the development package and run the NiViewer example program from the `x86-Release` folder under `OpenNI-Bin-Dev-Linux-x86-v1.5.4.0/Samples/Bin/`:

```
cd ../OpenNI-Bin-Dev-Linux-x86-v1.5.4.0
cd Samples/Bin/x86-Relelase/
./NiViewer
```

10. Place a human in front of the Kinect sensor and ask him/her to move. In the following screenshot, you can see the author move his coffee cup:

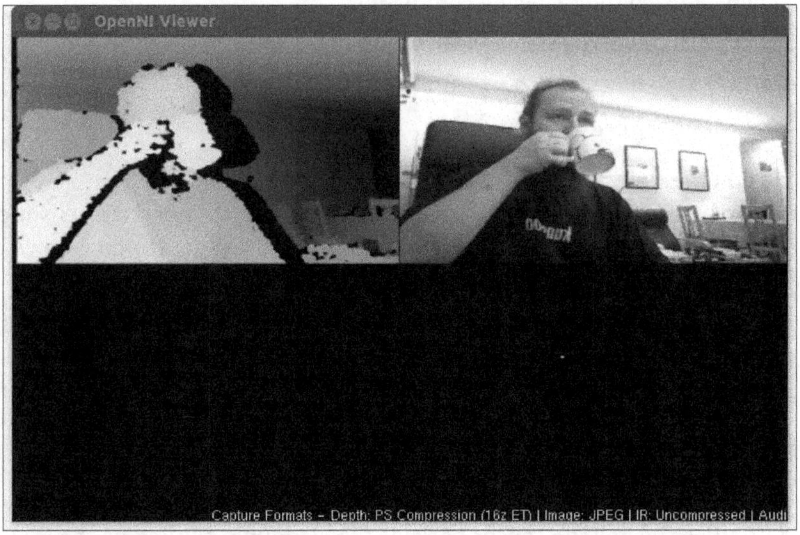

Objective Complete - Mini Debriefing

We just downloaded and installed the OpenNI open source drivers to access the Kinect sensor board. These drivers allow us to access infrared and RGB images from the Kinect controller. Kinect also does a depth scan using the infrared camera and is capable of tracking users.

After installing the development kit, the middleware drivers, and the sensor board for the Kinect controller, we used one of the example programs from the development kit to test the installation.

Classified Intel

There are also other sensor bars apart from Kinect that use the PrimeSense technology and are supported by the OpenNI package. To use these, you need to install the sensor packages from `http://www.openni.org`, which we had skipped in the *Engage Thrusters* section.

I have run and tested the programs in this project using a Kinect, but you could try them with other sensor bars such as **PrimeSense Sensors** or **ASUS Xtion**.

Making Processing see

Our next task is to install the SimpleOpenNI library. This library enables us to use the OpenNI API in Processing. At first, we will learn how to access and display the depth image of the Kinect controller. Then, we will use the user tracking capabilities of the SimpleOpenNI framework and define some callback functions to get notified when a user is detected or when the tracked user disappears. And finally, we will color all the pixels in the depth image that belong to the user to enable the user to see what is being tracked.

Engage Thrusters

Let's teach Processing how to see:

1. At the time of writing, the SimpleOpenNI framework could not be installed using the new Library Manager. To install it manually, download the SimpleOpenNI package for your operating system from `http://code.google.com/p/simple-openni/downloads/list`.
2. Unzip it to a folder named `library` in your `sketchbook` folder. You can find the path to the folder in the **Preferences** dialog.
3. Restart Processing if it is currently running, to make sure that the library is found by your installation.
4. Now, create a new sketch and click on **Import library ...** under the **Sketch** menu to include the SimpleOpenNI library.
5. Add a `setup()` and `draw()` method to your sketch.

```
import SimpleOpenNI.*;
void setup() {
}

void draw() {
}
```

6. In the `setup()` method, resize the sketch window to 640 x 480 pixels and define an OpenNI context object. We use the `enableDepth()` method to start capturing the depth image and `setMirror()` to activate the mirror function.

```
import SimpleOpenNI.*;

SimpleOpenNI context;

void setup() {
  size( 640,480 );
```

```
    context = new SimpleOpenNI( this );
    context.setMirror( true );
    context.enableDepth();
}
```

7. Now add the following lines to your `draw()` method to make SimpleOpenNI load the next frame and calculate the depth image. Then, use `context.depthImage()` to get the data as a `PImage` object, and use `image()` to draw it to your sketch window.

```
void draw() {
  context.update();
  image( context.depthImage(), 0, 0 );
}
```

8. Run your sketch and wave into the camera. You should see a depth image of yourself and your surroundings.

9. Turn on user detection in the setup method by adding the following line:

```
void setup() {
  size( 640,480 );
  context = new SimpleOpenNI( this );
  context.setMirror( true );
  context.enableDepth();
  context.enableUser( SimpleOpenNI.SKEL_PROFILE_ALL );
}
```

10. You also need a variable to store the `userId` of the first user that the SimpleOpenNI framework detects, so add a player variable and initialize it to `-1` at the beginning of your sketch.

```
int player = -1;
```

11. To get notified when SimpleOpenNI has detected a user, we add the following two callback methods to our sketch:

```
void onNewUser( int userId ) {
  println( "new user " + userId );
  player = userId;
}

void onLostUser( int userId ) {
  println( "lost user " + userId );
  if ( userId == player ) {
    player = -1;
  }
}
```

12. To see where Kinect has found a user, you need to make all the pixels that belong to the user appear in green in your image. You can do this by adding the following code to our `draw()` method:

```
void draw() {
  context.update();
  image( context.depthImage(), 0, 0 );

  loadPixels();
  if ( player != -1 ) {
    int[] userPixels = context.getUsersPixels( player );

    for( int p = 0; p < width * height; p++) {
      if ( userPixels[p] != 0 ) {
        pixels[p] = color( 0, green( pixels[p] ), 0 );
      }
    }
  }
  updatePixels();
}
```

13. If you run your code now, the detected user's pixels should turn green, like in the following screenshot:

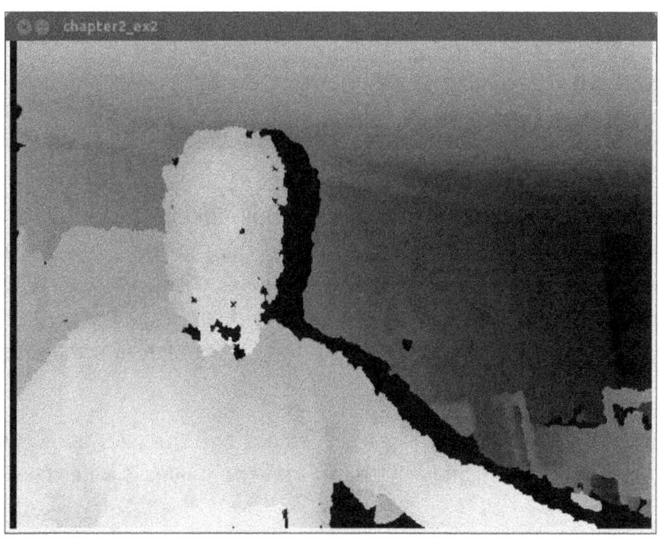

Objective Complete - Mini Debriefing

We have just learned how to access the depth image provided by Kinect using Processing. Starting with step 9, we used the tracking functions of the SimpleOpenNI framework. We added a callback function named `onNewUser()`, which gets called by the library every time a user is detected, and a second one named `onLostUser()` to receive a notification if the user isn't in the tracking range anymore.

In our `draw()` method, we used a pixel map that we got from the `getUsersPixels()` method to color all the pixels in the depth image green if they belong to the user and leave them unchanged if they don't. The array returned by the function `getUsersPixels()` contains a value of `0` for every non-user pixel and a `1` for the ones we want to color. For every `1` that is part of the user's pixels, we take the current gray value of the depth image and replace it with a green value of the same intensity.

Classified Intel

Apart from the infrared and RGB camera, the Kinect also comes with a motor control to allow for the adjustment of the camera tilt. Unfortunately, the OpenNI framework has no support for controlling the motor. There is a second open source framework called **libfreenect**, which can be used to access the Kinect. It lacks the user-tracking features of OpenNI but comes with support for motor control. So if you need to adjust the tilt level of your Kinect, because it's notorious for cutting off the heads or feet of your players, you can install the libfreenect library and the demo applications and use them to adjust your Kinect.

Making a dancer

In the previous section, we used the user-tracking capabilities of the OpenNI framework to locate the user in the depth image provided by the Kinect infrared camera. Now we will take it one step further and locate the body parts of the player. The feature we are going to use in this task is called **skeleton tracking**. The OpenNI skeleton tracker locates certain key points of a human body, which we will use to construct our stick figure. For each player, the Kinect can see and get the location of the head, neck, torso, shoulders, elbows, hands, hips, knees, and feet.

We are also showing the image of the infrared camera and the user pixels we used in the last section as a little heads-up display (HUD) so that the player is able to see what Kinect is tracking.

Engage Thrusters

1. We need to create a new Processing sketch and import the `SimpleOpenNI` library. Then we need to add a `setup()` and a `draw()` method.

```
import SimpleOpenNI.*;

void setup() {
}

void draw() {
}
```

2. We create three methods that are called by our `draw()` method and used to draw the HUD, the dancers, and the dancefloor.

```
void drawHUD() {
}

void drawDancer() {
}

void drawFloor() {
}
```

3. In our `draw()` method, we need to add calls to the three methods we just created. Since the Kinect returns coordinates using a different coordinate system than the one Processing uses (it does this by default), we need to rotate and scale our viewpoint before we call the `drawDancer()` and `drawFloor()` methods.

```
void draw() {
  background( 255 );
  context.update();

  drawHUD();

  translate( width/2, height/2, 0 );
  rotateX( PI );

  scale(0.5);
  translate(0, -100, -400);
  rotateY( radians( 30 ));

  drawDancer();
  drawFloor();
}
```

4. Now we need to add a SimpleOpenNI context to our script and initialize it in the `setup()` method. We also need to set the size of our sketch to 1024 x 768 pixels.

```
SimpleOpenNI context;
int player = -1;
boolean calibrated = false;void setup() {
  size( 1024, 768, P3D);
  context = new SimpleOpenNI( this );
  context.enableDepth();

  context.enableUser( SimpleOpenNI.SKEL_PROFILE_ALL);
}
```

5. To create the HUD, we need to add the `onNewUser()` and `onUserLost()` callback methods, like we did in the previous section. As we also want to use the skeleton tracker, we start the skeleton calibration in the `onNewUser()` function.

```
void onNewUser(int userId) {
  println("onNewUser - userId: " + userId);
  println("  start pose detection");
  if ( player == -1 ) {
    player = userId;
    calibrated = false;
    context.requestCalibrationSkeleton(userId, true);
  }
}

void onLostUser( int userId ) {
  if ( player == userId ) {
    println( "lost user" );
    player = -1;
    calibrated = false;
  }
}
```

6. We also add a `onEndCalibration()` callback function that gets called when the calibration is finished. If the calibration is not successful, we can try to find the user for the second time by starting pose detection.

```
void onEndCalibration(int userId, boolean successfull) {
  println("onEndCalibration - userId: " + userId + ",
successfull: " + successfull);
  if ( player == userId ) {
    if (successfull) {
      println("  User calibrated !!!");
      context.startTrackingSkeleton(userId);
```

```
            calibrated = true;
        } else {
            println("  Failed to calibrate user !!!");
            println("  Start pose detection");
            context.startPoseDetection("Psi", userId);
        }
    }
}
```

7. If SimpleOpenNI detects the requested pose, the `onStartPose()` function gets called. So let's add this function to our sketch to start the calibration again when pose detection is successful.

```
void onStartPose(String pose, int userId) {
  println("onStartPose - userId: " + userId + ", pose: " + pose);
  println(" stop pose detection");
  if ( player == userId ) {
    context.stopPoseDetection(userId);
    context.requestCalibrationSkeleton(userId, true);
  }
}
```

8. Now we display the image of the infrared camera and color the pixels we get from the `getUsersPixel()` method. We want the image of the infrared camera to be displayed only in the top-left corner this time, not the entire sketch window. We also need to adjust the pixel coloring code that we used in the previous sketch. We only take every fourth pixel of every fourth row to shrink the image. Add the following code to the `drawHUD()` method:

```
void drawHUD() {
  image( context.depthImage(), 0, 0, 160, 120);

  loadPixels();
  if ( player != -1 ) {
    int[] up = context.getUsersPixels( player );
    for ( int y = 0; y < 480; y += 4) {
      for ( int x = 0; x < 640; x += 4) {
        if ( up[ y * 640 + x ] != 0 ) {

          float g = green( pixels[ y * 1024 / 4 + x / 4 ]);

          if ( calibrated ) {
            pixels[ (y/4) * 1024 + x/4 ] = color( 0, g, 0 );
          } else {
            pixels[ (y/4) * 1024 + x/4 ] = color( g, g, 0 );
          }
```

```
          }
        }
      }
    }
    updatePixels();
  }
```

9. The next method we are going to implement is the `drawDancer()` method. Since we have activated the user skeleton tracker, we can now start using the coordinates of the limbs and joints and draw lines between them. For the head, we will use a sphere that is scaled down along the x and z axes to turn it into an ellipsoid, like in the following diagram:

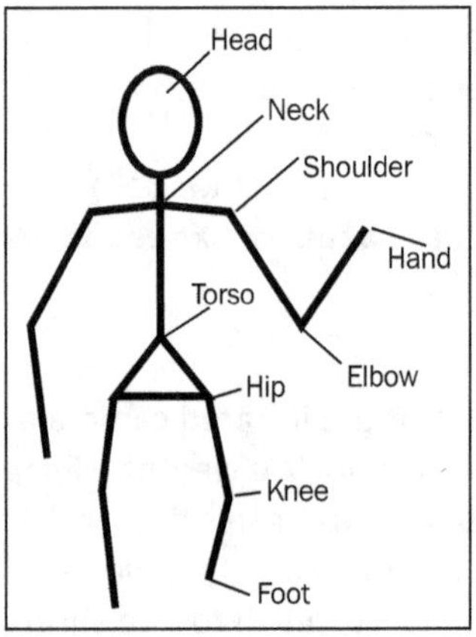

10. We need to add the following code to our sketch to draw the head and the torso:

```
void drawDancer() {
  if ( player != -1 && context.isTrackingSkeleton( player )) {
    pushMatrix();
    scale( .1 );
    stroke(0);
    strokeWeight(2);
    fill(0);
    PVector v1 = new PVector();
    PVector v2 = new PVector();
    context.getJointPositionSkeleton( player,
      SimpleOpenNI.SKEL_HEAD, v1 );
    context.getJointPositionSkeleton( player,
      SimpleOpenNI.SKEL_NECK, v2 );
    pushMatrix();
    translate( v1.x, v1.y, v1.z );
    scale( .5, .5, 1);
```

```
sphere( v1.dist( v2 ));
popMatrix();
line( v1.x, v1.y, v1.z, v2.x, v2.y, v2.z );

context.getJointPositionSkeleton( player,
  SimpleOpenNI.SKEL_NECK, v1 );
context.getJointPositionSkeleton( player,
  SimpleOpenNI.SKEL_LEFT_SHOULDER, v2 );
line( v1.x, v1.y, v1.z, v2.x, v2.y, v2.z );

context.getJointPositionSkeleton( player,
  SimpleOpenNI.SKEL_NECK, v1 );
context.getJointPositionSkeleton( player,
  SimpleOpenNI.SKEL_RIGHT_SHOULDER, v2 );
line( v1.x, v1.y, v1.z, v2.x, v2.y, v2.z );

context.getJointPositionSkeleton( player,
  SimpleOpenNI.SKEL_NECK, v1 );
context.getJointPositionSkeleton( player,
  SimpleOpenNI.SKEL_TORSO, v2 );
line( v1.x, v1.y, v1.z, v2.x, v2.y, v2.z );
```

11. We then add the following code to draw the arms:

```
context.getJointPositionSkeleton( player,
  SimpleOpenNI.SKEL_LEFT_SHOULDER, v1 );
context.getJointPositionSkeleton( player,
  SimpleOpenNI.SKEL_LEFT_ELBOW, v2 );
line( v1.x, v1.y, v1.z, v2.x, v2.y, v2.z );

context.getJointPositionSkeleton( player,
  SimpleOpenNI.SKEL_LEFT_ELBOW, v1 );
context.getJointPositionSkeleton( player,
  SimpleOpenNI.SKEL_LEFT_HAND, v2 );
line( v1.x, v1.y, v1.z, v2.x, v2.y, v2.z );

context.getJointPositionSkeleton( player,
  SimpleOpenNI.SKEL_RIGHT_SHOULDER, v1 );
context.getJointPositionSkeleton( player,
  SimpleOpenNI.SKEL_RIGHT_ELBOW, v2 );
line( v1.x, v1.y, v1.z, v2.x, v2.y, v2.z );

context.getJointPositionSkeleton( player,
  SimpleOpenNI.SKEL_RIGHT_ELBOW, v1 );
context.getJointPositionSkeleton( player,
  SimpleOpenNI.SKEL_RIGHT_HAND, v2 );
line( v1.x, v1.y, v1.z, v2.x, v2.y, v2.z );
```

12. And finally, we add the following code to draw the hips and legs:

```
        context.getJointPositionSkeleton( player,
          SimpleOpenNI.SKEL_TORSO, v1 );
        context.getJointPositionSkeleton( player,
          SimpleOpenNI.SKEL_LEFT_HIP, v2 );
        line( v1.x, v1.y, v1.z, v2.x, v2.y, v2.z );

        context.getJointPositionSkeleton( player,
          SimpleOpenNI.SKEL_TORSO, v1 );
        context.getJointPositionSkeleton( player,
          SimpleOpenNI.SKEL_RIGHT_HIP, v2 );
        line( v1.x, v1.y, v1.z, v2.x, v2.y, v2.z );

        context.getJointPositionSkeleton( player,
          SimpleOpenNI.SKEL_LEFT_HIP, v1 );
        context.getJointPositionSkeleton( player,
          SimpleOpenNI.SKEL_RIGHT_HIP, v2 );
        line( v1.x, v1.y, v1.z, v2.x, v2.y, v2.z );

        context.getJointPositionSkeleton( player,
          SimpleOpenNI.SKEL_LEFT_HIP, v1 );
        context.getJointPositionSkeleton( player,
          SimpleOpenNI.SKEL_LEFT_KNEE, v2 );
        line( v1.x, v1.y, v1.z, v2.x, v2.y, v2.z );

        context.getJointPositionSkeleton( player,
          SimpleOpenNI.SKEL_LEFT_KNEE, v1 );
        context.getJointPositionSkeleton( player,
          SimpleOpenNI.SKEL_LEFT_FOOT, v2 );
        line( v1.x, v1.y, v1.z, v2.x, v2.y, v2.z );

        context.getJointPositionSkeleton( player,
          SimpleOpenNI.SKEL_RIGHT_HIP, v1 );
        context.getJointPositionSkeleton( player,
          SimpleOpenNI.SKEL_RIGHT_KNEE, v2 );
        line( v1.x, v1.y, v1.z, v2.x, v2.y, v2.z );

        context.getJointPositionSkeleton( player,
          SimpleOpenNI.SKEL_RIGHT_KNEE, v1 );
        context.getJointPositionSkeleton( player,
          SimpleOpenNI.SKEL_RIGHT_FOOT, v2 );
        line( v1.x, v1.y, v1.z, v2.x, v2.y, v2.z );

         popMatrix();
    }
}
```

13. So far, our dancer is getting tracked and drawn, but if you run the code now, it will float in a void. To change this, add the following code to the `drawDancefloor()` method to give our dancer something to dance on:

```
void drawFloor() {
  noStroke();
  fill( 128 );

  beginShape(QUADS);
  vertex( -400, -100, -400 );
  vertex( -400, -100, 400 );
  vertex( 400, -100, 400 );
  vertex( 400, -100, -400 );
  endShape();
}
```

14. We need to run our sketch now. Our stick figure will follow our dance moves, like in this screenshot:

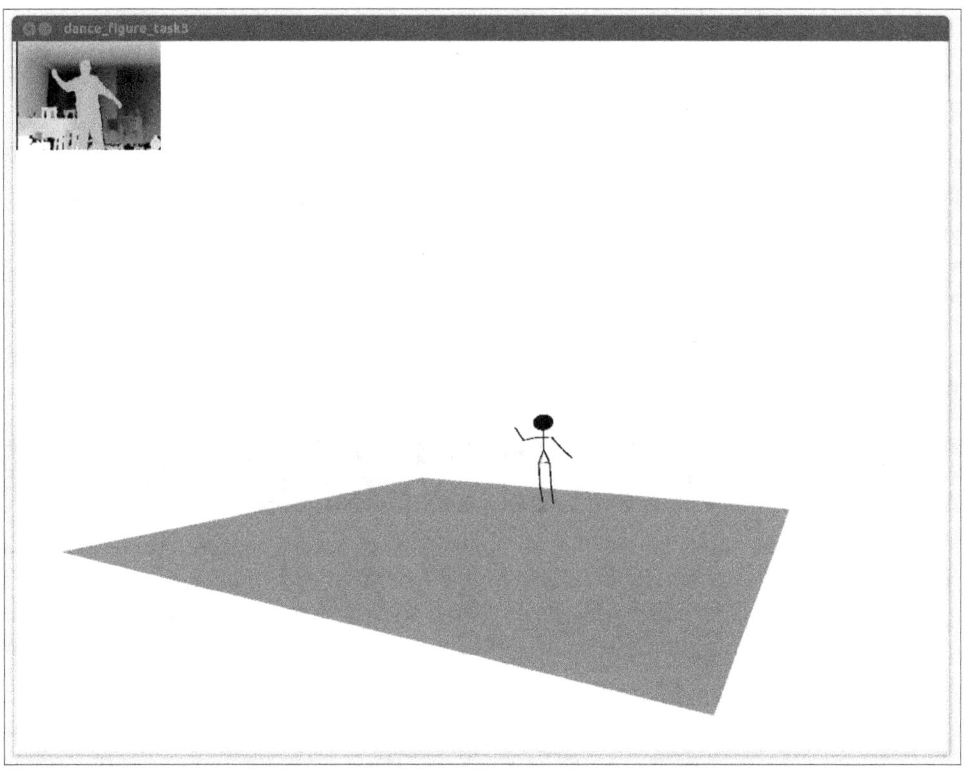

Objective Complete - Mini Debriefing

We have just learned how to use Kinect's skeleton tracking function. To get the coordinates of the limbs and joints, we added two new callback functions; one to be notified for when Kinect starts the calibration, and a second one when a user pose is detected.

To enable the user of our sketch to see the current status of the recognition and calibration, we added a little HUD display in step 5. Our HUD display is very similar to the sketch we created in the previous task, but because we don't want to use the entire window for displaying the depth map and user pixels, we need to convert the coordinates of our pixels and the indices of the pixel array.

We use the coordinates of the skeleton tracker in our `drawDancer()` method to draw a stick figure in step 8. The `jointPositionSkeleton()` method of the SimpleOpenNI context is used to load the joint positions into a `PVector` variable, which we use to draw the limbs with the `line()` method.

And finally, we made a simple dance floor for our stick figure to dance on in step 9 by drawing a gray rectangle. We used `beginShape()` and `endShape()` to define the shape, and added the coordinates of the corners using the `vertex()` method.

Classified Intel

The SimpleOpenNI context doesn't just provide the location of the joints, it also provides a direction vector. As we're only drawing a stick figure in this project to keep things simple, we haven't made use of this direction vector. But if you plan to control a more complicated figure like a rigged 3D model that you exported from a 3D modeling program like Blender, this information can be used to calculate the rotation and twist of the model's vertices.

You might also need this information if you need to test where an object got hit and in which direction it would fly away.

Dance! Dance! Dance!

In this final task of the stick figure dance company project, we finally come to the "company" part. So far, we've created one lonely stick figure dancer that is moving in its own little virtual world. And this is going out of fashion. We will now add some more dancers by cloning the one we've already created; to prevent our dancers from being indistinguishable, we will add a little variation here and there.

To make our code more readable, we will create a new class that holds our stick figure data and is responsible for drawing the body of one figure. This class is also used to store the color and size of each dancer.

We will place the dancers in the `draw()` method and use the `translate()` method to draw each dancer in another location on the dancefloor.

Engage Thrusters

Let's add more dancers:

1. Open the sketch you created in the *Making a dancer* task, and add a new class by clicking on the little arrow icon on the right and choosing **New Tab** from the menu. The new class is called `Figure`, so name the tab accordingly and add the following code:

   ```
   public class Figure {

   }
   ```

2. Now add an array of `PVector` objects to your class (which will store the coordinates you get from the Kinect) and an array with the same size containing the names of the `OpenNI` constants that identify each joint.

   ```
   public class Figure {
     PVector[] joints;
     int[] ni_names = new int[] {
       SimpleOpenNI.SKEL_HEAD,
       SimpleOpenNI.SKEL_NECK,
       SimpleOpenNI.SKEL_TORSO,
       SimpleOpenNI.SKEL_LEFT_SHOULDER,
       SimpleOpenNI.SKEL_LEFT_ELBOW,
       SimpleOpenNI.SKEL_LEFT_HAND,
       SimpleOpenNI.SKEL_RIGHT_SHOULDER,
       SimpleOpenNI.SKEL_RIGHT_ELBOW,
       SimpleOpenNI.SKEL_RIGHT_HAND,
       SimpleOpenNI.SKEL_LEFT_HIP,
       SimpleOpenNI.SKEL_LEFT_KNEE,
       SimpleOpenNI.SKEL_LEFT_FOOT,
       SimpleOpenNI.SKEL_RIGHT_HIP,
       SimpleOpenNI.SKEL_RIGHT_KNEE,
       SimpleOpenNI.SKEL_RIGHT_FOOT
     };
   }
   ```

3. To initialize the `joints` array, you need a constructor for your `Figure` class, which looks like this:

   ```
   public Figure() {
       joints = new PVector[15];
       for( int i=0; i<joints.length; i++ ) {
   ```

```
      joints[i] = new PVector();
    }
  }
```

4. You also need to add some constants to your class to be able to identify the entries in the array of coordinates without having to know the numerical indices in the array.

```
public class Figure {
  static final int HEAD=0;
  static final int NECK=1;
  static final int TORSO=2;
  static final int L_SHOULDER=3;
  static final int L_ELBOW=4;
  static final int L_HAND=5;
  static final int R_SHOULDER=6;
  static final int R_ELBOW=7;
  static final int R_HAND=8;
  static final int L_HIP=9;
  static final int L_KNEE=10;
  static final int L_FOOT=11;
  static final int R_HIP=12;
  static final int R_KNEE=13;
  static final int R_FOOT=14;
```

5. For each frame, the Kinect provides you with an updated set of coordinates; so you need to add an `update()` method that gets a reference to `SimpleOpenNI context` and `userId`. As you've added the names of the coordinates to an array, you can simply use a `for` loop to copy them to your `PVector` array.

```
  public void update( SimpleOpenNI context, int userId ) {
    for ( int i=0; i<joints.length; i++) {
      context.getJointPositionSkeleton( userId, ni_names[i], 
joints[i]);
    }
  }
```

6. You don't want every figure to look exactly the same, so you will have to scale each figure a little. Add the following variables to the class:

```
  float sx = 1;
  float sy = 1;
  float sz = 1;
  color c = 0;
```

7. Now add a function named `randomize()`, which initializes the values for scaling and chooses a color.

```
public void randomize() {
  sx = random( 0.9, 1.1 );
  sy = random( 0.9, 1.1 );
  sz = random( 0.9, 1.1 );

  colorMode( HSB );
  c = color( random( 255 ), 255, 255 );
  colorMode( RGB );
}
```

8. You have initialized your randomization values and updated your coordinates; now you need to draw your stick figure. To simplify the drawing, you need to add a new method called `drawLimb()`, which gets the index of the first and second coordinate for which you want the line to be drawn.

```
public void drawLimb(int idx1, int idx2 ) {
    line( joints[idx1].x, joints[idx1].y, joints[idx1].z,
      joints[idx2].x, joints[idx2].y, joints[idx2].z );
  }
```

9. To implement the actual drawing of the stick figures, you need to create a `draw()` method in your `Figure` class. First, you need to set the drawing color to the random color you generated for your figure in the `randomize()` method, and then set the scaling to your `sx`, `sy`, and `sz` values.

```
public void draw() {
  strokeWeight( 2 );
  stroke( c );
  fill( c );
  pushMatrix();
    scale( sx, sy, sz );
```

10. Now you need to add the code to draw the head and the lines for the body.

```
    pushMatrix();
  translate( joints[HEAD].x, joints[HEAD].y, joints[HEAD].z );
  scale( .5, .5, 1);
  sphere( joints[HEAD].dist( joints[NECK] ));
  popMatrix();
  drawLimb( NECK, HEAD );

  drawLimb( NECK, L_SHOULDER );
```

```
    drawLimb( L_SHOULDER, L_ELBOW );
    drawLimb( L_ELBOW, L_HAND );

    drawLimb( NECK, R_SHOULDER );
    drawLimb( R_SHOULDER, R_ELBOW );
    drawLimb( R_ELBOW, R_HAND );

    drawLimb( NECK, TORSO );
    drawLimb( TORSO, L_HIP );
    drawLimb( TORSO, R_HIP );
    drawLimb( L_HIP, R_HIP );

    drawLimb( L_HIP, L_KNEE );
    drawLimb( L_KNEE, L_FOOT );

    drawLimb( R_HIP, R_KNEE );
    drawLimb( R_KNEE, R_FOOT );
    popMatrix();
  }
```

11. Switch back to the main tab of the sketch and change the figure variable you defined in the last task to a two-dimensional array of `Figure` objects.

    ```
    Figure figures[][] = new Figure[5][4];
    ```

12. Now add the following lines in the `setup()` method to initialize the array. To make every little dancer look a bit different, call the `randomize()` method you added to the `Figure` class:

    ```
    void setup() {
      size( 1024, 768, P3D);
      context = new SimpleOpenNI( this );
      context.enableDepth();

      context.enableUser( SimpleOpenNI.SKEL_PROFILE_ALL);

      smooth();
      lights();

      for ( int i = 0; i<5; i++) {
        for ( int j=0; j<4; j++) {
          figures[i][j] = new Figure();
          figures[i][j].randomize();
        }
      }
    }
    ```

13. In the `drawDancer()` method, you need to call the `update()` function of every figure object that you have created. We need to use the `translate()` function to move each figure to a different position to make sure they aren't drawn on top of each other.

```
void drawDancer() {
  if ( player != -1 && context.isTrackingSkeleton( player )) {
    for ( int j=-2; j< 3; j++ ) {
      for ( int k = 0; k < 4; k++) {
        figures[j+2][k].update( context, player );
        pushMatrix();
        translate( 100*j, 0, -100*k);
        scale( .1 );
        figures[j+2][k].draw();
        popMatrix();
      }
    }
  }
}
```

14. Now start your music, stand in front of the Kinect, and start dancing. Your little stick figures will copy all your awesome dance moves without ever getting tired. You can see my dance company in this screenshot:

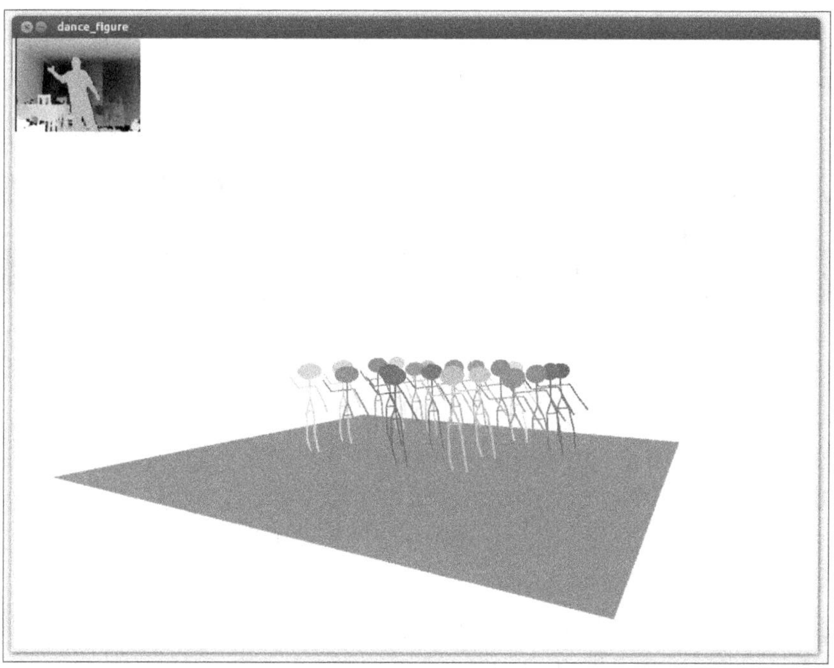

Objective Complete - Mini Debriefing

In this task, we defined a class for our stick figures. We moved the code that accesses the 3D coordinates and the drawing of the dancer to our class to simplify our `drawDancer()` method in the main sketch. The new class also enabled us to draw more than one dancer.

To prevent our dance company from looking like an army of clones, we added the `randomize()` method, which scales the stick figures a bit and chooses a random color for each one.

Mission Accomplished

In this project, we taught Processing how to see by connecting the Kinect and installing the OpenNI framework.

We used the depth image provided by the SimpleOpenNI framework and located the user in the image using the tracking capabilities of OpenNI. For every tracked user, the framework provides us with a bitmap defining which pixels belong to the tracked user and which don't. For the last two tasks, we used the depth image with the colored pixels that we created in the second task as an HUD display to enable the player to see what is currently being tracked.

Starting with our third task, we used the skeleton tracker to access the 3D coordinates of the player's limbs and joints and used the information to draw a stick figure that followed the player's moves.

In our final task, we refactored the drawing code for our stick figure to a class and used this class to draw multiple dancers so that our stick figure had some company while dancing.

You Ready to go Gung HO? A Hotshot Challenge

In this project, we only scratched the surface of the possibilities that Kinect offers. It's impossible to describe all of it in one project; you could write a whole book about it. So try to expand the knowledge you've gained in this project to try one of the following:

- Use the image of the RGB camera to display the player instead of one of the stick figures.
- Use a more complex 3D model rather than a stick figure for your dancers.
- Record the moves of the player and replay them after a short delay.
- Currently, our sketch supports only one player. The OpenNI framework can also track multiple users, so try to add multiplayer support.

Project 3

The Disco Dance Floor

In the previous project, we taught Processing how to see, and even more importantly how to dance. Our stick figure dance company is currently dancing on a very boring gray dance floor. This is going to change soon, because in this project we will create a proper disco dance floor for our dance company.

Illuminated disco dance floors were made popular in the late 70s by the film "Saturday Night Fever" with John Travolta, and we will simulate a dance floor made of 64 glass tiles that are illuminated by lights from below.

Mission Briefing

In this project, we will use Processing to play and analyze music using the Minim framework (developed by *Damien Di Fede*). We will also use it to access the music data in real time and implement some audio visualizations. Minim already comes bundled with Processing, so we don't need to install a library for this mission.

We will create multiple music and timer-controlled visualization patterns and we will make our sketch switch between them as the music plays. Then we will turn them into a disco dance floor by turning the graphics we are creating into a texture for a 3D object. Finally, we will add the texture to the somewhat boring dance floor we created in the previous project for our stick figure dance company.

Why Is It Awesome?

When it comes to music visualizations, Processing is a very smart choice. The Minim library simplifies the required access to things such as beat detection and fast Fourier transformation, and Processing offers access to the most awesome 3D and 2D graphic effects.

The default iTunes music visualizer started out as a Processing script called "Magnetosphere", and was written by the artist *Robert Hodgin*, also known as *Flight404*.

Your Hotshot Objectives

Our project consists of four tasks, namely:

- Can you hear me?
- Blinking to the music
- Making your disco dance floor
- Here come the dancers

Mission Checklist

This mission is about creating awesome visuals for music, so we obviously need some tunes to play and a sound card. These pre-requisites shouldn't be too hard to find. If you want to complete the final task of this mission, you will also need the final sketch from our previous mission and a Kinect, but the first three tasks can be followed independent of our previous mission.

At the time of writing, Processing 2.0 Beta doesn't support the Linux audio framework PulseAudio out of the box. If you are using a Linux distribution that uses PulseAudio, like for example, Ubuntu, you need to add the Java PulseAudio libraries to Processing. You can find detailed instructions on how to install the necessary libraries in the Processing ticketing system at `http://code.google.com/p/processing/issues/detail?id=930`.

Can you hear me?

In the first task for this mission, we will write a Processing sketch that plays an MP3 file and uses the Minim library to access the played samples. We will use this data to write an oscilloscope-like curve. We will then use the `fft` class of Minim to calculate the frequency spectrum of the currently played sound and generate a bar graph to visualize it.

Engage Thrusters

Let's give Processing ears:

1. Create a new Processing sketch and add a `setup()` and a `draw()` method.

   ```
   void setup() {
   }

   void draw() {
   }
   ```

2. Add the `import` statements for the Minim library by navigating to **Sketch** | **Import Library ...** | **minim**.

3. Now we need to add an MP3 file to our sketch by navigating to **Sketch** | **Add File ...** or by simply dropping it onto the sketch window.
4. Add an `AudioPlayer` object to your sketch and initialize it in the `setup()` method.

```
import ddf.minim.spi.*;
import ddf.minim.signals.*;
import ddf.minim.*;
import ddf.minim.analysis.*;
import ddf.minim.ugens.*;
import ddf.minim.effects.*;

Minim minim;
AudioPlayer player;

void setup() {
  size(600, 300 );
  minim = new Minim( this );

  player = minim.loadFile( "loop.mp3", 1024);
}

void draw() {
}
```

If you don't use the MP3 file provided with the example code, be sure to replace `"loop.mp3"` with the filename of the MP3 you want to use.

5. To start our player, we add a `mousePressed()` method that calls the `loop()` method if the player currently isn't running and `pause()` if otherwise.

```
void mousePressed() {
  if (player.isPlaying()) {
    player.pause();
  }   else {
    player.loop();
  }
}
```

6. Now we create an oscilloscope display by adding the following code to our `draw()` method:

```
void draw() {
  background(0);
  stroke(0, 255, 0);

  for ( int i=0; i< player.bufferSize()-1; i++) {
```

```
        float x1 = map( i, 0, player.bufferSize(), 0,
        width );
        float x2 = map( i+1, 0, player.bufferSize(), 0,
        width );
        line( x1, 75 + player.mix.get(i)*75, x2, 75 +
        player.mix.get(i+1)*75 );
    }
}
```

7. So far we have accessed the sample data of our audio data to generate visualizations. Another very useful tool for analyzing and visualizing audio data is the so called fast Fourier transformation—fft for short—which calculates the frequency spectrum of our sound at a given time. We use the `logAverages()` method to reduce the number of frequency bands we get. We add a new variable to our sketch and initialize it in the `setup()` method.

```
Minim minim;
AudioPlayer player;
FFT fft;

void setup() {
  size(600, 300 );
  minim = new Minim( this );

  player = minim.loadFile( "loop.mp3", 1024);

  fft = new FFT( player.bufferSize(), player.sampleRate());
  fft.logAverages(11, 1);
}
```

8. In our `draw()` method, we update the spectrum and iterate over the frequency bands the `fft` object has calculated for us by adding the following code:

```
void draw() {
  background(0);
  stroke(0, 255, 0);

  for ( int i=0; i< player.bufferSize()-1; i++) {
    float x1 = map( i, 0, player.bufferSize(), 0,
    width );
    float x2 = map( i+1, 0, player.bufferSize(), 0,
    width );
    line( x1, 75 + player.mix.get(i)*75, x2, 75 +
    player.mix.get(i+1)*75 );
  }
```

```
    noStroke();
    fill(255, 255, 0);
    fft.forward( player.mix );
    float step = width/8;
    for ( int i =0; i < 8; i++) {
      float value = fft.getAvg(i) * 3;
      rect( step * i, height - value, step, value );
    }
}
```

9. Now run the sketch and click inside the sketch window to start the music. The visualizers should look like in the following screenshot:

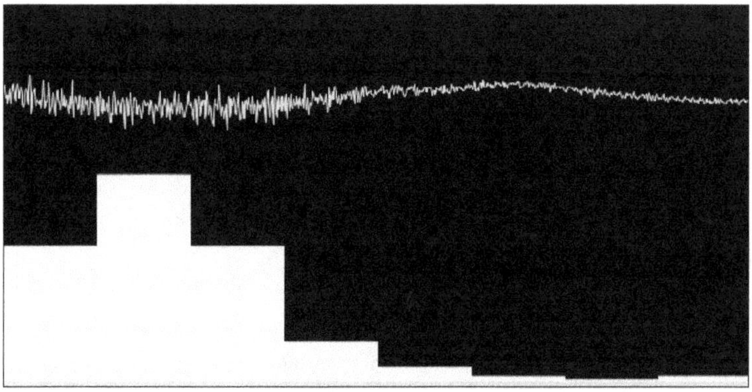

Objective Complete - Mini Debriefing

In this task, we have imported the Minim library into our sketch and added an MP3 loop. We used the sound player object to access and manage the starting and stopping of the music and used the mixer to access the samples and visualized them as an oscilloscope-like line.

In step 7, we added an `fft` object to get access to the frequency spectrum of the sample that's currently playing. In this sketch, we used the frequency data to generate a bar graph of the frequency spectrum. The number of frequency bands we can access using the `fft` object depends on the buffer size of our `AudioPlayer`. If you increase the buffer, you get a higher accuracy in the frequency domain, but you also need more samples to calculate the buffer, so your visualization will be less responsive. You also need more CPU power to calculate the spectrum if you increase the number of frequency bands. We need only eight bands for the visualizers we are creating in the next task, so we told Minim to calculate the average over several frequency bands.

Classified Intel

Minim is a very flexible and modular sound library. The methods we used to analyze the samples or frequencies of the sound are independent from the sound player. If you want to visualize the sound that's recorded via your sound card's line in a microphone, you can replace the `AudioPlayer` object with an input line like this:

```
AudioInput in;
in = minim.getLineIn();
```

Blinking to the music

The second task of our current mission is to create visualizers that generate an array of 8 x 8 tiles based on a timer or on the audio information we get from Minim. The array of tiles will be used by our `draw()` method to generate a top view of the dance floor.

To switch between the different visualizers, we are going to write a thread that runs in the background and chooses a new visualizer every *n* seconds.

Engage Thrusters

Let's blink to the music:

1. Let's start with a new sketch and import the Minim library. In our `setup()` method, we define a Minim context and an `AudioPlayer` object like we did in the previous task. This time, we start the looping of the player directly in the `setup()` method, so the loop starts as soon as the sketch is run.

```
import ddf.minim.spi.*;
import ddf.minim.signals.*;
import ddf.minim.*;
import ddf.minim.analysis.*;
import ddf.minim.ugens.*;
import ddf.minim.effects.*;

Minim minim;
AudioPlayer player;

void setup() {
  size(300,300);

  minim = new Minim( this );
  player = minim.loadFile( "loop.mp3", 1024);
  player.loop();
}
```

2. We add a new tab and name it `Visualizer`. An **interface** is like a class definition without the method implementation. This interface defines the method that all our visualizer classes have to implement.

```
interface Visualizer {
  public int[][] tiles = new int[8][8];
  public void init();
  public void tick();
  public void setActive( boolean active );
}
```

3. The first visualizer we are going to implement switches on and off after every second tile of our 8 x 8 tiles grid every time the `tick()` method gets called. Add a new tab, name it `Alternate`, and add the following code:

```
public class Alternate implements Visualizer {
  int p = 1;
  int count = 0;

  public Alternate() {
    init();
  }

  public void tick() {
    count ++;
    if ( count < 4 ) return;

    count =0;
    if ( p == 1 ) { p = 0; } else { p = 1; }
    for ( int x = 0; x < 8; x++ ) {
      for ( int y = 0; y< 8; y++) {
        tiles[x][y] = 255 * ( (x+y+p) % 2 );
      }
    }
  }

  public void init() {
    for ( int x = 0; x < 8; x++ ) {
      for ( int y = 0; y< 8; y++) {
        tiles[x][y] = 0;
      }
    }
  }

  public void setActive( boolean active ) {
  }
}
```

4. Now switch back to the main sketch tab and add a variable for the current visualizer, and then initialize it in our `setup()` method.

```
Visualizer viz;
Minim minim;
AudioPlayer player;

void setup() {
  size(300,300);

  minim = new Minim( this );
  player = minim.loadFile( "loop.mp3", 1024);

  viz = new Alternate();
  viz.setActive( true );

  player.loop();
}
```

5. To get the tick method called every 125 milliseconds, we need to add a timer. Add the following thread to the `setup()` method:

```
Visualizer viz;
Minim minim;
AudioPlayer player;

void setup() {
  size(300,300);

  minim = new Minim( this );
  player = minim.loadFile( "loop.mp3", 1024);

  viz = new Alternate();
  viz.setActive( true );
  Thread t = new Thread() {
    public void run() {
      for(;;) {
        viz.tick();
        delay(125);
      }
    }
  };
  t.start();

  player.loop();
}
```

6. Our visualizer is initialized and changes the tile pattern every *n* milliseconds, but the tiles have not been drawn yet. We change this by adding the following code to our `draw()` method:

```
void draw() {
  background(0);
  float w= 300/8;
  for( int x = 0; x < 8; x++ ){
    for( int y = 0; y< 8; y++) {
      stroke( 255 );
      fill( viz.tiles[x][y],0,0 );
      if ( viz.tiles[x][y] > 32 ) {
        viz.tiles[x][y] -= (viz.tiles[x][y]-32)/25;
      }
      rect( w * x, w*y, w, w );
    }
  }

}
```

The following screenshot shows what the pattern looks like:

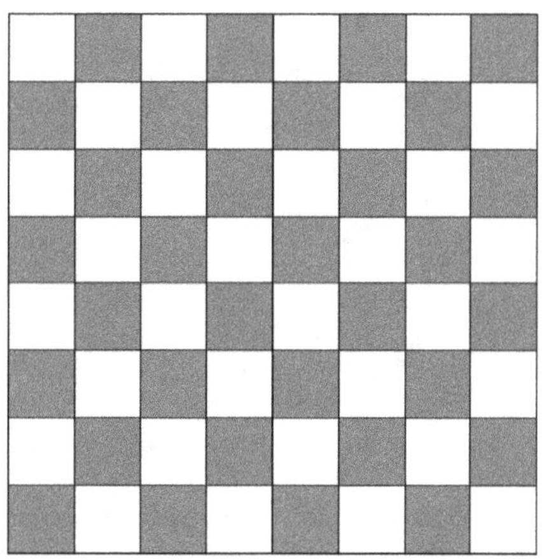

7. If we start our sketch now, the tiles blink like mad, but to be honest, it gets a bit boring after a while. So let's add another tab and implement a new visualizer. We name the class `BarHorizontal` and add the following code:

```
public class BarHorizontal implements Visualizer {
  int px = 0;
  int count = 0;

  public BarHorizontal() {
```

```
    init();
  }

  public void tick() {
    count++;
    if (count < 4) return;

    count = 0;
    for ( int i=0; i<8; i++) {
      tiles[min(7, px)][i] = 255;
    }

    if ( px >=  8 && tiles[7][7] != 0) {
      init();
    } else {
      px += 1;
    }
  }


  public void init() {
    px = 0;
    for ( int x = 0; x < 8; x++ ) {
      for ( int y = 0; y< 8; y++) {
        tiles[x][y] = 0;
      }
    }
  }

  public void setActive( boolean active ) {
  }
}
```

8. Switch back to the main tab and add an array for our visualizer classes. We also add a new timer similar to the first one, but this time we will make the delay longer, and instead of calling the `tick()` method we select a new visualizer from our array.

```
Visualizer viz;
Visualizer[] visualizers;

Minim minim;
AudioPlayer player;
```

```
void setup() {
  size(300,300);

  minim = new Minim( this );
  player = minim.loadFile( "loop.mp3", 1024);

  visualizers = new Visualizer[] {
    new BarHorizontal(),
    new Alternate()
  };

  viz = visualizers[0];
  viz.setActive( true );
  Thread t = new Thread() {
    public void run() {
      for(;;) {
        viz.tick();
        delay(125);
      }
    }
  };
  t.start();


  Thread t2 = new Thread() {
    public void run() {
      for(;;) {
        viz.setActive( false );
        viz = visualizers[ int(random
        ( visualizers.length))];
        viz.init();
        viz.setActive( true );
        delay(8000);
      }
    }
  };
  t2.start();
  player.loop();
}
```

The following screenshot shows what the `BarHorizontal` visualizer looks like:

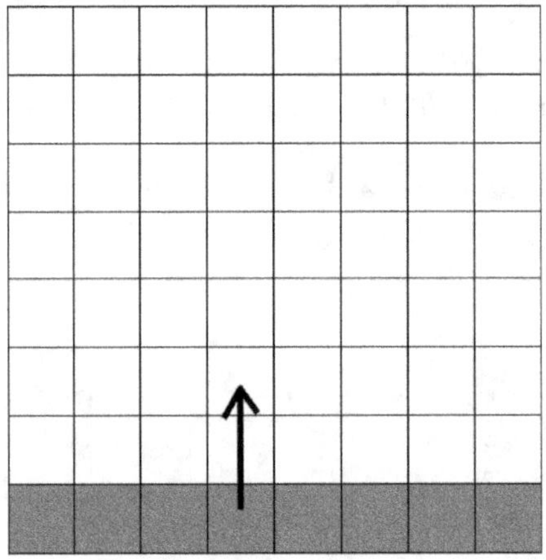

9. Now we are going to add a new visualizer that lights the panels in a spiral. We create a new tab, name it `SpiralIn`, and add the following code:

```
public class SpiralIn implements Visualizer {
  PVector p = new PVector(0,0);
  PVector d = new PVector(1,0);

  public SpiralIn() {
    init();
  }

  public void tick() {
    tiles[int(p.x)][int(p.y)] = 255;
    if ( d.x == 1 && ( p.x == 7 ||
      tiles[int(p.x+1)][int(p.y)] != 0)) {
      d = new PVector( 0, 1);
    } else if ( d.x == -1 && ( p.x == 0 ||
                  tiles[int(p.x-1)][int(p.y)] != 0 )) {
      d = new PVector( 0, -1 );
    } else if (  d.y == 1 && ( p.y == 7 ||
                  tiles[int(p.x)][int(p.y+1)] != 0 )) {
      d = new PVector( -1, 0 );
    } else if (d.y == -1 && ( p.y == 0 ||
                  tiles[int(p.x)][int(p.y-1)] != 0 )) {
      d = new PVector( 1, 0 );
    }
```

```
    if ( p.x == 3 && p.y == 3 && tiles[3][4] != 0 ) {
      init();
    } else {
      p.add( d );
    }
  }

  public void init() {
    p = new PVector( 0, 0 );
    d = new PVector( 1, 0 );
    for ( int x = 0; x < 8; x++ ) {
      for ( int y = 0; y< 8; y++) {
        tiles[x][y] = 0;
      }
    }
  }

  public void setActive( boolean active ) {
  }
}
```

10. To make the new visualizer available in our sketch, we switch to the main sketch and add the `SpiralIn()` class to the `visualizers` array:

```
visualizers = new Visualizer[] {
  new SpiralIn(),
  new BarHorizontal(),
  new Alternate(),
}
```

The pattern the `SpiralIn` visualizers generate is shown in the following screenshot:

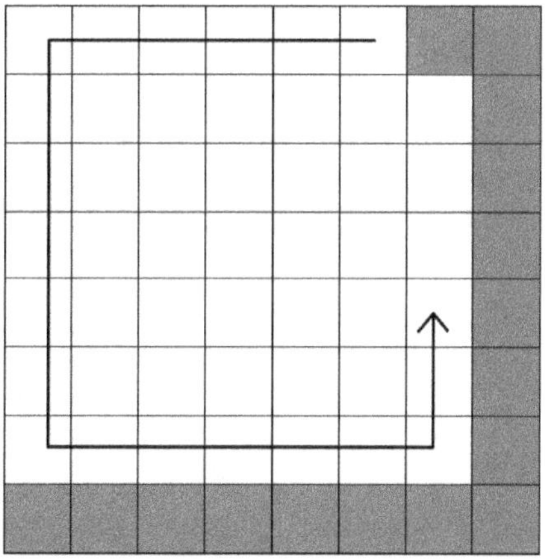

11. Now we add a visualizer that isn't controlled by our `tick()` method, but instead by the samples from the `AudioPlayer` object. Our class implements the `Visualizer` interface and additionally the `AudioListener` interface from Minim. The `tick()` method stays empty in this visualizer because we calculate our tiles in the `samples()` method. We add a new tab, name it `BeatVisualizer`, and add the following code:

```
public class BeatVisualizer implements Visualizer,
AudioListener {
  boolean active = false;
  public BeatVisualizer() {
    init();
  }

  public void tick() {
  }

  public void init() {
    for ( int x = 0; x < 8; x++ ) {
      for ( int y = 0; y< 8; y++) {
        tiles[x][y] = 0;
      }
    }
  }

  void samples(float[] samp) {
    samples( samp, samp );
  }

  void samples(float[] sampL, float[] sampR) {
    if ( active ) {
      for ( int x = 0; x < 8; x++ ) {
        float val = 0;
        for ( int i =0; i<5; i++) {
          val = sampL[x*5+i] * 8;
        }

        for ( int y = -4; y< 4; y++) {
          if (val > y && val < y+1) {
            tiles[x][4+y] = 255;
          }
          else {
            tiles[x][4+y] -= tiles[x][4+y]/4;
          }
        }
      }
```

```
    }
  }

  public void setActive( boolean active ) {
    this.active = active;
  }
}
```

12. Switch back to the main tab and add the `BeatVisualizer` class to the `visualizers` array. This time, we also need to register the visualizer as a callback function to the `AudioPlayer` object.

```
void setup() {
  size(300,300);

  minim = new Minim( this );
  player = minim.loadFile( "loop.mp3", 1024);

  BeatVisualizer bv = new BeatVisualizer();
  player.addListener( bv );

  visualizers = new Visualizer[] {
    new SpiralIn(),
    new BarHorizontal(),
    new Alternate(),
    bv
  };
```

The following screenshot shows the pattern that our `BeatVisualizer` class generates:

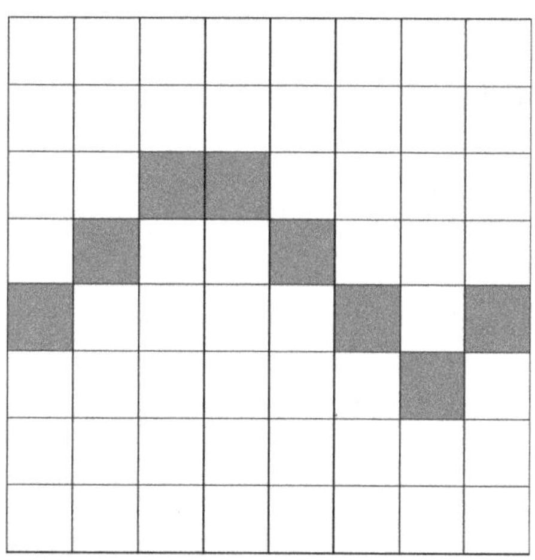

13. The final visualizer we are going to add uses the `fft` object to draw an 8-band frequency spectrum on our tiles. Add a new tab, name it `FFTVisualizer`, and add the following code:

```
public class FFTVisualizer implements Visualizer,
AudioListener {
  boolean active = false;
  FFT fft;
  public FFTVisualizer( AudioPlayer player ) {
    init();
    fft = new FFT( player.bufferSize(),
    player.sampleRate());
    fft.logAverages(11, 1);
  }

  public void tick() {
  }

  public void init() {
    for ( int x = 0; x < 8; x++ ) {
      for ( int y = 0; y< 8; y++) {
        tiles[x][y] = 0;
      }
    }
  }

  void   samples(float[] samp) {
    samples( samp, samp );
  }

  void samples(float[] sampL, float[] sampR) {
    if ( active ) {
      fft.forward( sampL );

      for ( int x = 0; x < 8; x++ ) {
        float val = fft.getAvg(x)/20;
        for ( int y = 0; y< 8; y++) {
          if (val > y) {
            tiles[x][7-y] = 255;
          } else {
            tiles[x][7-y] -= tiles[x][7-y]/4;
          }
        }
      }
    }
```

```
  }

  public void setActive( boolean active ) {
    this.active = active;
  }
}
```

14. Now add the new visualizer to the `visualizers` array in the main tab and register it as a callback.

```
void setup() {
  size(300,300);

  minim = new Minim( this );
  player = minim.loadFile( "loop.mp3", 1024);

  BeatVisualizer bv = new BeatVisualizer();
  player.addListener( bv );

  FFTVisualizer fv = new FFTVisualizer( player );
  player.addListener( fv );

  visualizers = new Visualizer[] {
    new SpiralIn(),
    new BarHorizontal(),
    new Alternate(),
    bv,
    fv
  };
```

The following screenshot shows the pattern that the `FFTVisualizer` class generates:

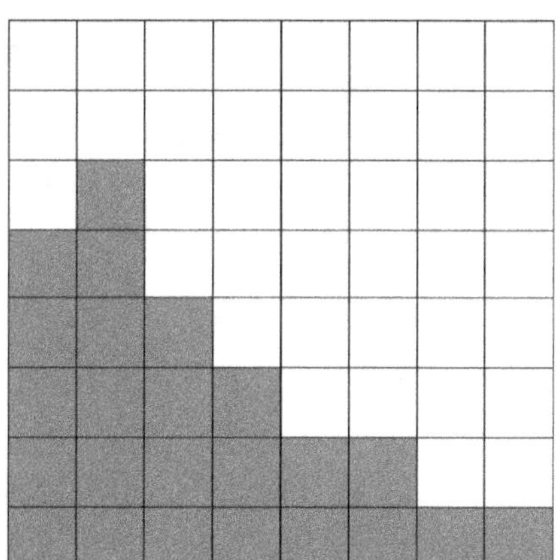

Objective Complete - Mini Debriefing

In this task, we created three time-based visualizers and two sound reactive ones that control an 8 x 8 tile pattern for our dance floor. We created two timer threads, one thread that calls the `tick()` method of our visualizers every 125 milliseconds, and one that changes the active visualizer.

The time-based visualizers we created are driven by the `tick()` method, which is where we update the tile pattern. These visualizers are added to an array of available visualizers from which our second thread chooses a new one by random.

The `BeatVisualizer` and `FFTVisualizer` classes don't use the `tick()` method at all. They change the visualized pattern in the `samples` method. We registered these two visualizers as listeners to our `AudioPlayer` object, which then calls the `samples()` method every time the player loads a new buffer.

The tile pattern we create in the visualizers is used by our `draw()` method. We also implemented a little afterglow effect for the tiles by reducing the color intensity in every frame after a tile has been lit instead of simply turning it off.

Making your disco dance floor

In this task, we will use the sketch we generated in the previous task and turn it into a texture for a 3D object. We will create a rectangle using the Processing shapes and texture it with our visualizer.

We will also implement the `playlist` functionality for our MP3 files and define a file format that allows us to control the sequence of the music and the visualizers.

Prepare for Lift Off

In this task, we are going to create a text file that controls our playlist and the sequence in which the visualizers are shown. Each playlist entry has two lines. The first line contains only the filename of the MP3 file and the second line contains the visualizer IDs and their length in seconds. The entries are separated using a "-". The following is an example of a playlist text file:

```
song1.mp3
0:4-1:2-3:2
song2.mp3
0:1-1:1:0:1-2:1
```

In this case, the `song2.mp3` file is played and the visualizers with IDs `0`, `1`, `0`, and `2` are shown for one second.

So, add some MP3 files to the data folder and create a playlist file for your songs. Add the visualizer sequences you like in the format described previously and put the playlist file in to the data folder by dropping it on the sketch window or by navigating to **Sketch** | **Add File...**.

Engage Thrusters

Let's create our dance floor:

1. To implement the playlist functionality, we are going to add a new class named `PlaylistItem`. Let's add a new tab to define our class.

   ```
   public class PlaylistItem {
   }
   ```

2. A `PlaylistItem` class needs to hold the song name, an array of visualizer IDs, and an array defining how long we want each visualizer to be shown. We also implement a variable named `current` and a `next()` method, which allows us to switch to the next visualizer.

   ```
     String songname;
     int[] visualizers;
     int[] delays;
     int current;
     public PlaylistItem( String songname, int[]
     visualizers, int[] delays ) {
       this.songname = songname;
       this.current = 0;
       this.visualizers = visualizers;
       this.delays = delays;
     }

     public void next() {
       current += 1;
       if ( current >= visualizers.length ) { current = 0; }
     }

     public int getVisualizer() {
       return visualizers[current];
     }

     public int getDelay() {
       return delays[current];
     }
   ```

3. To use our playlist, we need to make some changes to our setup method. We add a variable pointing to the current song and use the `songname` attribute from the `PlaylistItem` array to load the song for our player.

```
Visualizer viz;
Visualizer[] visualizers;
PlaylistItem[] playlist;
int currentSong = 0;
Minim minim;
AudioPlayer player;

void setup() {
  size(640,480, P3D);

  minim = new Minim( this );

  playlist = loadPlaylist( "playlist.txt" );
  player = minim.loadFile( playlist[currentSong].songname,
  1024);

  BeatVisualizer bv = new BeatVisualizer();
  player.addListener( bv );
  ...
```

4. We need to implement the `loadPlaylist()` function, which parses our playlist text file and generates an array of `PlaylistItem`. Add the following method to your sketch:

```
PlaylistItem[] loadPlaylist( String name ) {
  String[] str = loadStrings( name );

  PlaylistItem[] playlist = new PlaylistItem
  [ int( str.length / 2 ) ];

  for( int i =0; i < str.length; i+= 2 ) {
    String songname = str[i];
    String[] raw = str[i+1].split("-");

    int[] v = new int[raw.length];
    int[] d = new int[raw.length];

    for( int j =0; j<raw.length; j++) {
      String[] visdel = raw[j].split(":");
      v[j] = int(visdel[0]);
      d[j] = int(visdel[1]);
```

```
      }

      playlist[ i/2 ] = new PlaylistItem( songname, v, d );
    }
    return playlist;
  }
```

5. Now we need to change the thread that controls the switching of the visualizations and change the player start command from `loop()` to `play()`, since we don't want to loop the first song, but rather play through our whole playlist.

```
    Thread t2 = new Thread() {
      public void run() {
        for(;;) {
          viz.setActive( false );
          viz = visualizers
          [ playlist[currentSong].getVisualizer() ];
          viz.init();
          viz.setActive( true );

          int rest = player.length() - player.position();
          if ( rest > playlist[currentSong].getDelay() * 1000
          ) {
            delay( playlist[currentSong].getDelay() * 1000 );
          } else {
            delay( rest );
          }
          playlist[currentSong].next();
        }
      }
    };
    t2.start();
    player.play();
  }
```

6. If you run your sketch now, the first song starts playing and the visualizers change to the pattern we defined, but after the first song, the music simply stops. So we need a method to check if a song has completed and then start the next one. Add the following method to our sketch:

```
  void checkSongEnd() {
    if (player.position() == player.length()) {
      currentSong += 1;
      if (currentSong >= playlist.length)
      { currentSong = 0; }
```

```
        player = minim.loadFile
        ( playlist[currentSong].songname, 1024);
        player.play();
      }
    }
```

7. The method we just created gets called by the `draw()` method. Add the following line to make our sketch check for the end of the song at every frame:

```
void draw() {
  background(0);
  float w= 300/8;
  for( int x = 0; x < 8; x++ ){
    for( int y = 0; y< 8; y++) {
      stroke( 255 );
      fill( viz.tiles[x][y],0,0 );
      if ( viz.tiles[x][y] > 32 )
      { viz.tiles[x][y] -= ( viz.tiles[x][y] -32)/25; }
      rect( w * x, w*y, w, w );
    }
  }

  checkSongEnd();
}
```

8. The next thing we are going to do is change the graphics we are generating in our `draw()` method to a texture for a 3D object. To have a little more space, and to enable a 3D mode in Processing, we change the size of our sketch in the `setup()` method.

```
void setup() {
  size(640,480, P3D);
  ...
```

9. Now we are going to create a `PGraphics` object, and instead of calling the drawing commands from the main window, we use the one the new graphics object provides. The graphics object we just created contains the current frame of our visualizer in a buffer, which we can use as a texture. So, we are now going to add a 3D square and texture it.

```
void draw() {
  PGraphics g = createGraphics( 320, 320 );
  g.beginDraw();
  g.background(0);
  float w= 320/8;
  for( int x = 0; x < 8; x++ ){
```

```
    for( int y = 0; y< 8; y++) {
      g.stroke( 255 );
      g.fill( viz.tiles[x][y],0,0 );
      if ( viz.tiles[x][y] > 32 )
      { viz.tiles[x][y] -= ( viz.tiles[x][y] -32)/25; }
      g.rect( w * x, w*y, w, w );
    }
  }
  g.endDraw();

  background(0);

  translate( width/2, height/2 );
  rotateY( frameCount / 300.0 );
  beginShape(QUADS);
  texture( g );
  vertex( -200, 100, -200, 0,   0 );
  vertex( -200, 100,  200, 0, 320 );
  vertex(  200, 100,  200, 320, 320 );
  vertex(  200, 100, -200, 320, 0 );
  endShape();

  checkSongEnd();
}
```

Objective Complete - Mini Debriefing

In this task, we turned our visualizer from the previous task into a texture for a 3D shape. In our case, we used a simple plane that will act as a dance floor in our final task.

We also implemented a playlist for our disco. The song that's currently playing is controlled by a text file, and we select the next song from the list in the `checkSongEnd()` method. This method checks if the current song is completed, and if so, it advances to the next `PlaylistItem`.

The playlist text file doesn't only contain the list of songs we want to play, but it also allows us to control the sequence and the timing of our visualizers. Each playlist item holds two arrays of integers named `id` and `delay`. The first one stores the sequence of the visualizers and the second one stores how long we have to wait before switching to the next visualizer in our timing thread in step 6.

Here come the dancers

The final task for our mission is to add the disco dance floor we just created to the sketch from *Project 2, The Stick Figure Dance Company*. We will replace the boring gray dance floor our dancers are currently using with the awesome visualizers we have created in this mission.

We are going to use the `metaData` object we can get from a Minim player to display the title of the currently played MP3 file.

Engage Thrusters

Let's add our dancers:

1. The first thing we need to do for this task is copy all the visualizer classes from the previous sketch to the stick figure dance company sketch from our previous project. So, we open both the "visualizers" sketch from the previous task and the final sketch from the previous project.
2. We save the stick figure dance company sketch under a different name by navigating to **File | Save As**.
3. Now we switch to the "visualizer" sketch and open the sketch folder by navigating to **Sketch | Show Sketch Folder**.
4. Select all the files in this folder except for the `visualizers.pde` file, and drag them on to the sketch window of the dance figure sketch. Processing adds a new tab for every file you drop.
5. Copy the `loadPlaylist()` function to the dance figure sketch.

```
PlaylistItem[] loadPlaylist( String name ) {
  String[] str = loadStrings( name );

  PlaylistItem[] playlist = new PlaylistItem
  [ int( str.length / 2 ) ];

  for( int i =0; i < str.length; i+= 2 ) {
    String songname = str[i];
    String[] raw = str[i+1].split("-");

    int[] v = new int[raw.length];
    int[] d = new int[raw.length];

    for( int j =0; j<raw.length; j++) {
      String[] visdel = raw[j].split(":");
      v[j] = int(visdel[0]);
```

```
      d[j] = int(visdel[1]);
    }

    playlist[ i/2 ] = new PlaylistItem( songname, v, d );
  }
  return playlist;
}
```

6. Copy the following changes to our `setup()` method to initialize the playlist and the threads for changing the visualizers. We also have to rename the `AudioPlayer` variable to `aplayer`, since `player` has already been used in the stick figure dance company sketch:

```
SimpleOpenNI context;
int player = -1;
boolean calibrated = false;

Figure figures[][] = new Figure[5][4];

Visualizer viz;
Visualizer[] visualizers;
PlaylistItem[] playlist;
int currentSong = 0;
Minim minim;
AudioPlayer aplayer;

void setup() {
  size( 1024, 768, P3D);
  context = new SimpleOpenNI( this );
  context.enableDepth();
  context.setMirror( true );

  context.enableUser( SimpleOpenNI.SKEL_PROFILE_ALL);

  smooth();
  lights();

  for ( int i = 0; i<5; i++) {
    for ( int j=0; j<4; j++) {
      figures[i][j] = new Figure();
      figures[i][j].randomize();
    }
  }
```

```
minim = new Minim( this );

playlist = loadPlaylist( "playlist.txt" );
aplayer = minim.loadFile( playlist
[currentSong].songname, 1024);

BeatVisualizer bv = new BeatVisualizer();
aplayer.addListener( bv );

FFTVisualizer fv = new FFTVisualizer( aplayer );
aplayer.addListener( fv );

visualizers = new Visualizer[] {
  new SpiralIn(),
  new BarHorizontal(),
  new Alternate(),
  bv,
  fv
};

viz = bv;
viz.setActive( true );
Thread t = new Thread() {
  public void run() {
    for(;;) {
      viz.tick();
      delay(125);
    }
  }
};
t.start();

Thread t2 = new Thread() {
  public void run() {
    for(;;) {
      viz.setActive( false );
      viz = visualizers
      [ playlist[currentSong].getVisualizer() ];
      viz.init();
      viz.setActive( true );

      int rest = aplayer.length() - aplayer.position();
      if ( rest > playlist[currentSong].getDelay() *
      1000 ) {
```

```
            delay( playlist[currentSong].getDelay() * 1000 );
          } else {
            delay( rest );
          }
          playlist[currentSong].next();
        }
      }
    };
    t2.start();
    aplayer.play();

}
```

7. We now add our drawing code for the visualizers to the `drawFloor()` method so that we can use them as a texture on the floor square.

```
void drawFloor() {
  PGraphics g = createGraphics( 320, 320 );
  g.beginDraw();
  g.background(0);
  float w= 320/8;
  for( int x = 0; x < 8; x++ ){
    for( int y = 0; y< 8; y++) {
      g.stroke( 255 );
      g.fill( viz.tiles[x][y],0,0 );
      if ( viz.tiles[x][y] > 32 )
      { viz.tiles[x][y] -= ( viz.tiles[x][y] -32)/25; }
      g.rect( w * x, w*y, w, w );
    }
  }
  g.endDraw();


  noStroke();
  fill( 128 );

  beginShape(QUADS);
  texture( g );
  vertex( -400, -100, -400, 0, 0 );
  vertex( -400, -100, 400, 0, 320 );
  vertex( 400, -100, 400, 320, 320 );
  vertex( 400, -100, -400, 320, 0 );
  endShape();
}
```

8. Now we need to copy the `checkSongEnd()` method to check if the current song is completed.

```
void checkSongEnd() {
  if (aplayer.position() == aplayer.length()) {
    currentSong += 1;
    if (currentSong >= playlist.length) { currentSong = 0; }

    aplayer = minim.loadFile( playlist[currentSong].songname,
1024);

    aplayer.play();
  }
}
```

9. To make sure our `checkSongEnd()` method gets called after every frame, we add it to the `draw()` method.

```
void draw() {
  background( 255 );
  checkSongEnd();

  context.update();
  ...
```

10. The final item on our list for this task is to display the title and the artist of the currently played song. Fortunately, Minim provides a `MetaData` class that can extract this data from the `AudioPlayer` object. Define a variable named `meta` in our main sketch right above the `setup()` method.

```
AudioMetaData meta;
```

11. Add the following line to the `setup()` method:

```
  ...
  playlist = loadPlaylist( "playlist.txt" );
  aplayer = minim.loadFile
  ( playlist[currentSong].songname, 1024);
  meta = aplayer.getMetaData();
  textFont(createFont("Serif", 12));
  ...
```

12. Then we need to update the metadata in the `checkSongEnd()` method as well, as we need to update the `metaData` object when the current song is completed so we can start the next one.

```
void checkSongEnd() {
  if (aplayer.position() == aplayer.length()) {
    currentSong += 1;
```

```
      if (currentSong >= playlist.length)
      { currentSong = 0; }

      aplayer = minim.loadFile
      ( playlist[currentSong].songname, 1024);
      meta = aplayer.getMetaData();
      aplayer.play();
    }
  }
```

13. Add a `drawMeta()` method that uses the Minim `MetaData` object to get the title and artist of the song and uses the `text()` function to show them.

```
void drawMeta() {
  textAlign( RIGHT );
  fill(0);
  text( "Title: "+meta.title(), 1000, 40 );
  text( "Author: "+meta.author(), 1000, 65 );
}
```

14. Now we call our `drawMeta()` method from the `draw()` method.

```
void draw() {
  background( 255 );
  checkSongEnd();
  context.update();

  drawHUD();
  drawMeta();
  translate( width/2, height/2, 0 );
  ...
```

15. Add some MP3 files to our sketch and adjust the playlist text file. Run your sketch and start dancing.

Objective Complete - Mini Debriefing

In this task, we added the visualizers from our last task to the stick figure dance company sketch. We used the texture in the `drawFloor()` method to replace the gray colored square with our visualizers. We also added the playlist functionality and the visualizer sequencing to complete our disco.

In step 8, we added a new function to draw the song title and artist. This data is gathered using the Minim `metaData` object.

Mission Accomplished

In this project, we learned how to use the Minim framework to play MP3 files and how to access the sample data. We used the samples to generate a visualizer for the currently played sound. We used the `fft` class of the Minim framework to generate an equalizer visualizer.

In our second task, we wrote five classes that change a pattern consisting of an 8 x 8 grid of tiles. We used a timer thread that triggers the changes in three of the classes. We also added a visualizer that uses the sample data and the `fft` class to generate the pattern.

In the third task, we changed the `draw()` method and used the visuals we generated in the second task as a texture. We also added a playlist functionality. The playlist controls the sequence of played songs and also the sequence of our visualizers and how long they are shown.

In the final task of our mission, we merged our visualizer texture and the `playlist` classes to the stick figure dance company from *Project 2, The Stick Figure Dance Company*. We also added a new function to our `draw()` method to display the song title and the artist that we retrieved from the MP3 metadata.

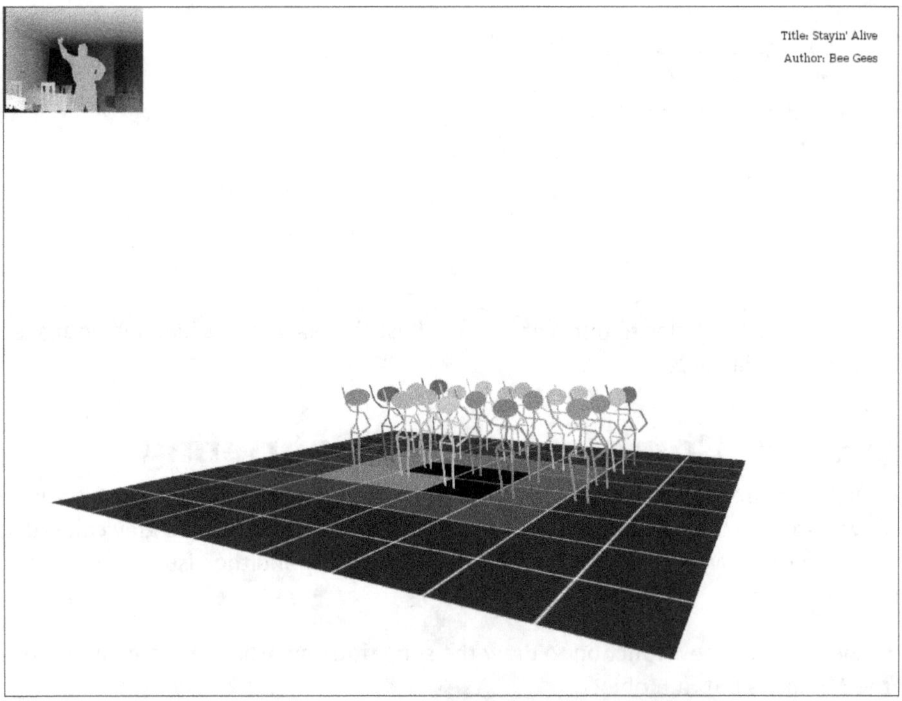

You Ready to go Gung HO? A Hotshot Challenge

In this mission, we created some very cool sound visualizations and we replaced the boring gray dance floor from the last mission with an awesome blinking disco dance floor. But even a very awesome disco dance floor can be made better! Why don't you try to take it to the next level by implementing one of the following ideas:

- Add some light-effects, a disco ball, or a stroboscope
- Add some firework effects using particles
- Change the red tiles to color-changing ones
- Connect some DMX-controlled lights and make the virtual dance floor control your real one too
- Add cross-fading to the playlist

Project 4

Smilie-O-Mat

When we communicate over a text-based medium like SMS, Twitter, or chat, it's somewhat hard to convey how we are currently feeling. It would be much easier and accurate to use pictures instead of a 140-character description. Humans have a lifelong training in reading emotions on faces, so our next mission is to create a Smilie-O-Mat. This little program allows us to adjust certain facial parameters of a smiley and then post the image on Twitter.

Mission Briefing

Our mission is to create the Smilie-O-Mat; a program that allows the user to create a smiley face that reflects his or her emotional state and posts it on Twitter. We will make three parameters adjustable: the angle of the eyebrows, the color of the face, and the position of the mouth (which is changeable, from frowning to smiling and vice-versa).

To post the image on Twitter, we are going to use a Java library named Twitter4J; we will also learn how to authorize a Processing sketch to change the status of a Twitter user using the OAuth authentication framework.

Why Is It Awesome?

You're feeling greenish-yellow today, with a little smile and neutral eyebrows. Don't know how to express that in 140 characters? No problem; adjust the face of the Smilie-O-Mat and tweet it. Life can be so easy when you have the right tools.

Besides that, accessing the Twitter data stream and then posting to it is a very rich data source for visualization projects or interactive Processing sketches.

Your Hotshot Objectives

To complete this mission, we have to accomplish four tasks. They are:

- Drawing your face
- Let me change it
- Hello Twitter
- Tweet your mood

Mission Checklist

For this mission, we don't need any additional hardware; however, in tasks 3 and 4, we are going to post status updates to Twitter, so you will need a working Internet connection and a Twitter account to finish these two tasks.

Drawing your face

The first task of our current mission is to draw a face using Processing. We will use drawing primitives such as ellipses and curves and learn how to change the fill and stroke styles. We want to make three parameters changeable in the next task, so we define variables for these parameters and use their values for drawing our face.

Engage Thrusters

Let's draw a face:

1. Open a new sketch and add a `setup()` and a `draw()` method:

```
void setup() {
}

void draw() {
}
```

2. In the `setup()` method, we set the window size to 300 x 300 pixels and turn on line smoothing. We also change the color mode to HSB (which stands for Hue, Saturation, and Brightness) instead of RGB to make changing the color of the face easier.

```
void setup() {
  size(300,300);
  smooth();
  colorMode(HSB);
}
```

3. The first thing we are going to draw is a colored circle. To make the color changeable, we will add an integer variable named `col` to our sketch, just above the `setup()` method.

```
int col = 150;

void setup() {
```

4. Our control variable `col` will store values ranging from `0` to `1023` to control the hue value of our smiley. The `color()` command expects a value between `0` and `255`, so we need to remap the value using the map command.

```
void draw() {
  background(255);
  strokeWeight(3);

  color c = color(map(col, 0, 1024, 0, 255), 255, 255 );
  fill(c);
  ellipse(150,150,250,250);
}
```

5. To create our eyes, we will add two white circles and two smaller black ones for the pupils.

```
void draw() {
  background(255);
  strokeWeight(3);

  color c = color(map(col, 0, 1024, 0, 255), 255, 255 );
  fill(c);
  ellipse(150,150,250,250);

  fill(255);
  ellipse( 120, 140, 60, 60);
  ellipse( 180, 140, 60, 60);
  fill(0);
  ellipse( 125, 150, 20, 20);
  ellipse( 175, 150, 20, 20);
}
```

6. To make the eyes more expressive, we are going to add eyebrows. Add a new variable to control the angle of the eyebrows.

```
int eye = 512;
int col = 150;

void setup() {
```

7. Now, for the eyebrows, add two lines to the code for your face by adding the following code to the `draw()` method:

```
void draw() {
  background(255);
  strokeWeight(3);

  color c = color(map(col, 0, 1024, 0, 255), 255, 255 );
  fill(c);
  ellipse(150,150,250,250);

  fill(255);
  ellipse( 120, 140, 60, 60);
  ellipse( 180, 140, 60, 60);
  fill(0);
  ellipse( 125, 150, 20, 20);
  ellipse( 175, 150, 20, 20);

  line( 100, 100 + map( eye, 0, 1024, -10, 10),
      140, 100 - map( eye, 0, 1024, -10, 10) );
  line( 160, 100 - map( eye, 0, 1024, -10, 10),
      200, 100 + map( eye, 0, 1024, -10, 10) );
}
```

8. We will add a third control variable to change the mouth from smiling to frowning.

```
int mouth = 1024;
int eye = 512;
int col = 150;

void setup() {
```

9. To draw the mouth, we are going to use a curve shape. The curve definition starts with the `beginShape()` method and ends with the `endShape()` method. Between these commands, we will define the control points of the curve using the `curveVertex()` command.

```
void draw() {
  background(255);
  strokeWeight(3);

  color c = color(map(col, 0, 1024, 0, 255), 255, 255 );
  fill(c);
  ellipse(150,150,250,250);

  fill(255);
```

```
    ellipse( 120, 140, 60, 60);
    ellipse( 180, 140, 60, 60);
    fill(0);
    ellipse( 125, 150, 20, 20);
    ellipse( 175, 150, 20, 20);

    line( 100, 100 + map( eye, 0, 1024, -10, 10), 140,
        100 - map( eye, 0, 1024, -10, 10) );
    line( 160, 100 - map( eye, 0, 1024, -10, 10),
        200, 100 + map( eye, 0, 1024, -10, 10) );

    noFill();
    beginShape();
    curveVertex(100, 200);
    curveVertex(100, 200);
    curveVertex(150, 180 + map( mouth, 0, 1024, 0, 50));
    curveVertex(200, 200);
    curveVertex(200, 200);
    endShape();
}
```

10. Now run the sketch and change the values of our control variables to see how they affect the resulting face. The parameters we used in the example so far result in the smiley that you see in the following screenshot:

Objective Complete - Mini Debriefing

For the first task of our current mission, we created a Processing sketch that draws our basic face. We added three variables that control the facial features we are enabling the user to change. We changed the color mode to HSB to make it easier for the user to select the desired color tone. Like RGB, the HSB color mode has three parameters, but instead of mixing red, green, and blue, you choose the basic color (hue), the brightness, and the saturation. We keep the brightness and saturation value fixed for the sake of simplicity and let the user change the hue value.

All the control variables store a value between `0` and `1023`, which are than mapped to the value range we need for drawing using the `map()` command.

Let me change it

Nobody feels like smiling all the time, but it is currently somewhat cumbersome to change the facial parameters of our smiley, which could have an impact on your current state of emotion. To prevent our Smilie-O-Mat from increasing the user's level of frustration or annoyance, our second task for this mission is to make the facial parameters adjustable using the mouse by adding three sliders below the smiley.

Engage Thrusters

Let's now change our face:

1. Open the Smilie-O-Mat sketch and change the size of our sketch window in the `setup()` method to add more room for the sliders below the smiley face.

   ```
   void setup() {
     size(300,390);
     smooth();
     background(255);
     colorMode(HSB);
   }
   ```

2. Now add a new method named `drawSliders()` and draw three black rectangles for the bases of our sliders.

   ```
   void drawSliders() {
     fill(0);
     strokeWeight(1);
     rect( 20,315,width-40,2 );
     rect( 20,345,width-40,2 );
     rect( 20,375,width-40,2 );
   }
   ```

3. The first slider will change the mouth position, so we add a smaller rectangle and map the value of the `mouth` variable to the x-coordinate of our rectangle.

```
void drawSliders() {
  fill(0);
  strokeWeight(1);
  rect( 20,315,width-40,2 );
  rect( 15 + map( mouth, 0, 1024, 0, width-40 ), 310, 10, 12 );

  rect( 20,345,width-40,2 );
  rect( 20,375,width-40,2 );
}
```

4. Add a slider for the eyebrow angle and one for the color of our face, the same way you did for the `mouth` variable.

```
void drawSliders() {
  fill(0);
  strokeWeight(1);
  rect( 20,315,width-40,2 );
  rect( 15 + map( mouth, 0, 1024, 0, width-40 ), 310, 10, 12 );

  rect( 20,345,width-40,2 );
  rect( 15 + map( eye, 0, 1024, 0, width-40 ), 340, 10, 12 );

  rect( 20,375,width-40,2 );
  rect( 15 + map( col, 0, 1024, 0, width-40 ), 370, 10, 12 );
}
```

5. Now we call our `drawSliders()` method from the `draw()` method.

```
void draw() {
  background(255);

  drawSliders();

  color c = color(map(col, 0, 1024, 0, 255), 255, 255 );
  fill(c);
  ellipse(150,150,250,250);
  strokeWeight(3);
```

6. Run your sketch, then make changes to the control variables and check whether the position of the slider changes.

7. To make the slider react to the mouse, we add a new method named `mousePressed()` and a Boolean variable named `mclick`. This method gets called every time the mouse button is pressed; we will now test whether the mouse click occurred on our mouth slider.

```
boolean mclick = false;
void mousePressed() {
  if ( mouseY > 310 && mouseY < 322 ) {
    mclick = true;
    mouth = constrain( int( map( mouseX, 20, width - 20, 0, 1024
)), 0, 1024 );
  }
}
```

8. We need to add another callback method that gets called when the user drags the mouse. We change the position of the slider only if the `mclick` variable is set to `true` by our `mousePressed()` method.

```
void mouseDragged() {
  if (mclick) mouth = constrain( int( map( mouseX, 20, width - 20,
0, 1024 )), 0, 1024 );
}
```

9. We set the `mclick` variable to `true` when the slider is clicked on. When the mouse button is released, we need to set the variable back to `false`. Add a `mouseReleased()` method to our sketch.

```
void mouseReleased() {
  mclick = false;
}
```

10. Run the sketch, drag the first slider, and check whether the position of the mouth changes accordingly.

11. To make our eye and color sliders work, we need two more Boolean variables, and we need to add the following code to our `mousePressed()` method:

```
boolean mclick = false;
boolean eclick = false;
boolean cclick = false;

void mousePressed() {
  if ( mouseY > 310 && mouseY < 322 ) {
    mclick = true;
    mouth = constrain( int( map( mouseX, 20, width - 20, 0, 1024
)), 0, 1024 );
  }
  if ( mouseY > 340 && mouseY < 352 ) {
```

```
    eclick = true;
    eye = constrain( int( map( mouseX, 20, width - 20, 0, 1024 )),
0, 1024 );
  }
  if ( mouseY > 370 && mouseY < 382 ) {
    cclick = true;
    col = constrain( int( map( mouseX, 20, width - 20, 0, 1024 )),
0, 1024 );
  }
}
```

12. We also need to handle the dragging and releasing of the mouse button by adding the following code to the `mouseDragged()` and `mouseReleased()` methods:

```
void mouseDragged() {
  if (mclick) mouth = constrain( int( map( mouseX, 20, width - 20,
0, 1024 )), 0, 1024 );
  if (eclick) eye = constrain( int( map( mouseX, 20, width - 20,
0, 1024 )), 0, 1024 );
  if (cclick) col = constrain( int( map( mouseX, 20, width - 20,
0, 1024 )), 0, 1024 );
}

void mouseReleased() {
  mclick = false;
  eclick = false;
  cclick = false;
}
```

13. Now run our sketch and use the sliders to adjust the facial parameters to match your current mood. In this screenshot, you can see one of the smileys that can be generated:

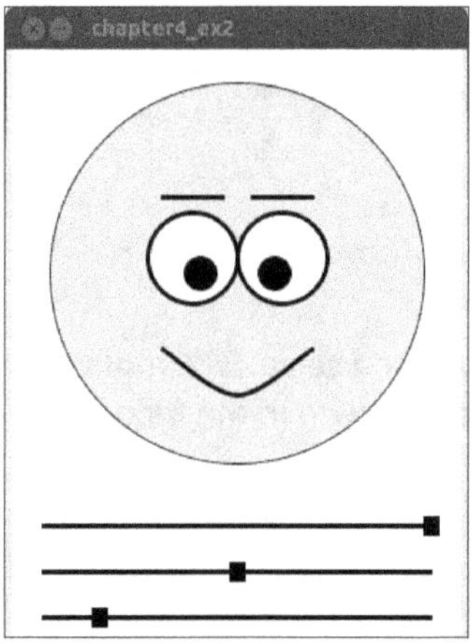

Objective Complete - Mini Debriefing

For this task, we added three sliders that change the values of our control variables. We didn't use any existing GUI libraries; we created the sliders from scratch by mapping the values of our variables that fall within the interval `0` to `1024` to the length of the slider and drawing two rectangles.

We also implemented three callback functions to make the sliders react to mouse events. In the `mousePressed()` method, we test whether the mouse pointer is on one of our sliders, and if it is, we set the Boolean variable for this slider to `true`. In the `mouseDragged()` method, we change the value of our control variables if the Boolean variable for this parameter is `true`. When the mouse button is released, we set all Boolean variables to `false` in the `mouseReleased()` method.

Hello Twitter

Task 3 of our mission is to create a Processing sketch that is able to change our current Twitter status. We will use the Java library Twitter4J from `twitter4j.org`, which encapsulates all the Twitter API calls into convenient Java objects to set the status. We will also use the Twitter developer website to create the necessary application keys and learn how to ask the user for permission to post a status update.

Prepare for Lift Off

To complete this and the following task of our current mission, you will need a Twitter account to post the tweets and access to the Twitter developer site. If you are already using Twitter, you are fulfilling the prerequisites for this task, as Twitter doesn't distinguish between normal and developer accounts; every Twitter user has the permission to create and register applications. If you have no Twitter account yet, go to `twitter.com` and register for one.

Engage Thrusters

Let's tweet a bit:

1. Go to the Twitter developer pages at `https://dev.twitter.com/` and log in with your Twitter account.
2. Now click on your account and select **My applications** from the pop-up menu in the upper-right corner, as can be seen in the following screenshot:

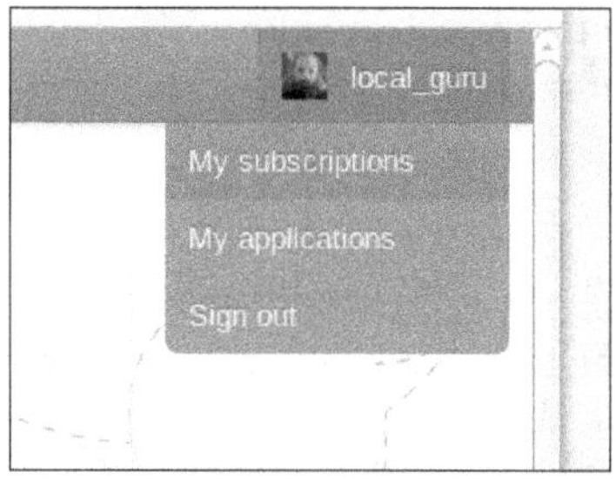

3. Now register a new application by clicking on **Create a new Application** and filling out the registration form.
4. Switch to the **Settings** tab and change the **Application Type** to **Read and Write** to allow our app to post tweets.
5. Now switch back to the **Details** tab and create the consumer key in **Consumer key** and the **Consumer Secret** key by clicking on **Recreate my access token**. The following screenshot shows the **Details** page for my Smilie-O-Mat application:

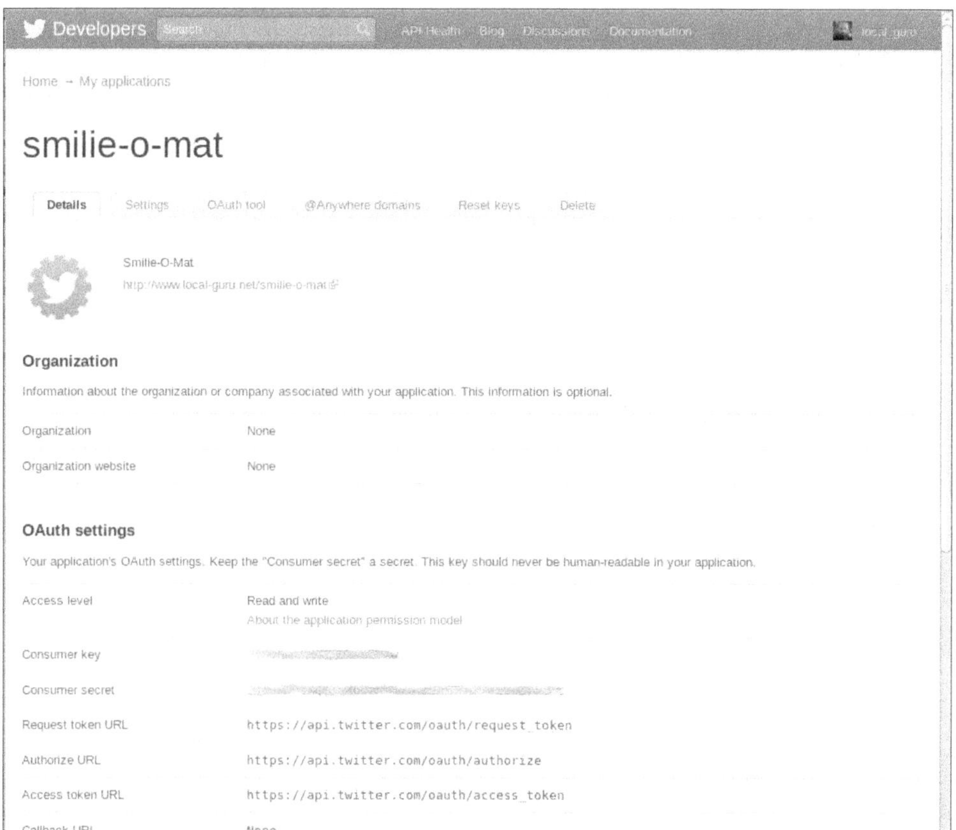

6. Copy the two keys to a text file named `keys.txt`; place each key on a new line and make sure that there are no blank spaces at the end of each line.
7. For this task, we need the Twitter4J library. Go to `http://twitter4j.org`, download the `twitter4j-3.0.3.zip` file, and unzip it. We need the `twitter4j-core.jar` file from the `lib` folder of the ZIP package.
8. Create a new Processing sketch and add the `jar` file you just extracted from the ZIP file by dragging it to the sketch window or by using the **Add File ...** option under the **Sketch** menu.
9. Drag the `keys.txt` file we created in step 6 to the sketch window, or add it using the **Add File ...** option under the **Sketch** menu.
10. Now add a `draw()` and a `setup()` method to our sketch.

```
void setup() {
}

void draw() {
}
```

11. To use the Twitter4J library, we need to import it and define a `twitter` object. We also need to define a string array, which will contain some Twitter messages that we want to send.

```
import twitter4j.*;

Twitter twitter;
String[] tweets = {
  "tweet tweet #test",
  "test 1 2 3 #test",
  "microphone test #test"
};
```

12. In our `setup()` method, we need to initialize the `twitter` object and provide the consumer key and the consumer secret key that we stored in the `keys.txt` file. We also need an access token and an access token secret to get the permission to post to a user's feed. To get these two access keys, we need to trigger a browser window to open to ask the user for his/her permission.

```
void setup() {
  size(300,100);
  noLoop();
  textFont( createFont( "Georgia", 24 ));

  String[] keys = loadStrings( "keys.txt" );
```

```
    try {
      twitter = TwitterFactory.getSingleton();
      twitter.setOAuthConsumer( keys[0], keys[1] );
      RequestToken requestToken =
               twitter.getOAuthRequestToken();
      AccessToken at = null;
      if ( System.getProperty("os.name").toLowerCase().
indexOf("win")>=0) {
        link(requestToken.getAuthorizationURL());
      }
      else {
        open(requestToken.getAuthorizationURL());
      }

      } catch ( Exception e ) {
        e.printStackTrace();
      }
}
```

This is the page that opens when our sketch doesn't find a key:

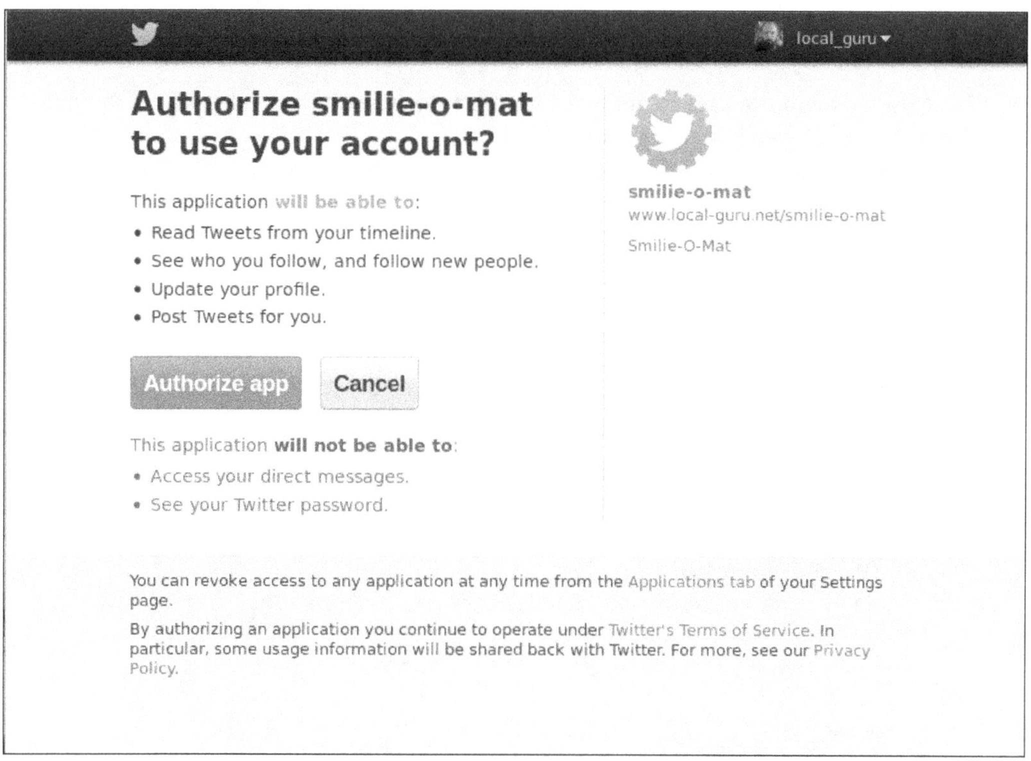

13. When the user clicks on **Authorize app**, Twitter generates a pin like the one shown in this screenshot:

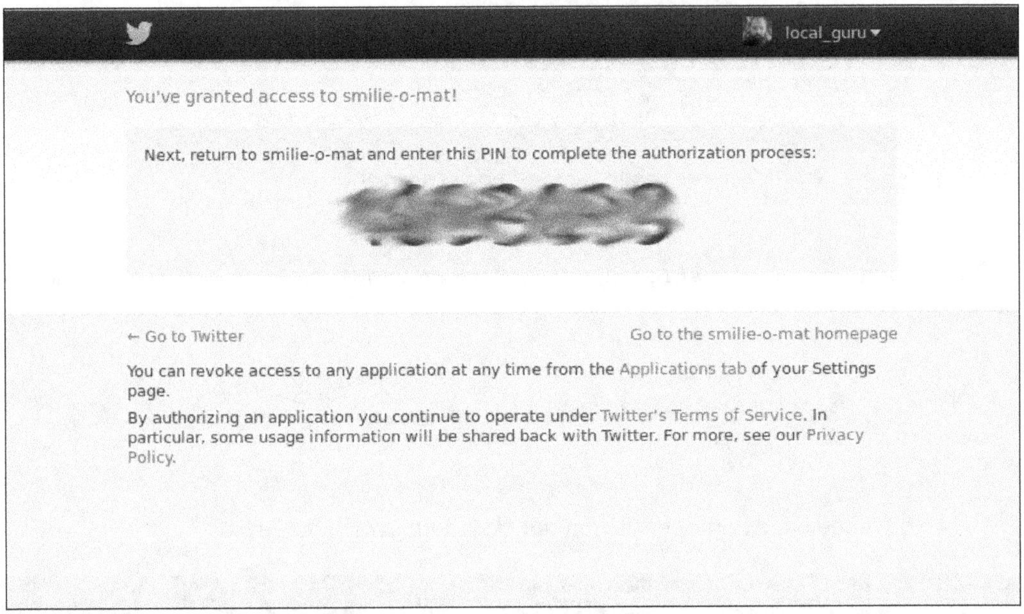

14. Now we need the user to enter the pin from the website and use this pin to fetch our access token keys from Twitter.

```
void setup() {
  size(300,100);
  noLoop();
  textFont( createFont( "Georgia", 24 ));

  String[] keys = loadStrings( "keys.txt" );

  try {
    twitter = TwitterFactory.getSingleton();
    twitter.setOAuthConsumer( keys[0], keys[1] );
    RequestToken requestToken =
           twitter.getOAuthRequestToken();
    AccessToken at = null;
    if ( System.getProperty("os.name").toLowerCase().
indexOf("win")>=0) {
      link(requestToken.getAuthorizationURL());
    }
    else {
```

```
      open(requestToken.getAuthorizationURL());
    }


    String preset="";
    String
pin=javax.swing.JOptionPane.showInputDialog(frame,
      "Enter your pin",preset);
    at = twitter.getOAuthAccessToken(requestToken, pin);

    } catch ( Exception e ) {
      e.printStackTrace();
    }
}
```

15. Here you can see a screenshot of the dialog we created in the previous step:

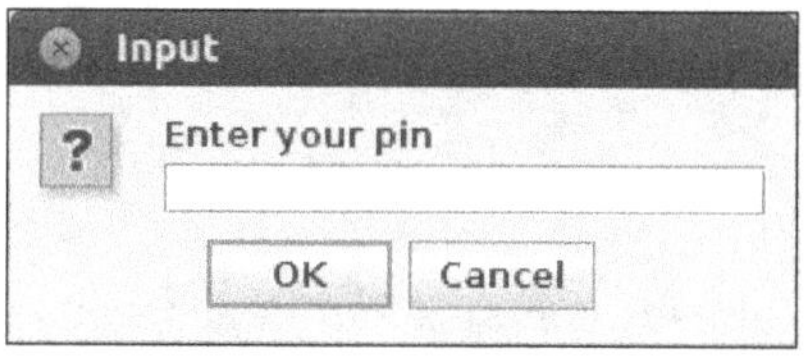

16. We need to ask for the user's permission only once. If we already have access to the keys, we can reuse them. We store the consumer keys and the access token keys in the `keys.txt` file and use them when our sketch is run the next time.

```
void setup() {
  size(300,100);
  noLoop();
  textFont( createFont( "Georgia", 24 ));

  String[] keys = loadStrings( "keys.txt" );
  try {
    twitter = TwitterFactory.getSingleton();
    twitter.setOAuthConsumer( keys[0], keys[1] );
    RequestToken requestToken= twitter.getOAuthRequestToken();
    AccessToken at = null;
    if ( System.getProperty("os.name").toLowerCase().
indexOf("win")>=0) {
      link(requestToken.getAuthorizationURL());
    }
    else {
```

```
      open(requestToken.getAuthorizationURL());
    }

    String preset="";
    String pin=javax.swing.JOptionPane.showInputDialog(frame,
      "Enter your pin",preset);
    at = twitter.getOAuthAccessToken(requestToken, pin);

    String[] newKeys = new String[4];
    newKeys[0] = keys[0];
    newKeys[1] = keys[1];
    newKeys[2] = at.getToken();
    newKeys[3] = at.getTokenSecret();

    saveStrings( "data/keys.txt", newKeys   );

    } catch ( Exception e ) {
      e.printStackTrace();
    }
}
```

17. If the `keys.txt` file already contains four keys because we already have the user's permission to tweet, we can use a configuration builder to create the Twitter object.

```
void setup() {
  size(300,100);
  noLoop();
  textFont( createFont( "Georgia", 24 ));

  String[] keys = loadStrings( "keys.txt" );

  if (keys.length <= 2) {
    try {
    twitter = TwitterFactory.getSingleton();
    twitter.setOAuthConsumer( keys[0], keys[1] );
    RequestToken requestToken = twitter.getOAuthRequestToken();
    AccessToken at = null;
    if ( System.getProperty("os.name").toLowerCase().
indexOf("win")>=0) {
      link(requestToken.getAuthorizationURL());
    }
    else {
      open(requestToken.getAuthorizationURL());
    }
```

```
    String preset="";
    String pin=javax.swing.JOptionPane.showInputDialog(frame,
      "Enter your pin",preset);
    at = twitter.getOAuthAccessToken(requestToken, pin);

    String[] newKeys = new String[4];
    newKeys[0] = keys[0];
    newKeys[1] = keys[1];
    newKeys[2] = at.getToken();
    newKeys[3] = at.getTokenSecret();

    saveStrings( "data/keys.txt", newKeys   );

    } catch ( Exception e ) {
      e.printStackTrace();
    }

  } else {
    ConfigurationBuilder cb = new ConfigurationBuilder();
    cb.setOAuthConsumerKey( keys[0] );
    cb.setOAuthConsumerSecret( keys[1] );
    cb.setOAuthAccessToken( keys[2] );
    cb.setOAuthAccessTokenSecret( keys[3] );

    twitter = new TwitterFactory( cb.build()).getInstance();
  }
}
```

18. In our `draw()` method, we set the background and fill color and display a text message to make sure the user knows what to do.

```
void draw() {
  background(255);
  fill(0);
  text( "click here to tweet", 40, 60 );
}
```

19. Now we add a `mouseClicked()` method to our sketch and create a `StatusUpdate` object. We choose a random tweet from the list of messages we created at the beginning and use the `updateStatus()` method of our Twitter object to send it.

```
void mouseClicked() {
  try {
    StatusUpdate status = new StatusUpdate(
            tweets[ int(random( tweets.length ))] );
```

```
      twitter.updateStatus( status );
    } catch ( Exception e ) {
      e.printStackTrace();
    }
  }
```

20. Run the sketch and click on the window to generate some tweets. This is what the application window looks like:

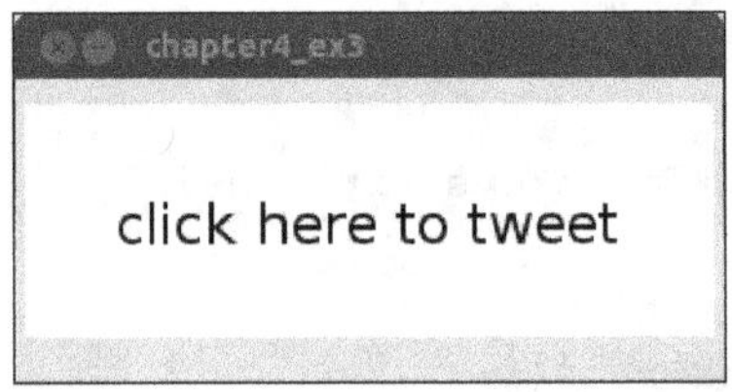

Objective Complete - Mini Debriefing

Task 3 of our current mission was to implement a tweeting sketch. In steps 1 to 5, we registered our application on the Twitter developer site and generated the required consumer and consumer secret keys. To actually post on behalf of a Twitter user, we need two more keys: an access token and an access token secret. To get these, we opened a browser window in step 12.

After the user grants the requested permission to our application, we need the pin that is shown in the browser window to finish our authorization process. We therefore open a swing input dialog and ask the user to enter the pin.

The access token keys are reusable, so we only need to acquire them once and then store them to the same text file where our consumer keys are kept. If this file already contains the four keys, we can create our Twitter objects directly and start tweeting right away.

We used Twitter4J to access the Twitter API, and to actually tweet something, we implemented a `mouseClicked()` method, which sends a random tweet to the world. We defined an array of strings for these tweets and chose a random one every time, because Twitter doesn't allow the exact same text to be posted twice via the API (for spam prevention).

Tweet your mood

The final task in this mission is to combine tweeting with the mood faces we created earlier to tell the world how we currently feel. We extend the GUI section of our Smilie-O-Mat with a button and implement a status update method that doesn't just tweet a text message, but also uploads our current smiley.

Engage Thrusters

Let's tweet our mood:

1. Open the Smilie-O-Mat sketch from task 2, *Let me change it*.
2. The first thing we are going to add is a button to tweet the face, so let's reduce the size of the sliders to make room for it. Change the `drawSliders()` method like this:

   ```
   void drawSliders() {
     fill(0);
     strokeWeight(1);
     rect( 20,315,width-130,2 );
     rect( 15 + map( mouth, 0, 1024, 0, width-130 ), 310, 10, 12 );

     rect( 20,345,width-130,2 );
     rect( 15 + map( eye, 0, 1024, 0, width-130 ), 340, 10, 12 );
     rect( 20,375,width-130,2 );
     rect( 15 + map( col, 0, 1024, 0, width-130 ), 370, 10, 12 );
   }
   ```

3. We also need to adjust our `mousePressed()` and `mouseDragged()` methods to make the mapping of the mouse coordinates work with the shorter sliders.

   ```
   void mousePressed() {
     if ( mouseY > 310 && mouseY < 322 ) {
       mclick = true;
       mouth = constrain( int(
         map( mouseX, 20, width - 110, 0, 1024 )), 0, 1024 );
     }
     if ( mouseY > 340 && mouseY < 352 ) {
       eclick = true;
       eye = constrain( int(
           map( mouseX, 20, width - 110, 0, 1024 )), 0, 1024 );
     }
     if ( mouseY > 370 && mouseY < 382 ) {
       cclick = true;
       col = constrain( int(
         map( mouseX, 20, width - 110, 0, 1024 )), 0, 1024 );
     }
   }

   void mouseDragged() {
     if (mclick) mouth = constrain(
        int( map( mouseX, 20, width - 110, 0, 1024 )), 0, 1024 );
   ```

```
    if (eclick) eye = constrain(
        int( map( mouseX, 20, width - 110, 0, 1024 )), 0, 1024 );
    if (cclick) col = constrain(
        int( map( mouseX, 20, width - 110, 0, 1024 )), 0, 1024 );
}
```

4. Now add a `drawButton()` method and a Boolean variable that will indicate if the button is currently being pressed.

```
boolean bclick = false;
void drawButton() {
  fill( bclick ? 128 : 255);
  stroke( 0 );
  strokeWeight(2);
  rect( width - 90, 310, 70, 70 );
  fill(0);
  text( "tweet", width-83, 353 );
}
```

5. Call the `drawButton()` method from the `draw()` method to make our button show up.

```
void draw() {
  background(255);
  color c = color(map(col, 0, 1024, 0, 255), 255, 255 );
  fill(c);
  ellipse(150,150,250,250);
  strokeWeight(3);

  fill(255);
  ellipse( 120, 140, 60, 60);
  ellipse( 180, 140, 60, 60);
  fill(0);
  ellipse( 125, 150, 20, 20);
  ellipse( 175, 150, 20, 20);

  line( 100, 100 + map( eye, 0, 1024, -10, 10), 140, 100 - map(
eye, 0, 1024, -10, 10) );
  line( 160, 100 - map( eye, 0, 1024, -10, 10), 200, 100 + map(
eye, 0, 1024, -10, 10) );

  noFill();
  beginShape();
  curveVertex(100, 200);
  curveVertex(100, 200);
  curveVertex(150, 180 + map( mouth, 0, 1024, 0, 50));
```

```
    curveVertex(200, 200);
    curveVertex(200, 200);
    endShape();

    drawSliders();
    drawButton();
}
```

6. To make the button clickable, we need to handle the mouse events; so add the following code to our `mousePressed()` method:

```
void mousePressed() {
  if ( mouseY > 310 && mouseY < 380
       && mouseX > width - 90 && mouseX < width - 20 ) {
    bclick = true;
    return;
  }
  if ( mouseY > 310 && mouseY < 322 ) {
    mclick = true;
    mouth = constrain( int(
         map( mouseX, 20, width - 110, 0, 1024 )), 0, 1024 );
  }
  if ( mouseY > 340 && mouseY < 352 ) {
    eclick = true;
    eye = constrain( int(
        map( mouseX, 20, width - 110, 0, 1024 )), 0, 1024 );
  }
  if ( mouseY > 370 && mouseY < 382 ) {
    cclick = true;
    col = constrain( int(
       map( mouseX, 20, width - 110, 0, 1024 )), 0, 1024 );
  }
}
```

7. The click event is generated when the mouse button is released again. So, add the following code to the `mouseReleased()` method:

```
void mouseReleased() {
  if (bclick) {
      println( "button clicked" );
  }
  bclick = false;
  mclick = false;
  eclick = false;
  cclick = false;
}
```

8. Now drag the `twitter4j-core.jar` file and the `keys.txt` file that we generated in the last task for our Smilie-O-Mat.
9. We need to import the Twitter4J library; we also need an array of tweets to send. Add the `import` statement and the variable definitions to the beginning of the sketch.

```
import twitter4j.*;

Twitter twitter;
String[] tweets = {
  "I feel like so #SmilieOMat",
  "I currently feel like this #SmilieOMat",
  "This is how I feel #SmilieOMat"
};
```

10. Add an `initTwitter()` method and copy the initialization code from our Twitter test application.

```
void initTwitter()  {
  String[] keys = loadStrings( "keys.txt" );

  if (keys.length <= 2) {
    try {
    twitter = TwitterFactory.getSingleton();
    twitter.setOAuthConsumer( keys[0], keys[1] );
    RequestToken requestToken = twitter.getOAuthRequestToken();
    AccessToken at = null;
    if ( System.getProperty("os.name").toLowerCase().
indexOf("win")>=0) {
      link(requestToken.getAuthorizationURL());
    }
    else {
      open(requestToken.getAuthorizationURL());
    }

    String preset="";
    String pin=javax.swing.JOptionPane.
showInputDialog(frame,"Enter your pin",preset);
    at = twitter.getOAuthAccessToken(requestToken, pin);

    String[] newKeys = new String[4];
    newKeys[0] = keys[0];
    newKeys[1] = keys[1];
    newKeys[2] = at.getToken();
```

```
    newKeys[3] = at.getTokenSecret();

    saveStrings( "data/keys.txt", newKeys   );

    } catch ( Exception e ) {
      e.printStackTrace();
    }

  } else {
    ConfigurationBuilder cb = new ConfigurationBuilder();
    cb.setOAuthConsumerKey( keys[0] );
    cb.setOAuthConsumerSecret( keys[1] );
    cb.setOAuthAccessToken( keys[2] );
    cb.setOAuthAccessTokenSecret( keys[3] );

    twitter = new TwitterFactory( cb.build()).getInstance();
  }
}
```

11. Now we call the `initTwitter()` method from our `setup()` method.

```
void setup() {
  size(300,390);
  smooth();
  background(255);
  colorMode(HSB);
  textFont( createFont( "Georgia", 20 ));
  initTwitter();
}
```

12. To tweet the current smiley, we add a new method named `tweet()`. Since we only want to tweet the image of the smiley and not the GUI elements, we need to copy the section of the window we want to a `PImage` object and then save it to a file. We will use this file as a media object for our status updates to upload to Twitter.

```
void tweet() {

  PImage image = get( 0, 0, 300,300);
  image.save( "smilie.png");

  java.io.File f = new java.io.File( sketchPath( "smilie.png" ));
  StatusUpdate status = new StatusUpdate( tweets[int(random(
tweets.length ))]);
  status.setMedia(f);
  try {
    twitter.updateStatus(status);
```

```
    }
    catch ( Exception e ) {
      e.printStackTrace();
    }
  }
```

13. Now change the `mouseReleased()` method to make it call the new `tweet()` method instead of making it print a message.

```
void mouseReleased() {
  if (bclick) {
    tweet();
  }
  bclick = false;
  mclick = false;
  eclick = false;
  cclick = false;
}
```

14. Run your sketch, create a smiling happy smiley, and tweet it using our tweet button. In the following screenshot, you can see our Smilie-O-Mat and the resulting tweet:

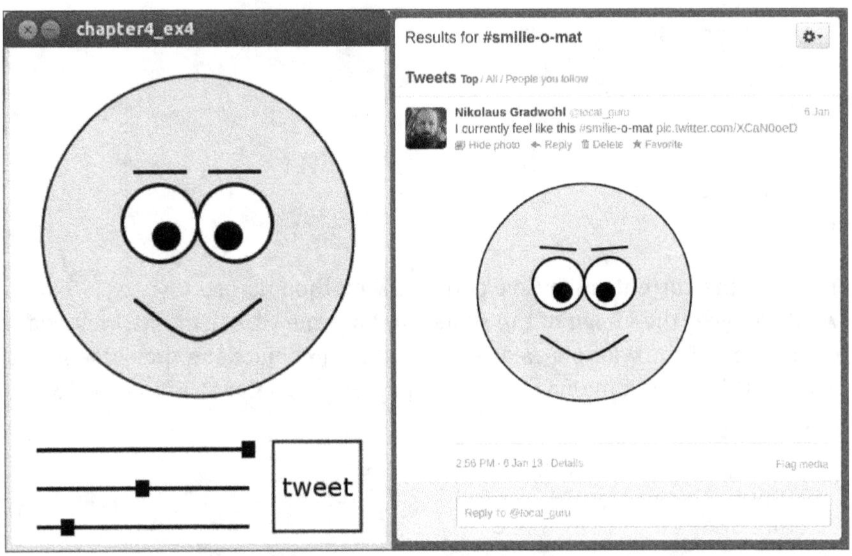

Objective Complete - Mini Debriefing

In task 4, we combined all the sketches we have written for this mission and added the Twitter functionality to our Smilie-O-Mat. We added a button to trigger the tweeting and added the key setup mechanism we implemented in task 3.

We also learned how to add a media file to our Twitter status update. In this sketch, the media file was the image of the smiley that we created.

Mission Accomplished

Our mission was to implement a sketch that makes it easier to communicate the current emotional status of a user. We have accomplished this by creating a smiley that has various controllable facial parameters. In task 1, we implemented the drawing routine that generates our smiley, but changing the parameters meant changing a variable and running the sketch again.

To tackle this problem, we added some GUI elements to our sketch in task 2 to simplify the interaction with our sketch for the user. We didn't use any existing GUI libraries, but instead created the sliders from scratch by implementing the mouse event callback functions and drawing some rectangles.

In task 3, we created the necessary code to authenticate our app with `twitter.com` and created a method that allows our app to post status updates for a Twitter user. We created a consumer key and a consumer secret key on the Twitter developer site and asked the user for permission to tweet using a request URL and pin code.

And finally, we combined the two sketches in task 4 by adding a button to our GUI that tweets a status message on Twitter and adds the face the user has adjusted. We created an image containing the smiley by sparing the GUI elements and copying only a section of the sketch window to a new `PImage` object; we then saved this file and added it as a media object to the status update.

You Ready to go Gung HO? A Hotshot Challenge

The Smilie-O-Mat is finished, but this doesn't mean you have to stop here. Why don't you try to take it to the next level and implement one of the following suggestions:

- Parse the Twitter stream for the `#SmilieOMat` messages of people you follow
- Make additional facial features changeable
- Create a mobile version
- Publish your smiley on other social networks

Project 5
The Smilie-O-Mat Controller

The invention of mouse and graphical user interfaces at Xerox PARC was a groundbreaking event in computer history. The mouse is a very versatile mechanism of interacting with a computer, and it enabled a whole range of new methods for data entry and controlling the program flow. But if a tool is usable on a very broad range of problems, it generally means that it isn't optimized for any of them. Some programs are easier, faster, or more ergonomically usable with a specialized controller. In this mission, we are going to create a customized controller for our Smilie-O-Mat sketch, which we created in *Project 4, Smilie-O-Mat*.

Mission Briefing

Our current mission is to build a custom controller for the Smilie-O-Mat sketch we wrote in the previous project. We will make use of an Arduino board (an inexpensive board using an AVR microcontroller), a button, and some variable resistors. We will connect the Arduino board to our computer through USB and create a simple protocol for controlling the facial parameters of our smiley.

Why Is It Awesome?

As already mentioned in the introduction, the mouse is a great and versatile input device, but sometimes it's not the best one available. Drawing an image is far more fun with a pressure-sensitive tablet, playing racing games is more fun with a steering wheel and some pedals, and making music is far easier with a keyboard controller, just to name a few examples. Sometimes we need a specialized controller to interact in a faster or more natural way with our data or our processes.

Knowing how to interface sliders, buttons, and knobs with a computer, enables us to optimize our workspace and workflow exactly the way we need and want it.

Your Hotshot Objectives

Our current mission consists of four tasks. We are starting with a simple "hello world" circuit and extending it until we have a working controller board for our Smilie-O-Mat sketch, and then building a housing for it. The task list for our current mission is as follows:

- Connecting your Arduino
- Building your controller
- Changing your face
- Putting it in a box

Mission Checklist

To build the controller, we will need an Arduino board, a solderless breadboard, and a handful of electronic components, as follows:

- Arduino
- Breadboard
- Wires
- A push button
- A resistor (10 kOhm)
- Three variable resistors (100 kOhm)

In the final task of this mission, we will create a permanent housing for the controller using a box and some fancy knobs. I will also provide a list of materials that I have used in this section, but similar to the robots in *Project 1, Romeo and Juliet*, the housing is very much a matter of taste.

Connecting your Arduino

Say hello to your Arduino. The first task of our current mission is to write a sketch that runs on Arduino and reads the value of a variable resistor. Since this is a book about Processing, we are going to write a Processing sketch that receives the resistor values from our Arduino board and prints the value.

Prepare for Lift Off

In this task, we are going to write code that runs on Arduino, so we need the Arduino IDE installed. You can download it from `www.arduino.cc` and install it by unzipping the package that matches your operating system.

Engage Thrusters

Let's hook up our Arduino:

1. The first thing we need to do for this task is to build a little circuit, so take one of your variable resistors and hook it up to the solderless breadboard like in the following diagram:

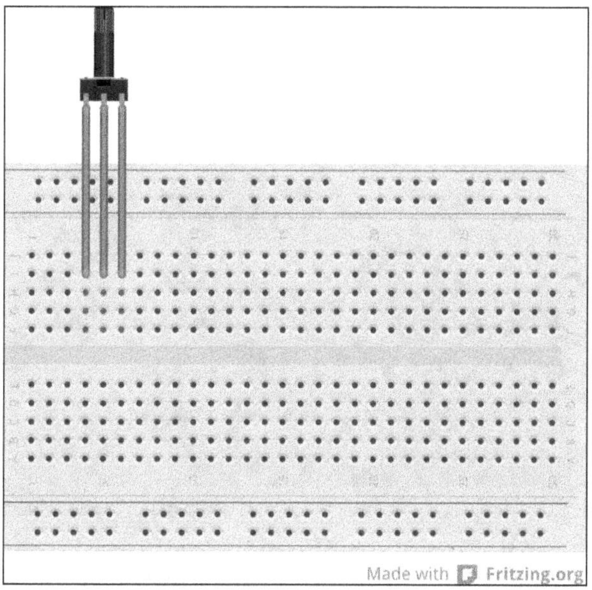

2. Now connect a red wire from the **5V** pin of your Arduino board to one of the outer leads of our resistor.
3. The middle pin of the resistor gets connected to the pin labeled **ANALOG IN 0** on your Arduino board.

4. Connect a black wire from the **Gnd** pin of your Arduino to the remaining pin of your resistor. Your connections should look as shown in the following diagram:

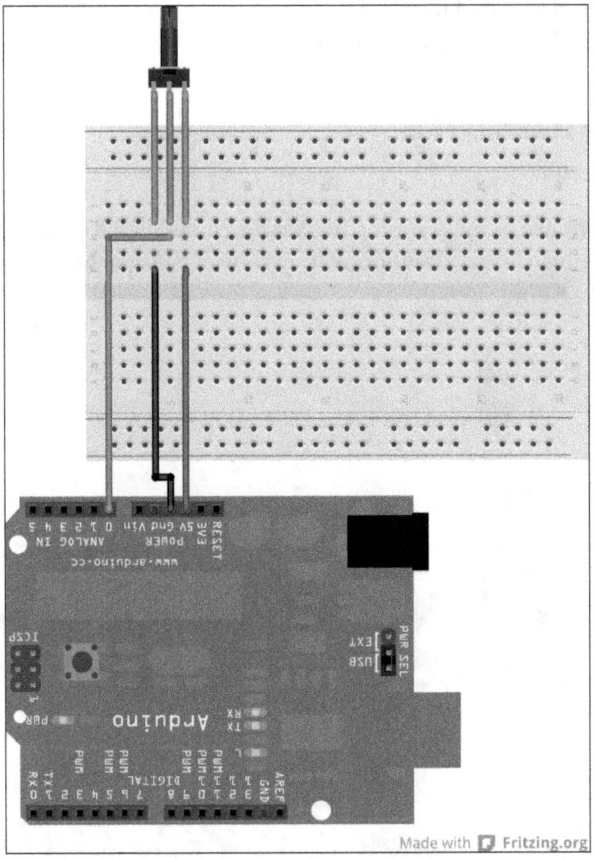

5. Now connect your Arduino board to a USB port in your computer and start the Arduino IDE.
6. Make sure that the correct serial port is selected by checking the **Tools** | **Serial Port** menu, and the correct Arduino board type is selected by checking the **Tools** | **Board** menu.
7. Our first Arduino sketch will use the built-in LED of Arduino. We'll use the variable resistor that we've just added to control the blinking speed of the LED. Now, we will add the following code to the Arduino sketch and save it:

```
int del = 5;
boolean state = true;
```

```
void setup() {
  pinMode( 13, OUTPUT );
  Serial.begin( 9600 );
}

void loop() {
if ( state ) {
  digitalWrite( 13, HIGH );
} else {
 digitalWrite( 13, LOW );
}
  delay( del );
  state = !state;

  del = analogRead( 0 );
}
```

8. Verify the code by clicking on the verify icon, and if everything compiles well, click on the upload button to install the code on your Arduino.
9. Turn the knob of your variable resistor and check the blinking speed of the LED.
10. Now we want Arduino to send the value of the variable resistor to the computer using a serial port. Add the following line of code to the `setup()` method of the Arduino sketch to initialize the serial port and set its speed as follows:

```
void setup() {
  pinMode( 13, OUTPUT );
  Serial.begin( 9600 );
}
```

11. In our `loop()` method, we print the value of the resistor using the `println()` method of the `Serial` object. We also remove the LED blinking code and the delay from our sketch:

```
void loop() {
  del = analogRead( 0 );
  Serial.println( del );
}
```

12. Compile and install the sketch on Arduino by clicking on the verify and upload icon.
13. Now we need to open the serial console to see what values the Arduino is sending. Use the **Tools** | **Serial Monitor** menu to see the serial console and turn the knob of your resistor, and then watch the values change on the console.

14. Currently, the resistor value is sent every time the Arduino runs through the main loop, but most of the time the value hasn't changed. So let's send the value only if there is a change by storing the last value we have sent and comparing it to the current value.

```
int del = 5;
int lastDel = d;

void loop() {
  del = analogRead( 0 );
  if (abs( del - lastDel ) > 10 ) {
    Serial.println( del );
    lastDel = del;
  }
}
```

15. Compile and upload the code to Arduino and open the serial console. If you turn your knob now, you will see the changed values, but if you leave it as it is then no values will be sent.

16. Now we have finished the Arduino part of our first task, let's switch to the Processing half of it. Open Processing, create a new sketch, and add the `setup()` and `draw()` methods:

```
void setup() {
}

void draw() {
}
```

17. To communicate with our Arduino, we need to import the `serial` library, which enables us to use the serial port in our processing sketch. So, use the **Sketch** | **Import Library ...** | **serial** menu to import the library.

    We create an instance of the serial port object and define a string where we can store the text lines we read from the serial port:

```
import processing.serial.*;

Serial port;
String str = "";
```

18. Then, we add the following code to our `setup()` method to initialize the serial port and define a font. Be sure to use the same name for the serial board we have used in the Arduino IDE in step 6. In this case, it's `/dev/ttyUSB0`.

```
void setup() {
  size( 300,300 );
```

```
    port = new Serial( this, "/dev/ttyUSB0",", 9600);
    textFont( createFont( "Sans", 64 ));
  }
```

19. In our `draw()` method, we simply write out the content of the string variable:

```
void draw() {
  background( 255 );
  fill(0);
  text( str, 20, 100 );
}
```

20. Now, we add a callback method named `serialEvent()` that gets called every time the serial port detects an activity. We are reading a string from the current buffer until we find a newline character, and then we store it in our string variable:

```
void serialEvent( Serial p ) {
  String in = p.readStringUntil( '\n' );
  if ( in != null ) {
    str = in;
  }
}
```

21. Now, connect your Arduino and start your Processing sketch. Turn the knob and watch the values change. Your sketch window should look like the following screenshot:

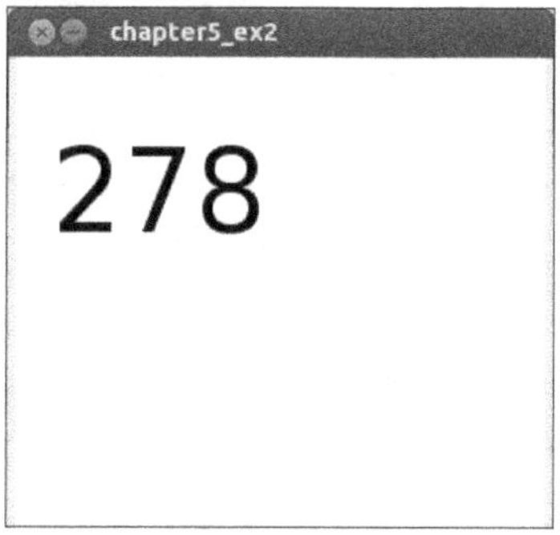

Objective Complete - Mini Debriefing

For this first task of our current mission, we created an Arduino sketch that runs on a microcontroller and reads the value of a variable resistor. We created a simple circuit to hook up the resistor to Arduino. Then, from step 1 to step 9, we made our sketch read the value of the resistor and use this value to change the blinking speed of the built-in LED. Once this code is installed on the microcontroller, it runs independently from any computer and uses the USB cable only as a power source. If you would disconnect the USB cable and power the Arduino board using an AC adapter or a battery, your sketch still would run.

Starting from step 10, we removed the blinking code and replaced it with a call to the `println()` method of the `Serial` object, which uses the built-in serial port to send the resistor value to the computer. To read the values, we used a serial monitor that the Arduino IDE provides.

In step 16, we started writing a Processing application that listens to the serial port instead of the serial monitor and displays the values it reads on the serial port using the Processing's `serial` library.

Classified Intel

Arduino sends values from the variable resistor in a range from 0 to 1,023. Usually, we expect the values to be zero on the left-hand side of the knob and the maximum on the right-hand side. If your controller sends the value the other way around, you have two possibilities to fix this. On the hardware side, you can switch the leads that go to **Gnd** and **5V** on the Arduino board. On the software side, you can calculate the value by subtracting it from the maximum value:

```
val = 1023 - val;
```

The software side is especially helpful if you have already soldered your circuit.

Building your controller

In the first task of this mission, we learned how to connect a variable resistor to Arduino and send its value to the computer using the serial port. Our next task is to extend this basic circuit and add two more resistors, because we want to use them to control all the facial parameters of our Smilie-O-Mat sketch in the next task.

We will also add a button to our circuit and learn how to detect the click events and send them to our sketch. We will extend our communication protocol a bit and write a new Processing sketch that parses the messages—our Arduino generates—and displays the values we send.

Engage Thrusters

Let's build our controller:

1. For this task, we need to expand our circuit and add two more variable resistors. So let's start by connecting the **5V** pin to one of the outer power rails of the breadboard and the **Gnd** pin to the other one. Connect your three resistors to the breadboard as shown in the following diagram:

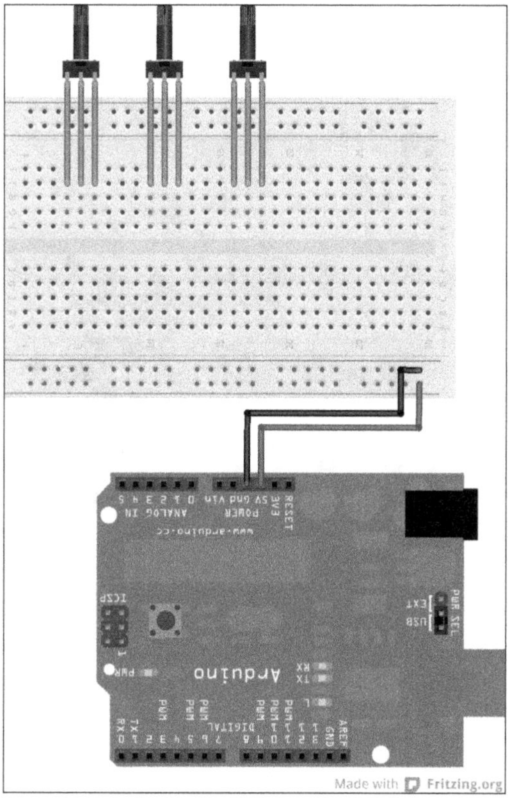

2. Connect the left-outer lead of each resistor to the **5V** rail and the other one to **Gnd**, as shown in the following diagram:

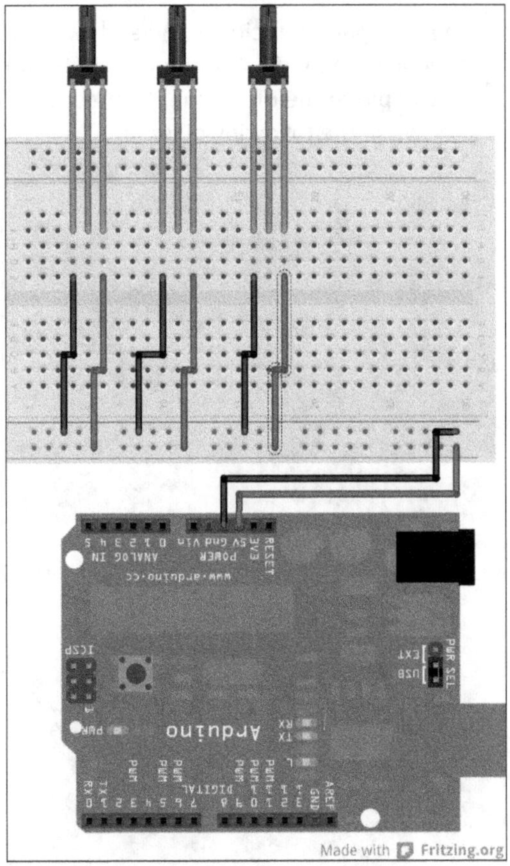

3. Now connect the Arduino pins, analog inputs **0**, **1**, and **2** to the middle pins of your resistors. Your wiring should look as shown in the following diagram:

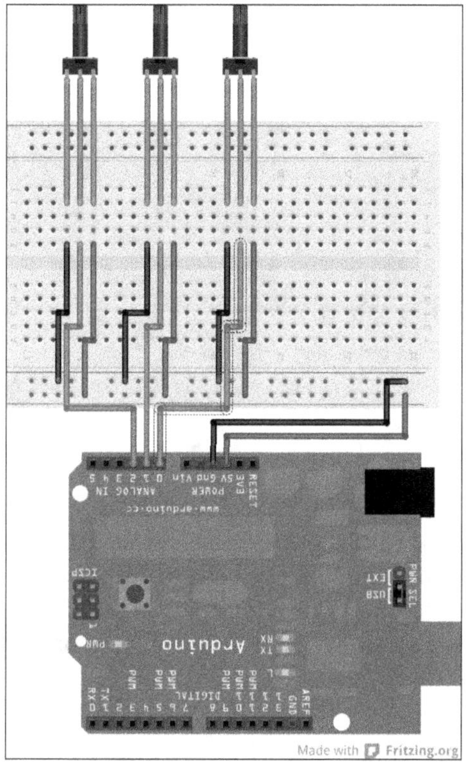

4. In our `loop()` method, we need to copy the code that reads the value and sends it to the serial port to read the other two ports as well:

```
int a = 0;
int lastA = a;

int b = 0;
int lastB = b;

int c = 0;
int lastC = c;

void setup() {
  Serial.begin( 9600 );
}
```

```
void loop() {
  a = analogRead( 0 );
  if (abs( a - lastA ) > 10 ) {
    Serial.println( a );
    lastA = a;
  }
  b = analogRead( 1 );
  if (abs( b - lastB ) > 10 ) {
    Serial.println( b );
    lastB = b;
  }
  c = analogRead( 2 );
  if (abs( c - lastC ) > 10 ) {
    Serial.println( c );
    lastC = c;
  }
}
```

5. Compile the code and upload it to your Arduino.
6. Now run the processing sketch we created for the first task, *Connecting your Arduino*, and turn the knobs of the resistors. We see that the value changes, but our Processing sketch isn't able to recognize which resistor sent the value. So, switch back to the Arduino IDE and let's add the letter `A`, `B`, or `C` in front of the value:

```
void loop() {
  a = analogRead( 0 );
  if (abs( a - lastA ) > 10 ) {
    Serial.print("A");
    Serial.println( a );
    lastA = a;
  }
  b = analogRead( 1 );
  if (abs( b - lastB ) > 10 ) {
    Serial.print("B");
    Serial.println( b );
    lastB = b;
  }
  c = analogRead( 2 );
  if (abs( c - lastC ) > 10 ) {
    Serial.print("C");
    Serial.println( c );
    lastC = c;
  }
}
```

7. Compile and upload the code to your Arduino.
8. Now run the Processing sketch and turn the knobs. Each knob controls one corresponding variable in our processing sketch. Here you can see the value of the input `B` has changed:

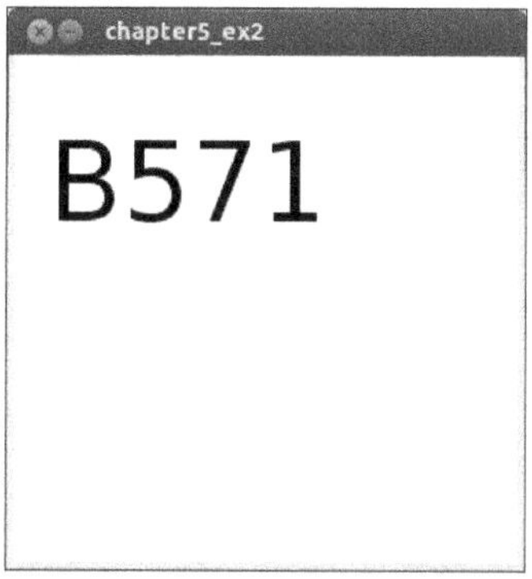

9. To complete the circuit of our controller, we need to add a button. Connect the two leads of your push button to the breadboard and add the 10 kOhm resistor as shown in the following diagram:

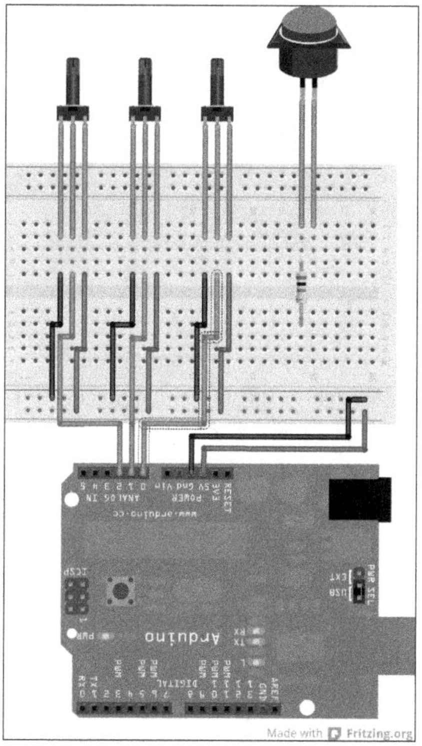

10. Now make a connection from the **Gnd** line to the resistor you just added and a connection from the **5V** line to the second leg of your button.
11. Connect the digital **2** pin of your Arduino board between the resistor and the button, as shown in the following diagram:

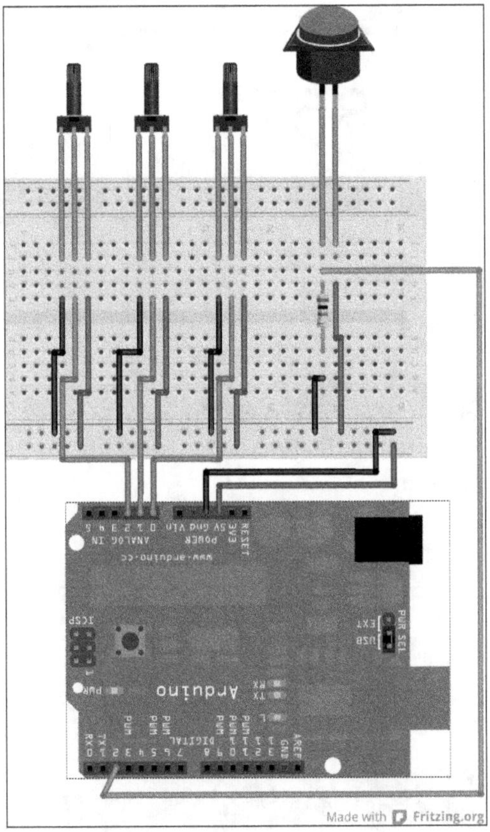

12. The digital pins of your Arduino can be configured for input and output, so add the following highlighted code line to the `setup()` method of your Arduino sketch to configure the pin **2** for being used as an input:

```
void setup() {
  pinMode( 2, INPUT );
  Serial.begin( 9600 );
}
```

13. Now add a variable to store the last state of our button and initialize it to `LOW`:

```
int  button = LOW;
int buttonLast = LOW;
```

14. In our `loop()` method, we are going to read the current state of the button and compare it to the last value we saved. If the button state changes from *pressed* to *released*, we are going to send a message to the serial bus:

```
void loop() {
  a = analogRead( 0 );
  if (abs( a - lastA ) > 10 ) {
    Serial.print( "A" );
    Serial.println( a );
    lastA = a;
  }
  b = analogRead(1);
  if (abs( b - lastB ) > 10 ) {
    Serial.print( "B" );
    Serial.println( b );
    lastB = b;
  }
  c = analogRead(2);
  if (abs( c - lastC ) > 10 ) {
    Serial.print( "C" );
    Serial.println( c );
    lastC = c;
  }

  button = digitalRead( 2 );
  if ( buttonLast == HIGH && button == LOW ) {
      Serial.println( "click" );
  }
  buttonLast = button;
}
```

15. Compile and upload the code to your Arduino and switch to Processing.
16. Run our Processing sketch, turn the knobs, and press the button. Each knob sends its own message now, and when the button is pressed, we receive a message on the Processing side. This is what our Processing sketch looks like when a button is pressed:

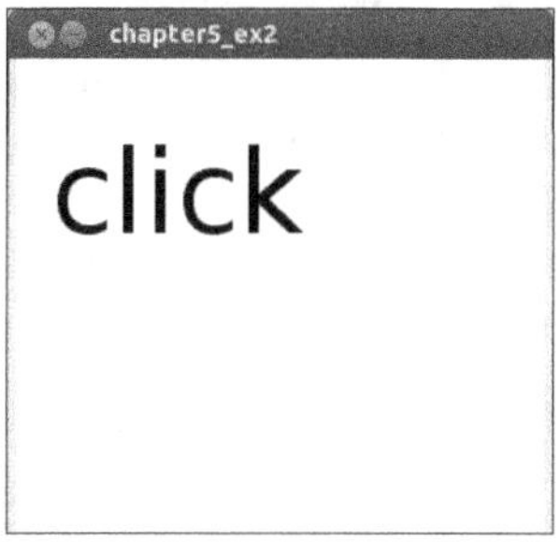

17. And this is what your wiring currently should look like the following picture:

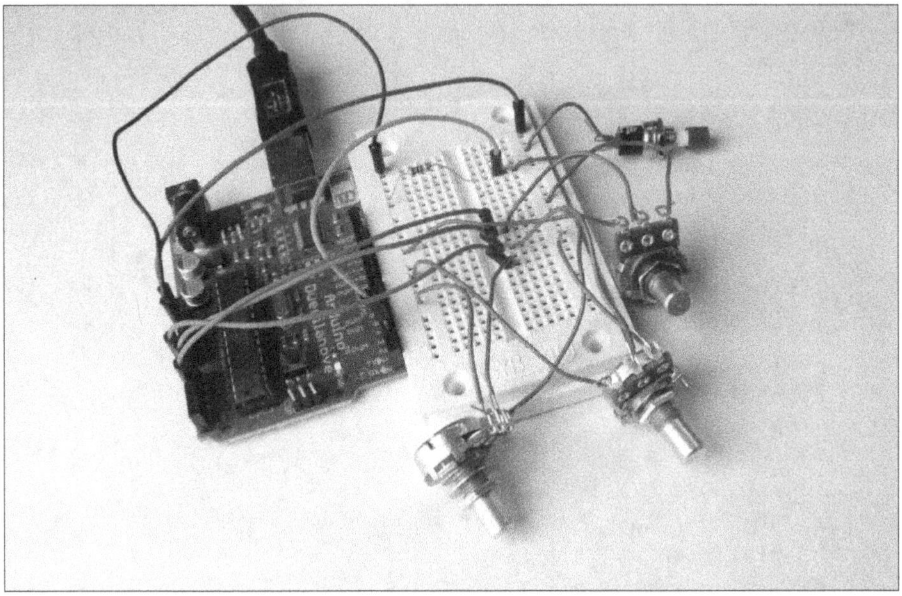

Objective Complete - Mini Debriefing

For this task of our current mission, we have created a prototype version of the hardware we need for our Smilie-O-Mat controller. We have added three variable resistors, and in step 8 we defined a protocol to send the values of these inputs to a computer via the serial port. The protocol also allows us to detect which input knob has been turned.

Starting with step 11, we extended the circuit and added a button to it. We also extended the messages we send to the computer with a **click** message. This message gets transmitted when the value of the button changes from pressed to released, and we will use it to trigger our `tweet()` method in the next task.

Changing your face

The current task of our mission is to integrate the prototyped hardware controller we have just created into the Smilie-O-Mat controller. We will extend the program to parse the messages that our Arduino-based controller is sending via the serial port and adjust the sliders to match the values of the hardware knobs. When the user of our controller presses the button on the board, we are going to call the `tweet()` method.

Engage Thrusters

Let's change our smiley using our controller:

1. Open the Smilie-O-Mat sketch from our previous mission.
2. To get access to the serial port, we need to import the `serial` library, so use the **Sketch** | **Import library ...** | **serial** menu to import it.
3. Now add a `Serial` object to your sketch:

```
import twitter4j.*;
import processing.serial.*;

Serial port;

Twitter twitter;
String[] tweets = {
  "I feel like so #SmilieOMat",
  "I currently feel like this #SmilieOMat",
  "This is how I feel #SmilieOMat"
};
...
```

4. In the `setup()` method, we need to initialize the serial port. Be sure to change the port name of your serial port like you did in the first task of this mission:

```
void setup() {
  size( 300,390 );
  smooth();
  background( 255 );
  colorMode( HSB );
  textFont( createFont( "Georgia", 20 ));
  initTwitter();
  port = new Serial( this, "/dev/ttyUSB1", 9600);
}
```

5. We need to parse the messages from the serial port; so let's add the `serialEvent()` method to get notified every time a message is available. We are checking the first letter of the string we get, and if it starts with a capital `A`, `B`, or `C`, then we will parse the rest of the string and store it in the control variables for the facial parameters:

```
void serialEvent( Serial p ) {
  String in = p.readStringUntil( '\n' );
  if ( in != null ) {
    if ( in.charAt( 0 ) == 'A' ) {
      eye = int(in.substring( 1,in.length()-2 ));
```

```
    } else if ( in.charAt( 0 ) == 'B' ) {
      mouth = int(in.substring( 1,in.length()-2 ));
    } else if ( in.charAt( 0 ) == 'C' ) {
      col = int(in.substring( 1,in.length()-2 ));
  }
}
```

6. Connect your Arduino board to the USB port and start your Smilie-O-Mat sketch. Each variable resistor controls one facial parameter.
7. Now we are going to add support for the button, so add the following code to the `serialEvent()` method to make it react to the `click` messages we send from our Arduino:

```
void serialEvent( Serial p ) {
  String in = p.readStringUntil( '\n' );
  if ( in != null ) {
    if ( in.charAt(0) == 'A' ) {
      eye = int(in.substring(1,in.length()-2));
    } else if ( in.charAt(0) == 'B' ) {
      mouth = int(in.substring(1,in.length()-2));
    } else if ( in.charAt(0) == 'C' ) {
      col = int(in.substring(1,in.length()-2));
    } else if ( "click".equals( in.trim() )) {
      tweet();
    }
  }
}
```

8. If we would run the code now, every now and then our Arduino would send two or three `click` messages in quick succession, because when a button closes or opens, there is a short phase where it has very little contact and switches very fast between the open and closed state. This behavior is called **bouncing**. To prevent multiple messages from being sent to Twitter, we are going to implement a little countermeasure in our Arduino sketch called **debouncing**. Open the Arduino sketch for our controller and add the following two variables:

```
int a = 0;
int lasta = a;

int b = 0;
int lastb = b;

int c = 0;
int lastc = c;
```

```
int  button = LOW;
int buttonLast = LOW;

long buttonTime = 0;
long debounceDelay = 50;
```

9. In our `loop()` method, we are going to save the time we use sending a click event and check the button's state only if some time has passed. In our case, we have set the `debounceDelay` variable to `50` milliseconds:

```
void loop() {
  a = analogRead(0);
  if (abs( a - lasta ) > 10 ) {
    Serial.print("A");
    Serial.println( a );
    lasta = a;
  }
  b = analogRead(1);
  if (abs( b - lastb ) > 10 ) {
    Serial.print("B");
    Serial.println( b );
    lastb = b;
  }
  c = analogRead(2);
  if (abs( c - lastc ) > 10 ) {
    Serial.print("C");
    Serial.println( c );
    lastc = c;
  }

  if ( millis() > buttonTime + debounceDelay ) {
    button = digitalRead( 2 );
    if ( buttonLast == HIGH && button == LOW ) {
      Serial.println("click");
    }
    buttonLast = button;
    buttonTime = millis();
  }
}
```

10. Compile and upload the Arduino code and switch back to our Processing sketch.

11. Now start the Smilie-O-Mat sketch and change the facial parameters using the knobs of your controller and send some tweets using the button. Create a smiling face as shown in the following screenshot and post it on Twitter:

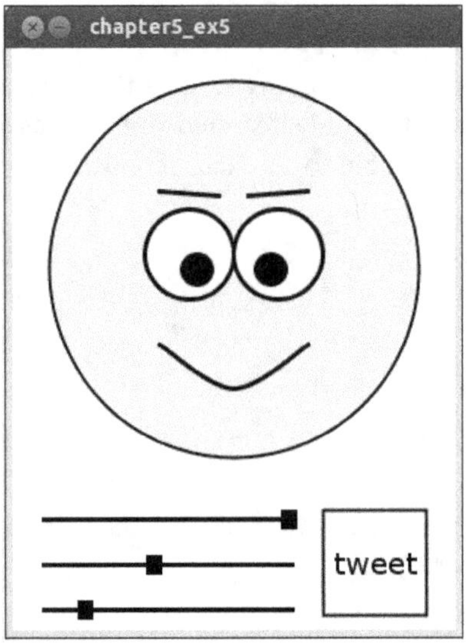

Objective Complete - Mini Debriefing

The third task of our current mission was to connect our prototyped controller to the Smilie-O-Mat sketch and to extend the sketch to parse the messages from the serial port. In step 5, we added a `serialEvent()` callback method to get notified when messages arrive on the serial port, and we checked the first letter of the message to see which of the knobs have been turned. Then, we converted the rest of the string to a number and used it to control the facial parameters of our smiley.

Starting with step 7, we added support for the `click` messages our Arduino sketch is sending when the button was pressed. Since our button sometime triggers more than one **click** message, we debounced the button by adding a little delay to the Arduino sketch so that our controller doesn't fire the messages on accident.

Putting it in a box

Now we have prototyped the controller, changed the Smilie-O-Mat sketch to support it, and tested it, but it is still a little bit brittle and hard to use. The current task is to create a customized controller that is easier and faster to use than a mouse, which we currently do not have.

What we need to do is put the controller into a more stable housing and add some knobs to the variable resistors. We will use an aluminum box to house our controller, drill some holes for the resistors, and then switch and solder the connections to prevent them from losing contact. We will also add a sheet of paper to prevent our Arduino from touching the metal directly and causing a short circuit.

Like the robots in *Project 1, Romeo and Juliet*, the version of the controller shown in this task is how I solved the problem, and this is by no means the only valid solution. You want to use a pink lunch box or a little plastic dinosaur instead of the aluminum box? No problem! This is your controller—feel free!

Engage Thrusters

Let's build a housing for our controller:

1. Take off the lid of our box and mark the spots where you want your input elements to be.
2. Drill four holes; three for our variable resistors and one for the push button, as shown in the following picture:

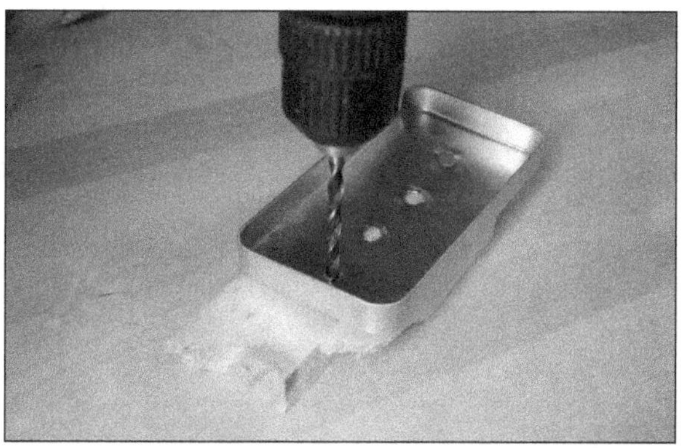

3. Screw off the nut of your resistors, stick them through the holes you just made, and fix them with the nut again.
4. Turn the lid around and solder the wires to the middle connectors.
5. Now, prepare three pieces of wire and solder them to all the left legs of our resistors.
6. Solder the wire from the second resistor to the left leg of the first one, and the wire from the third resistor to the left leg of the second one.
7. Now, take three more pieces of wire and solder them to the right legs of the resistors.

8. Solder the wire from the second resistor to the right leg of the first one, and the wire from the third resistor to the right leg of the second one. Your circuit should look like the following picture:

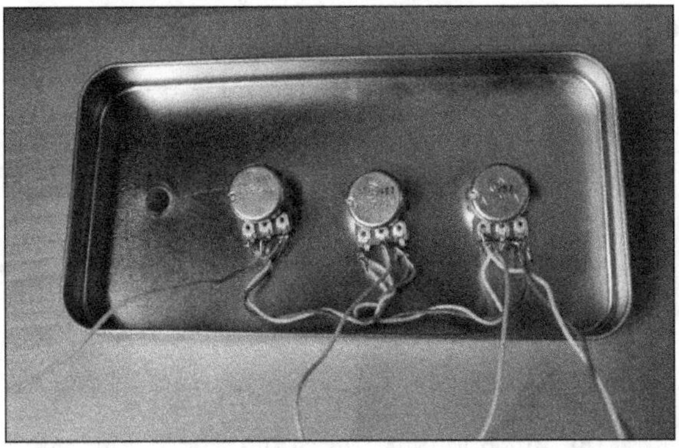

9. Now unscrew the nut of your push button and place it in the remaining hole.
10. Fix it with the nut, and then solder the fixed resistor to one of the legs and also solder a wire to the second leg.
11. Now solder the remaining leg of the resistor to the right leg of the nearest variable resistors and solder the wire to the left leg.
12. We need to solder one final piece of wire to the leg of the push button where the resistor is soldered to. Your wiring should look as shown in the following diagram:

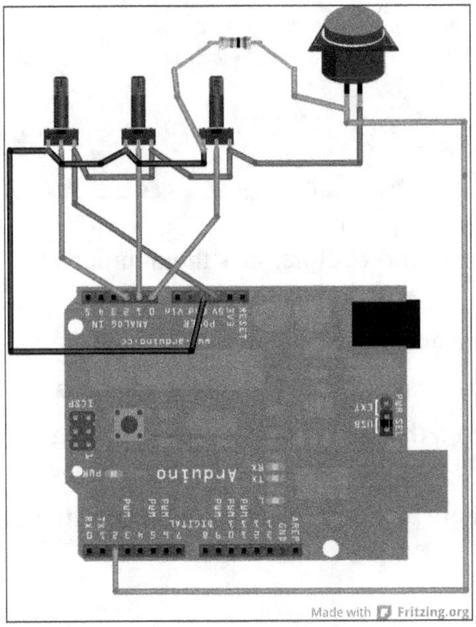

13. Take a metal cutter and cut an opening for the USB cable to the bottom half of our box. Make sure your gap is deep enough to support the cable, even when the lid is closed like as shown in this picture:

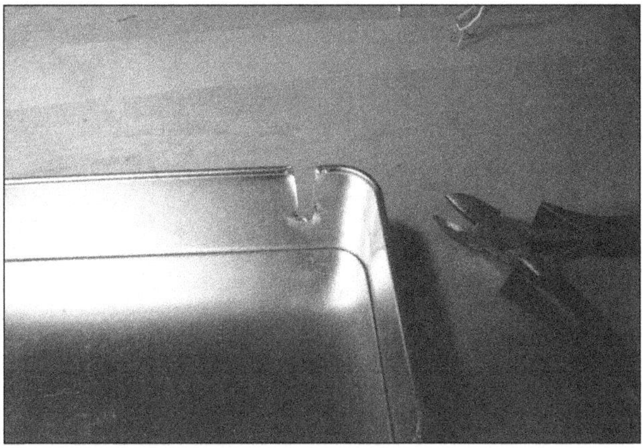

14. Place the Arduino in the box and connect the wire dangling from the left leg of the first resistor to the **5V** pin of the Arduino board.
15. Now connect the wire from the right leg to the **Gnd** pin.
16. Hook the middle wires of the resistors to analog inputs **0**, **1**, and **2**, and connect the wire we soldered to the push button to digital **2**. The next picture shows how I connected my lid to the Arduino:

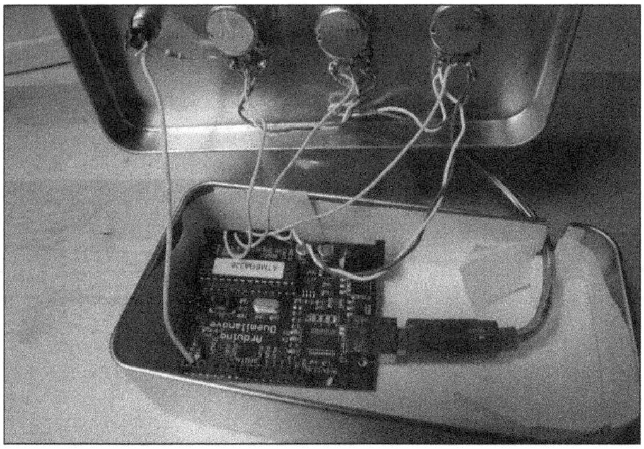

17. Close the lid of your box and stick some knobs to the turnable shaft of the variable resistors.

18. If you like you can label the knobs and the button using a sharpie pen. The next picture shows my finished controller board:

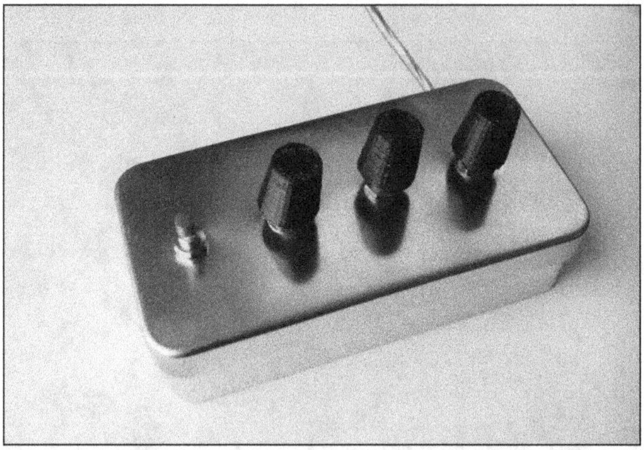

Objective Complete - Mini Debriefing

In our final task for this mission, we removed the solderless breadboard from our circuit and soldered the components together. We didn't use a circuit board, but since our circuit is very simple, we directly connected the pars using a technique sometimes called **rat nest wiring**. We also created a housing for our controller by mounting the input controllers to a box.

As I already said in the introduction to this task, how your controller housing looks and how you lay out the input elements is mainly a matter of taste. Make this controller as personal or wierd as you like.

Mission Accomplished

Our current mission was to build a custom input controller for our Smilie-O-Mat. We started with a variable resistor and connected it to the Arduino—an AVR microcontroller development board. Arduino is programmed in C++, but the API is very similar to the Processing language, and the Arduino IDE uses the same framework as the Processing IDE. We created a program in the Arduino IDE that reads the value of our resistor and sends it to the computer via a serial port. On the Processing side, we used the serial library to read the messages and display them.

In the second task, *Building your controller*, we created a prototype of the controller by connecting three variable resistors and a button to a solderless breadboard. We created a simple protocol for the messages we send to the computer, which allowed us to send the value of the input and also which controller has changed. The button sends a **click** message to the computer every time the push button's state changes from pressed to released.

In the third task, *Changing your faces*, we extended the Smilie-O-Mat sketch we created in Project 4 to parse the messages from our controller. We implemented a `serialEvent()` callback method that gets called every time a message arrives at the serial port. In this method, we checked the first letter of the message, and if it starts with `A`, `B`, or `C`, we parsed the rest of the string to an integer. These integers are used to control the facial parameters of our smiley. If the message is **click**, then we triggered the `tweet()` method, which sends the current smiley to the tweeter.

When a button is pressed or released, there is a short period of time where the contacts are very near to each other but not fully closed. In this time, short contacts of the button can trigger multiple click events accidentally. To prevent this from happening, we created a 50 millisecond time slot where we don't send a second click message. This technique is called **debouncing**, and is very common when dealing with switches or buttons.

In the final task, *Putting it in box*, we created a housing for the controller and made the connections between our components permanent by soldering them together. We didn't use a circuit board, but soldered the components together directly. We used an aluminum box for housing and laid out the knobs in a straight line, but the layout of the elements and the material of the box are a matter of taste. This controller should reflect your workflow and your personal preferences. Make it as traditional or as crazy as you like it.

You Ready to go Gung HO? A Hotshot Challenge

Arduino is an incredibly cool platform for electronic prototypes for beginners and professionals alike. In this project, we have certainly only scratched the surface of its possibilities. If you like tinkering with electronics, try to extend your Smilie-O-Mat sketch in one of the following ways:

- Add additional knobs for more facial parameters
- Add a potentiometer or a rotary encoder to choose the text message to tweet
- Add an LCD display to show the last tweet
- Connect some servos and RGB LEDs to Arduino and create an animatronics' version of the face

Project 6
Fly to the Moon

Ever since people got their hands on computers, they have used them for playing games. One of the first games was a simulation game named *Lunar Lander*, where the player had to land a lunar-landing capsule on the moon. The first version was written in 1969 and was text-based. The first graphical version of this game was written four years later for DEC Terminals. The moon-landing simulation games have been ported to nearly every computer system ever since, which makes it a perfect game for our current mission, since we are going to use the Processing modes to make a game run in the browser using `Processing.js` and on Android devices.

Mission Briefing

Our current mission is to create a moon-lander game. The first version of the game will be a Processing sketch running on your computer like the ones we have created in the previous missions. Then, we will use the various Processing modes and make the game run in the browser using the JavaScript mode, and on Android devices using the Android mode.

For each of these modes, we will adjust the game controls to fit the platform if necessary.

Why Is It Awesome?

This project is awesome for two reasons: first, we are writing a game, and this has been on the official list of computer project awesomeness since the invention of computers, and second, we write a game that runs on your computer, your Android-powered mobile device, and in your browser. This allows us to cover nearly every Internet-capable platform that currently exists, from desktop computers and laptops to mobile phones, tablets, and smart TV's. When Java arrived, it made the promise of *write once, run everywhere*. Processing is taking this promise to the next level.

Your Hotshot Objectives

This mission is split into four tasks. We will write a moon-lander simulation game in the first two tasks, and make it run in the browser and on Android devices in the remaining two tasks. The following is the list of objectives for our current task:

- Drawing a sprite
- Initiating the landing sequence
- Running your sketch in the browser
- Running the game on an Android phone

Mission Checklist

The first two tasks of this mission are implemented using only Processing. In the third task, you will need a browser that supports the `canvas` element, like Firefox, Chrome, Safari, or Internet Explorer starting with Version 8.

For the last task, we will need to download and install the Android SDK, which is described in detail later.

Drawing a sprite

The first task for our current mission is to create a sprite showing a spaceship and make it move and rotate on the screen. We will make use of the `translate()` and `rotate()` methods that Processing provides. We will also generate the level design for our game and generate a landing platform for our spaceship.

To make the game more interesting, these levels will be recreated every time the game is restarted.

Engage Thrusters

Let's start creating the level design:

1. Create a new Processing sketch and add the `setup()` and `draw()` methods, as shown in the following code snippet:

```
void setup() {
}

void draw() {
}
```

2. Now we set the size of the window to `300` by `300` and define an array of integers, which we will use to draw our moon.

```
int[] moon;

void setup() {
  size( 300, 300 );
  moon = new int[width/10+1];
  for ( int i=0; i < moon.length; i++) {
    moon[i] = int( random( 10 ));
  }
}
```

3. In our `draw()` method, we add a light blue grid that fills a white page to make it look like we made our level on a page from our mathematics notebook.

```
void draw() {
  background(255);
  stroke(200, 200, 255);
  for ( int i=0; i<height/10; i++) {
    line( 0, i*10, width, i*10);
  }
  for ( int i=0; i<width/10; i++) {
    line( i*10, 0, i*10, height );
  }
}
```

4. To draw our moon, we iterate over the array we initialized in the `setup()` method and fill it with a transparent yellow color. We will add a `drawMoon()` method to our `draw()` method and create our yellow polygon using `beginShape()` and `endShape()`.

```
void draw() {
  background(255);
  stroke(200, 200, 255);
  for ( int i=0; i<height/10; i++) {
    line( 0, i*10, width, i*10);
  }
  for ( int i=0; i<width/10; i++) {
    line( i*10, 0, i*10, height );
  }

  drawMoon();
}

void drawMoon() {
```

```
    stroke(0);
    fill(255, 200, 0, 60);
    beginShape();
    vertex(0, height);
    for ( int i=0; i < moon.length; i++) {
      vertex( i * 10, height - 20 - moon[i] );
    }
    vertex(width, height);
    endShape(CLOSE);
}
```

5. Run your sketch; it should look like the following screenshot:

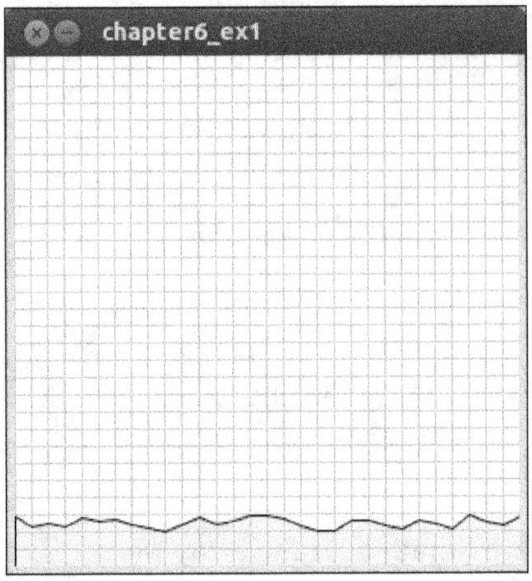

6. In this game, the player should land a rocket on a landing platform. We are going to align the platform to the grid we created in step 3 to make it look like we colored some of the boxes of our grid. Add a variable to store the landing platform's x coordinate and initialize it in the `setup()` method.

```
int[] moon;
int landingX = 0;

void setup() {
  size( 300, 300 );
  moon = new int[width/10+1];
  for ( int i=0; i < moon.length; i++) {
    moon[i] = int( random( 10 ));
  }
  landingX = int( random(3, moon.length-4))*10;
}
```

7. Now, we add a `drawLandingZone()` method to our `draw()` method and implement it by drawing a rectangle and two lines for the feet. We will use the `moon` array to calculate where our feet will touch the ground.

```
void draw() {
  background(255);
  stroke(200, 200, 255);
  for ( int i=0; i<height/10; i++) {
    line( 0, i*10, width, i*10);
  }
  for ( int i=0; i<width/10; i++) {
    line( i*10, 0, i*10, height );
  }

  drawMoon();
  drawLandingZone();
}

void drawLandingZone() {
  fill(128, 200);
  rect( landingX - 30, height - 50, 60, 10);
  line( landingX - 30, height - 20 - moon[landingX/10-3], landingX
- 20, height - 40 );
  line( landingX + 30, height - 20 - moon[landingX/10 +3],
landingX + 20, height - 40 );
}
```

8. We have our moon and a landing zone, but we still don't have a ship to land. So, draw an image of a rocket or download the image from the book's support material and add it to your sketch by dropping it on the sketch window or by using the **Sketch | Add File ...** menu.

9. Now we will add a `PImage` variable and load the image in our `setup()` method.

```
int[] moon;
int landingX = 0;
PImage ship;

void setup() {
  size( 300, 300 );
  moon = new int[width/10+1];
  for ( int i=0; i < moon.length; i++) {
    moon[i] = int(random(10));
  }
  landingX = int( random(3, moon.length-4))*10;
  ship = loadImage( "ship.png" );
}
```

10. In our `draw()` method, add a call to a method named `drawShip()` and implement this method.

```
void draw() {
  background(255);
  stroke(200, 200, 255);
  for ( int i=0; i<height/10; i++) {
    line( 0, i*10, width, i*10);
  }
  for ( int i=0; i<width/10; i++) {
    line( i*10, 0, i*10, height );
  }

  drawMoon();
  drawLandingZone();
  drawShip();
}

void drawShip() {
  image(ship, 150, 100);
}
```

11. Currently, we are able to position the ship where we want it by changing the x and y coordinates, but we also need to be able to rotate the ship, since in our game the player has to turn the ship and fire the thruster to steer it to the platform and land as smoothly as possible. To fix this, we will use the `rotate()` and `translate()` commands. We will also use `pushMatrix()` and `popMatrix()` to make sure our `rotate()` method only affects the image and not the whole window.

```
void drawShip() {
  pushMatrix();
  translate(150, 100);
  rotate(PI/6);
  image( ship, -ship.width/2, -ship.height/2, ship.width, ship.
height );

  popMatrix();
}
```

12. If you run your sketch now, the rocket is hovering above the moon at an angle of 30 degrees, but the moon, the landing platform, and our grid are unchanged.

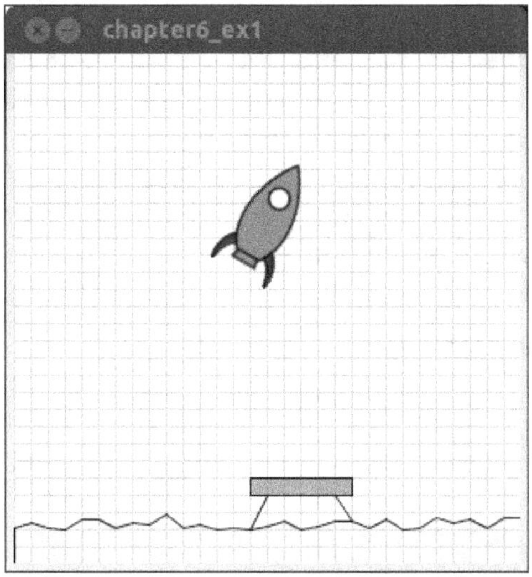

Objective Complete - Mini Debriefing

For the first task of our current mission, we created all the graphical elements we needed for our game. In steps 1 to 3, we created a grid that looks like a math notebook to make the game look like it has been drawn in class (during a break of course!).

In step 4, we added a randomly generated lunar landscape. We randomly generated the moon's ground level offsets in our `setup()` method and stored it in an array. This way, we can make sure that the moon stays the same during one game, but can be recreated without a hassle when the player has finished a level and restarts it. To draw the moon, we created a complex polygon using the `beginShape()` and `endShape()` methods and defined the vertices of the polygon using the `vertex()` command.

The landing platform consists of a rectangle that is aligned to the grid to make it look like we have colored some of the squares. We also added feet to the platform and made them touch the ground level of the moon by using the array from the previous section.

Finally, we used an image of the ship and created a transformation context to be able to rotate it. We need the new context to make sure that our calls to `translate()` and `rotate()` only affect the drawing operations we use for the ship, and not all the other sections of our screen. A new context is started with `pushMatrix()` and ends with `popMatrix()`. Every scale, translate, or rotate operation we use in this context only affects the drawing operations of it. Our grid, moon, and landing platform are unaffected by them.

Initiating the landing sequence

The second task of our current mission is to implement the physics simulation and the game controls for our moon-lander game. In this task, the game should able to run on desktop computers and laptops running Java. We will add keyboard controls to enable the player to turn the rocket left and right, and when the player hits the up cursor key, the thruster will fire and accelerate the rocket a bit in the direction it has been turned.

Engage Thrusters

Let's start implementing the physics by adding moon gravity:

1. The first thing we need to implement for our moon physics simulation are the variables to store the ship's position, the direction, the current speed, and the strength of the moon's gravity.

   ```
   int[] moon;
   int landingX = 0;
   PImage ship;

   PVector pos = new PVector( 150, 20 );
   PVector speed = new PVector( 0, 0 );
   PVector g = new PVector( 0, 1.622 );
   ```

2. Now we need to update the position of our ship at every frame, so we add an `update()` method to our sketch and call it from our `draw()` method.

   ```
   void draw() {
     background(255);
     stroke(200, 200, 255);
     for ( int i=0; i<height/10; i++) {
       line( 0, i*10, width, i*10);
     }
     for ( int i=0; i<width/10; i++) {
       line( i*10, 0, i*10, height );
     }

     drawMoon();
     drawLandingZone();
     drawShip();

     update();
   }

   void update() {
   }
   ```

3. We also need to change the call to the `translate()` command in our `drawShip()` method to use the new `pos` variable.

```
void drawShip() {
  pushMatrix();
  translate(pos.x, pos.y);
  rotate(PI/6);
  image( ship, -ship.width/2, -ship.height/2, ship.width, ship.
height );

  popMatrix();
}
```

4. In this `update()` method, we are going to implement all our physics calculations. So let's implement the influence of the gravity on our ship.

```
void update() {

  PVector gDelta = new PVector( g.x / frameRate, g.y / frameRate);
  speed.add( gDelta );
  pos.add( speed );
}
```

5. Since the moon's surface is quite solid, we also add a test that stops the ship once it reaches the surface.

```
void update() {

 PVector gDelta = new PVector( g.x / frameRate, g.y / frameRate);

  speed.add( gDelta );
  pos.add( speed );

  if ( pos.x > landingX - 40 && pos.x < landingX + 40  && pos.y >
height-50 - ship.height/2 ) {
     pos.y = height - 50 - ship.height/2;
  } else if (pos.y > height - 20 - ship.height/2 ) {
 pos.y = height - 20 - ship.height/2;

}
}
```

6. Run your sketch now. The rocket should start from the top of our window, drop to the floor, and stop there as shown in the following screenshot:

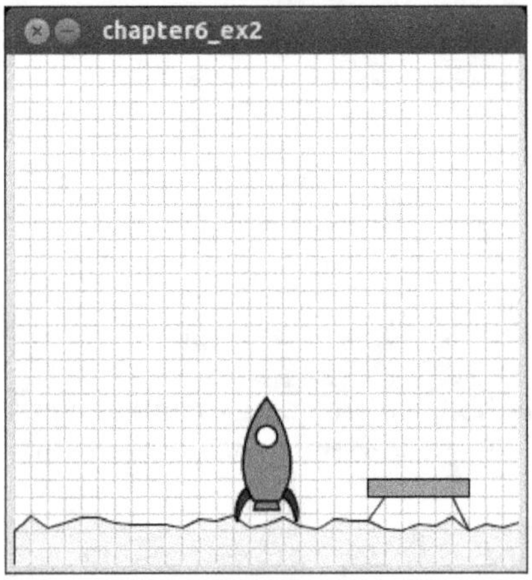

7. Since the game is not about crashing rockets into the moon but rather about landing them, we need to implement a method to slow down the rocket. The game will be controlled using the keyboard, so let's add a variable for the acceleration and the rotation angle.

```
int[] moon;
int landingX = 0;
PImage ship;

PVector pos = new PVector( 150, 20 );
PVector speed = new PVector( 0, 0 );
PVector g = new PVector( 0, 1.622 );

float a = 0;
float acc = 0;
```

8. Also, add a `keyPressed()` method to enable the player to change the rotation and acceleration of the rocket.

```
void keyPressed() {
  if ( keyCode == LEFT ) {
    a -= 0.1;
  }
  if ( keyCode == RIGHT ) {
    a += 0.1;
  }
  if ( keyCode == UP ) {
    acc += 0.04;
```

```
    acc = max( acc, 1/frameRate);
  }
}
```

9. Now, we need to adapt our `drawShip()` method and use the rotation variable to change the ship's rotation.

```
void drawShip() {
  pushMatrix();
  translate(pos.x, pos.y);
  rotate(a);
  image( ship, -20, -40, 40, 75 );
  popMatrix();
}
```

10. We also need to adapt our `update()` method to make the acceleration and the rotation angle influence our ship's speed and position.

```
void update() {
  PVector f = new PVector( cos( a+PI/2 ) * -acc,
    sin( a+PI/2 ) * -acc );
  if ( acc > 0 ) {
    acc *= 0.95;
  }


 PVector gDelta = new PVector( g.x / frameRate, g.y / frameRate);

  speed.add( gDelta );
  speed.add( f );
  pos.add( speed );

  if ( pos.x > landingX - 40 && pos.x < landingX + 40
    && pos.y > height-50 - ship.height/2 ) {
    pos.y = height - 50 - ship.height/2;
  } else if (pos.y > height - 20 - ship.height/2 ) {
    pos.y = height - 20 - ship.height/2;
  }
}
```

11. Our ship can now be turned and also reacts to the acceleration commands. Now, we add some code to the `drawShip()` method to make flames come out of the thruster when the user accelerates the ship.

```
void drawShip() {
  pushMatrix();
  translate(pos.x, pos.y);
```

```
    rotate(a);
    noFill();
    for ( int i=4; i >= 0; i--) {
      stroke(255, i*50, 0);
      fill(255, i*50, 20);
      ellipse( 0, 30, min(1, acc*10) *i*4, min(1, acc*10)* i*10);
    }

  image( ship, -ship.width/2, -ship.height/2, ship.width, ship.
  height );
    popMatrix();
  }
```

12. After the ship has landed on the platform or crashed to the moon surface, the game can only be played again by restarting the sketch. We are now going to fix this by adding a game state to our sketch. Add a variable named `state` to store the current state and define three constants named `WAITING`, `RUNNING`, and `FINISHED`. We initialize the `state` variable to `WAITING` and extract the level generation code from our `setup()` method to a method called `reset()`.

```
int[] moon;
int landingX = 0;

PVector pos = new PVector( 150, 20 );
PVector speed = new PVector( 0, 0 );
PVector g = new PVector( 0, 1.622 );

float a = 0;
float acc = 0;

PImage ship;

int WAITING =1;
int RUNNING = 2;
int FINISHED = 3;

int state = WAITING;

void setup() {
  size(300, 300);
  ship = loadImage( "ship.png" );
  reset();
}

void reset() {
```

```
  moon = new int[width/10+1];
  for ( int i=0; i < moon.length; i++) {
    moon[i] = int(random(10));
  }
  landingX = int( random(3, moon.length-4))*10;

  pos = new PVector( 150, 20 );
  a = 0;
  acc = 0;
  speed = new PVector(0,0);
}
```

13. In our `draw()` method, we will check the `state` variable and only call the `update()` method when the state is `RUNNING`. We will also add the `drawWaiting()` and `drawFinished()` methods that get called in the corresponding states.

```
void draw() {
  background(255);
  stroke(200, 200, 255);
  for ( int i=0; i<height/10; i++) {
    line( 0, i*10, width, i*10);
  }
  for ( int i=0; i<width/10; i++) {
    line( i*10, 0, i*10, height );
  }

  drawMoon();
  drawLandingZone();
  drawShip();

  if ( state == WAITING ) {
    drawWaiting();
  }
  else if ( state == RUNNING ) {
    update();
  }
  else if ( state == FINISHED ) {
    drawFinished();
  }
}

void drawWaiting() {
  textAlign( CENTER );
  fill(0);
```

```
    text( "Click mouse to start", width/2, height/2);
}

void drawFinished() {
  textAlign( CENTER );
  fill( 0 );
  if ( pos.x > landingX - 40 && pos.x < landingX + 40 ) {
    text( "you landed the ship!", width/2, height/2);
  } else {
    text( "you missed the platform!", width/2, height/2);
  }
  text( "click to restart", width/2, height/2 + 20 );
}
```

14. Now we add a `mouseClicked()` method that changes the state to `RUNNING` if the state was `WAITING` or `FINISHED`. In the latter case, we also call the `reset()` method we created in step 12 to generate a new level.

```
void mousePressed() {
  if ( state == WAITING ) {
    state = RUNNING;
  } else if ( state == FINISHED ) {
    reset();
    state = RUNNING;
  }
}
```

15. In our `update()` method, we change the state of the game to `FINISHED` if our rocket lands on the platform or crashes to the moon surface.

```
void update() {
  PVector f = new PVector( cos( a+PI/2 ) * -acc,
    sin( a+PI/2 ) * -acc );
  if ( acc > 0 ) {
    acc *= 0.95;
  }


 PVector gDelta = new PVector( g.x / frameRate, g.y / frameRate);

  speed.add( gDelta );
  speed.add( f );
  pos.add( speed );

  if ( pos.x > landingX - 40 && pos.x < landingX + 40  && pos.y >
height-50 - ship.height/2 ) {
    pos.y = height - 50 - ship.height/2;
    state = FINISHED;
```

```
      acc = 0;
    } else if (pos.y > height - 20 - ship.height/2 ) {
      pos.y = height - 20 - ship.height/2;
      state = FINISHED;
      acc = 0;
    }
  }
```

16. Run your sketch now and try to land the rocket on the platform by using the arrow keys. Your game window should look as shown in the following screenshot when the rocket is accelerated:

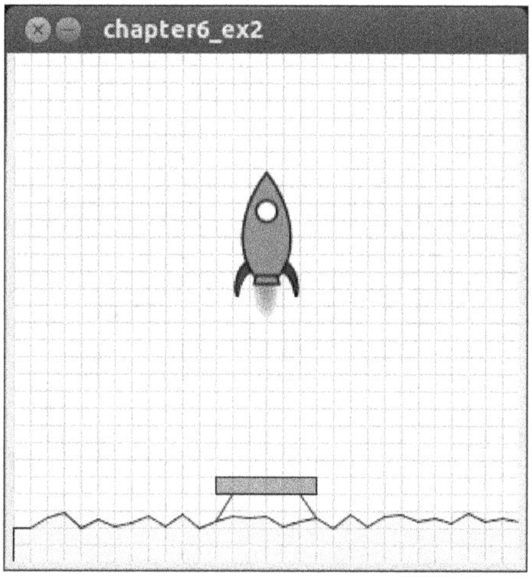

Objective Complete - Mini Debriefing

In this task of our current mission, we have completed the game for desktop and laptops running Mac OS X, Linux, or Windows. From step 1 to step 5, we implemented moon gravity to our sketch and made the rocket drop to the ground. We used a very simple physics simulation that adds a fraction of the moon's gravitational force to a speed variable at every frame and then adds the updated speed to the current position.

From step 6 to step 10, we implemented another force that influences our ship by implementing some keyboard control, allowing the player to turn the ship and to fire the thruster. We also made some flames come out of the thruster in step 11 to give some visual clues to the player on how strong the rocket is being accelerated.

Starting with step 12, we implemented a game-state system to prevent the rocket from dropping to the floor as soon as the game has been started. It also enables the player to restart the game after the rocket has landed on the platform or crashed to the moon by clicking on the program window.

Running your sketch in the browser

The next task of our current mission is to take the game we have created in the previous task and make it run in the browser using JavaScript. We will use the `Processing.js` mode to make our script run and we will create a customized HTML template for our game. The `Processing.js` mode allows us to run sketches that don't use any external libraries with little to no change in a modern browser.

Engage Thrusters

Let's convert the game to a browser application:

1. Open our sketch and switch from the Processing mode to the **JavaScript** mode by clicking on the icon above the **New Tab** icon and selecting **JavaScript** , as shown in the following screenshot:

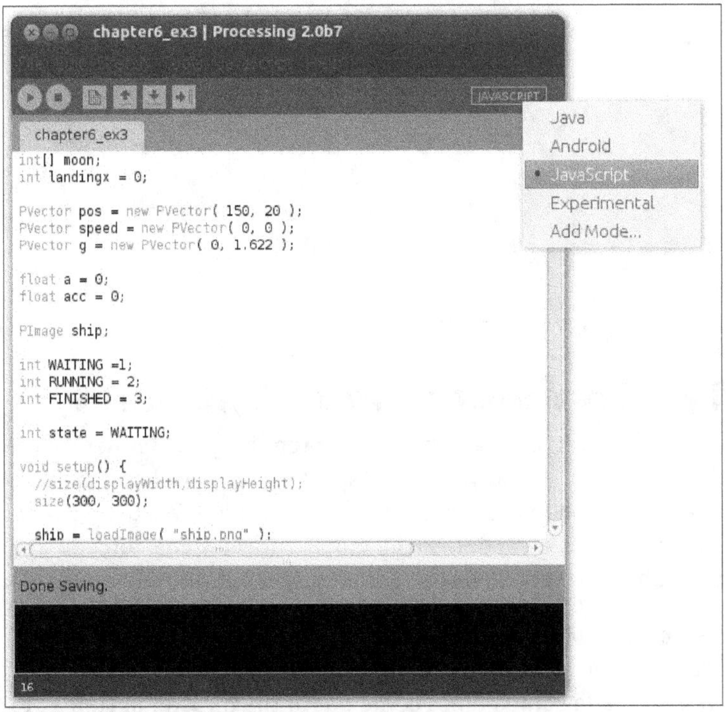

2. Now run the sketch. Processing starts a small web server in the background and opens the default browser with an HTML page running our game. This following screenshot shows the game running in a Firefox browser:

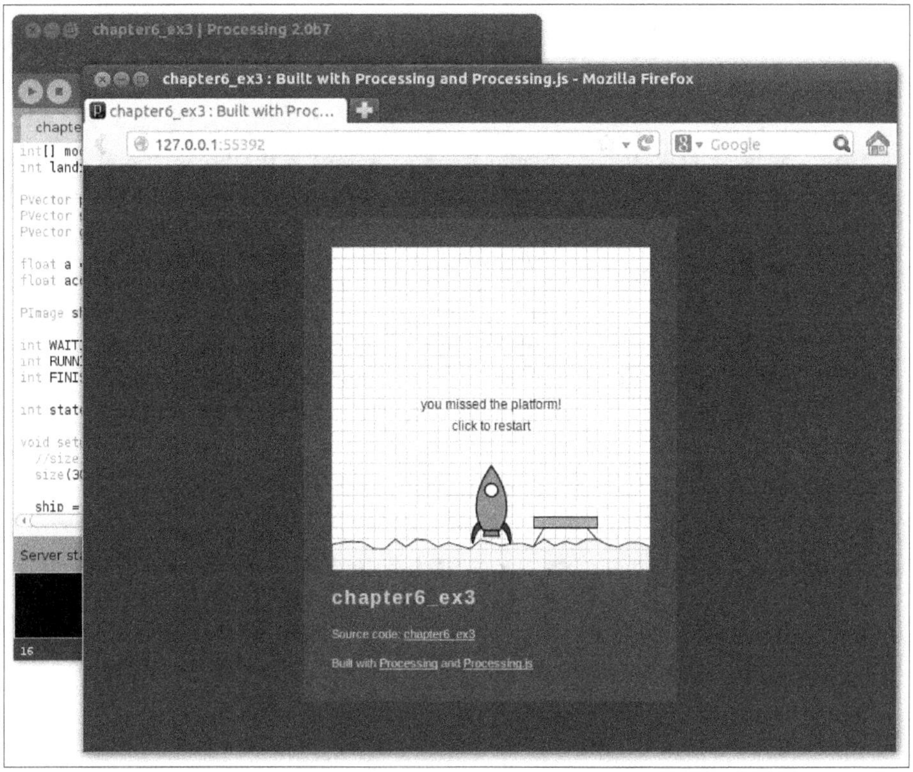

3. `Processing.js` is implementing a little workaround to make the image loading work. If we run our code as it is, it works perfectly on a local machine or on a very fast Internet connection, but we can make things easier for Processing by activating the preloading of the images we need. Click on the **JavaScript** | **Playback Settings (Directives)** menu, and then on the dialog that opens click on the **scan** button next to **"preload": images**, as shown in the following screenshot:

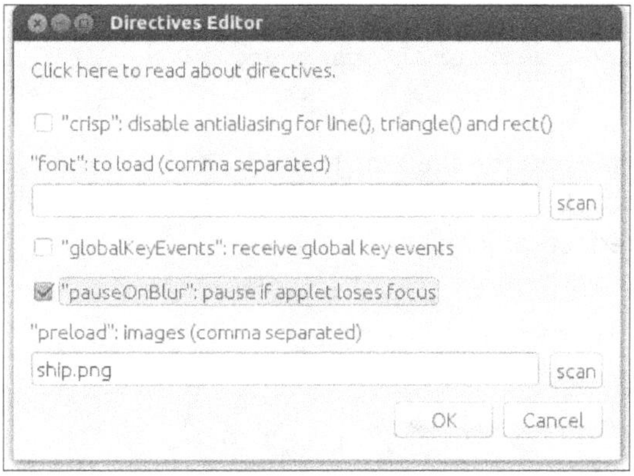

4. We also check the **"pauseOnBlur"** checkbox to make our sketch pause when the browser window is switched to the background and loses the focus, since we don't want the player's rockets to crash into the moon just because another application window opened a dialog.
5. After we click on **OK**, Processing inserts a comment at the beginning of our sketch and defines some directives for `Processing.js`, which are ignored by the other Processing modes.
6. When we run our sketch in the `Processing.js` mode, Processing generates an HTML page and draws the program's output on a `canvas` element. This HTML page is generated from a default template. We are now going to edit this template and add a little PNG graphic with a star pattern as our background image. So, click on the **JavaScript | Start Custom Template** menu to generate a copy of the template for our program.
7. Now, click on the **JavaScript | Show Custom Template** menu to open the folder containing the template Processing uses for the HTML page.
8. We need an image we can use as our background, so either create a black image with white dots, or download my version from the book's support file at `www.packtpub.com/support` and drop it into the `template` folder next to the `template.html` and `procesing.js` files.
9. Open the `template.html` file using a text editor of your choice. The `template.html` file is a normal HTML file containing some special placeholder variables that get replaced by Processing when the sketch gets started. Find the CSS section at the beginning of the file and add a `background` directive to the style definition of the `body` element.

```
body {
    background-color: #333; color: #bbb; line-height: normal;
    font-family: Lucida Grande, Lucida Sans, Arial,
    Helvetica Neue, Verdana, Geneva, sans-serif;
    font-size: 11px; font-weight: normal; text-decoration: none;
      line-height: 1.5em;
    background-image:url('stars.png');
  }
```

10. Save the template and run the sketch again. The background of our HTML page is now sprinkled with stars like a cloudless night, as shown in the following screenshot—perfect for flying to the moon:

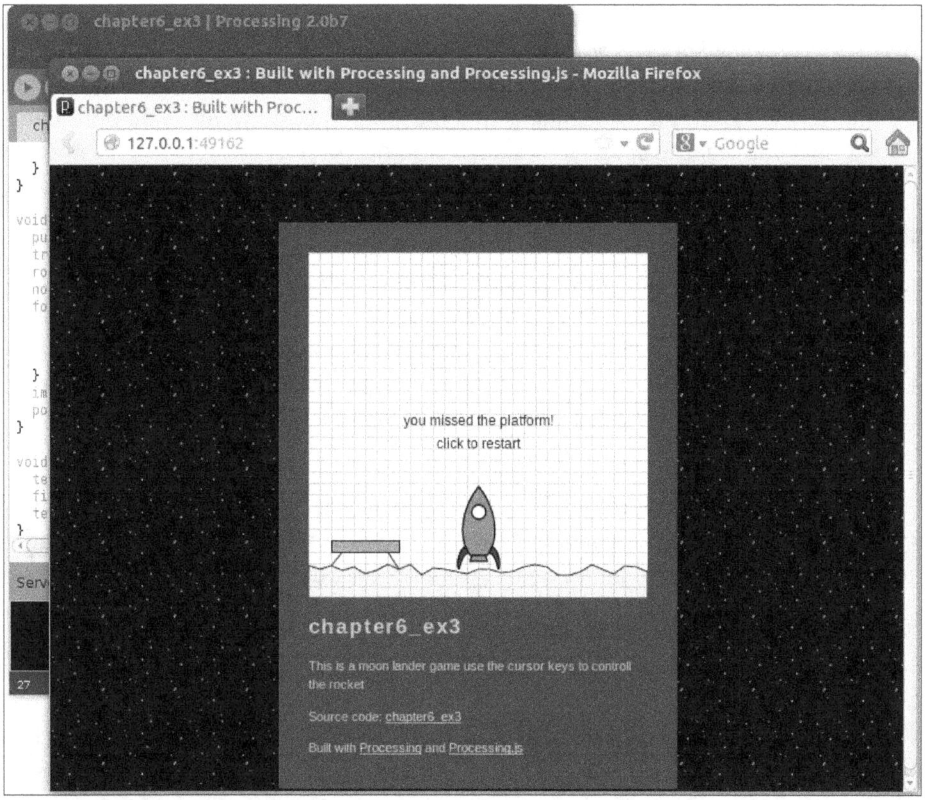

11. Currently, the HTML page shows the program name and a link to the source code of our sketch. Now we add a special comment to the beginning of our program that gets inserted in the template between these two. Add a comment like this to your sketch right after the `Processing.js` directives:

```
/* @pjs pauseOnBlur=true;
preload="ship.png";
 */

/**
This is a moon lander game use the cursor keys to control the
rocket
*/

int[] moon;
int landingX = 0;
...
```

12. When we have tested our JavaScript version and are sure that everything works as expected, we want to export the sketch so that we can deploy it on a web server. Save the sketch and click on the **File** | **Export** menu. Processing generates a folder named `web-export` containing all the files that need to be installed on a web server if you want to share your sketch with the world.

Objective Complete - Mini Debriefing

Our current task for this mission was to run the moon-lander game in the browser using Processing's **JavaScript** mode, which was accomplished in step 1 and 2. For some tasks, like loading images, `Processing.js` has to rely on the network handling of the browser, which might cause delays in our sketch when we load an image for the first time. Fortunately, `Processing.js` provides a method to preload our image before the sketch gets started, which we activated from step 3 to step 5.

Starting with step 6, we changed the HTML template where Processing embeds our sketch when we run or export it. We activated a custom template for our game and added a background image to the style definition of our template's CSS section.

Finally, we exported the sketch and all the needed files to enable the installation on a real web server.

Running the game on an Android phone

Our final task of this mission is to make our moon-lander game run on Android devices. We will install the Android SDK and use the **Android** mode of Processing to turn our game into an Android app. We will use the Android emulator and make the sketch run on devices connected via USB. Since most Android devices come without a keyboard but do have a touch screen, we will adapt our game controls and then run in full-screen mode.

Engage Thrusters

Let's convert the game to an Android app:

1. Go to `http://developer.android.com/sdk/index.html` and download the Android SDK for your computer. We don't need the bundled version that comes with Eclipse. Since we already have an IDE (Processing), we need to scroll down to the **SDK Tools Only** section and download the SDK package for our operating system.
2. Unpack the downloaded file and run the Android command from the `tools` folder.
3. Processing creates apps that run on Android starting with Version 2.3.3, since this was the first Android version with a hardware-accelerated OpenGL support. So let's select the SDK package and the Google API for this platform. If you are using Windows, you also need the Google USB driver package from the `Extras` folder. Linux and Mac OS X need no special driver. Select the packages as shown in the following screenshot and click on **Install**:

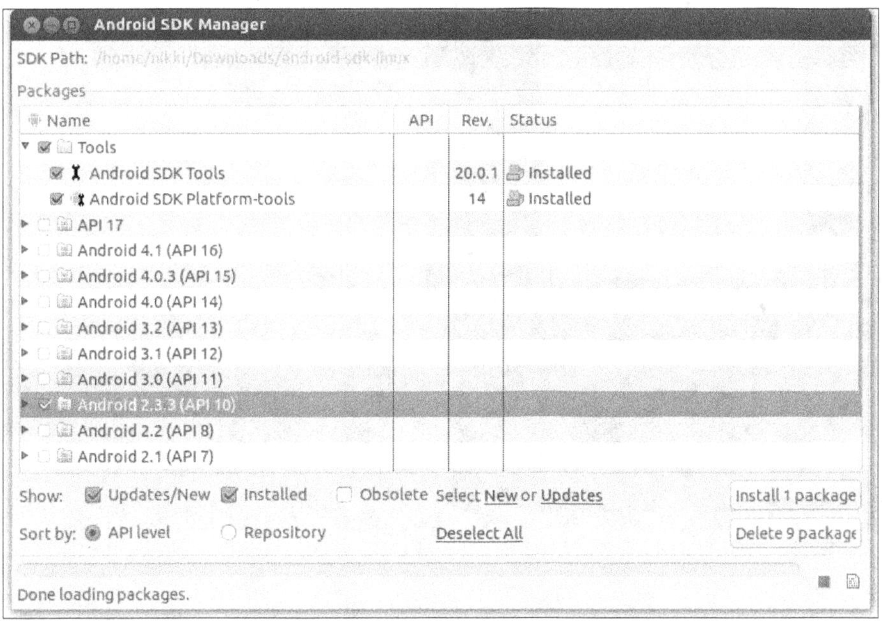

4. Now we need to tell Processing where it can find the Android SDK. Open our Processing game and switch to the **Android** mode on the right. When you do this for the first time, Processing asks you where it can find the Android SDK, so point it to the folder you have unpacked in step 2. A detailed install instruction can be found in the Processing wiki at `http://wiki.processing.org/w/Android`.

5. We are now going to run our sketch in an emulator. Click on the **Sketch** | **Run in Emulator** menu item. Processing now compiles the sketch to an Android app, creates a virtual device for the Android emulator, and then starts it. Since starting the Android emulator can take a while, especially when it's run for the first time, it's possible that you get a timeout error. In this case, simply repeat the step. After a while, you should see our sketch running in an emulator window like this:

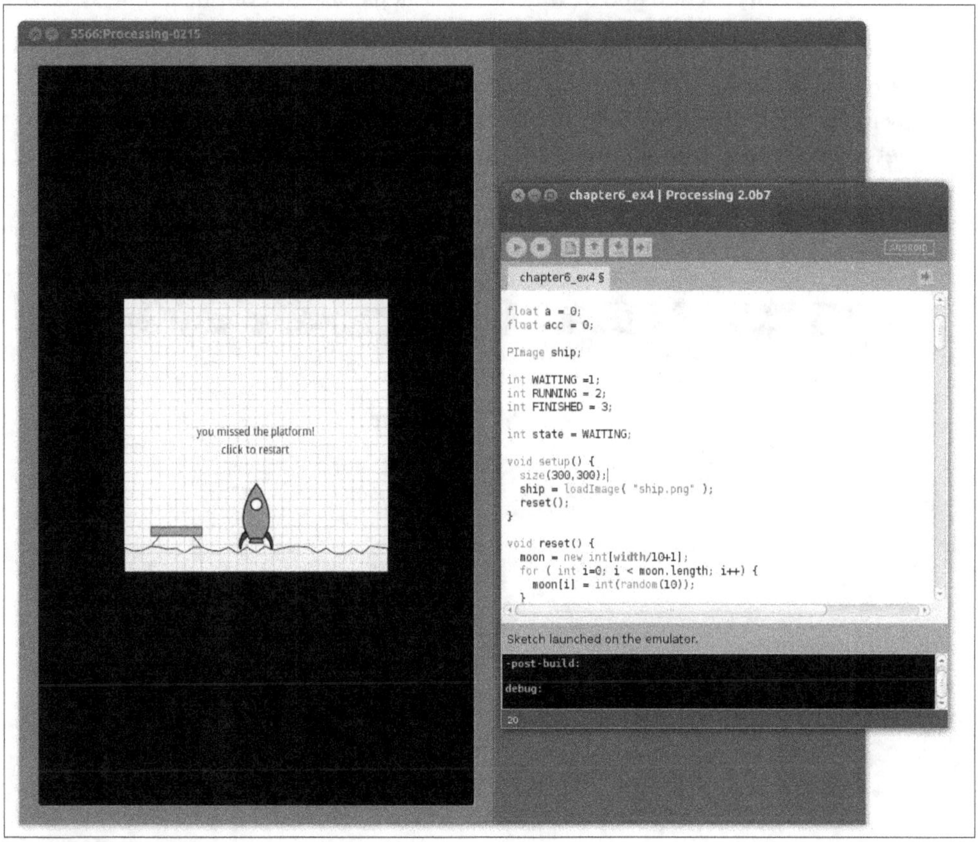

6. On a mobile device, applications usually run in full-screen mode since there are now windowing systems. We will now tell our sketch to make use of the entire screen. We also tell our sketch to run in landscape mode by using the `orientation()` method.

```
void setup() {
  size(displayWidth,displayHeight);
  orientation(LANDSCAPE);
  ship = loadImage( "ship.png" );
  reset();
}
```

7. Now the sketch runs in full-screen mode, but it is still unplayable on most Android devices because very few of them come with a hardware keyboard. To fix this, we need to implement controls that can be used with a touchscreen. The **Android** mode maps touch events to the mouse handling callbacks, so all we have to do is add some code to our `mousePressed()` method to control the ship. If our player touches the bottom third of the screen, we fire the thruster. If the upper part of the screen gets touched, we turn the ship left or right.

```
void mousePressed() {
  if ( state == WAITING ) {
    state = RUNNING;
  } else if ( state == RUNNING ) {
    if ( mouseY > height * 2 / 3) {
    acc += 0.04;
    acc = max( acc, 1/frameRate);
    }
    else if ( mouseX < width / 2 ) {
      a -= 0.1;
    }
    else {
      a += 0.1;
    }
  } else if ( state == FINISHED ) {
    reset();
    state = RUNNING;
  }
}
```

8. Run the sketch in the emulator again by clicking on the **Sketch** | **Run in Emulator** menu, and then play the game by clicking on the window.
9. With Processing in the **Android** mode, we can run our sketches on hardware devices too. So, if you have a mobile phone or a tablet running on Android, you can connect them to your computer using an USB cable and enable USB debugging in the **Developer** options section of your phone settings. Now you can run the sketch on the device by clicking on the **Sketch** | **Run on Devices** menu. Here is a picture of my mobile phone running the moon-lander game:

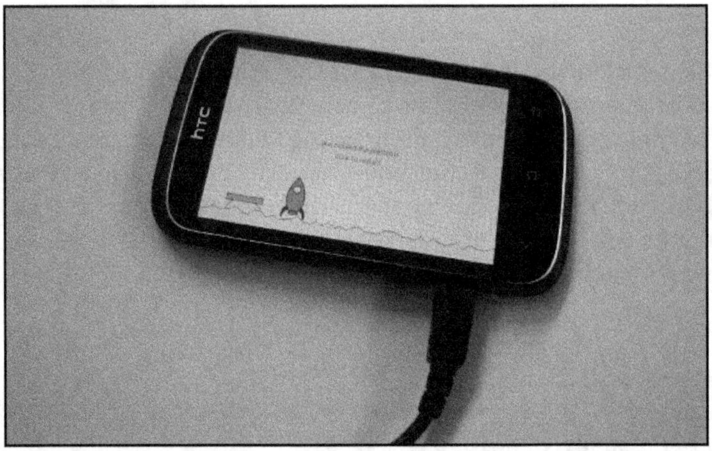

Objective Complete - Mini Debriefing

For this task of our current mission, we made our moon-lander game run on Android devices. From step 1 to step 4, we downloaded and installed the Android SDK, which is needed by Processing to compile the Android apps. We then made the game run in an emulator.

In step 6, we tweaked our code a little bit to make the game run in full-screen mode and to fix the device orientation to landscape mode. Since most Android devices come without a keyboard, we also added support for touchscreen input.

Finally, we made our app run on a real device.

Classified Intel

The Android mode also allows you to export your sketch as an Android project that can be used to create a signed APK file that can then be used to upload the app to Google Play or if you want to distribute it on your own. You can find detailed instructions on how to do this in the Processing Wiki at `http://wiki.processing.org/w/Android#Distributing_Apps`.

Mission Accomplished

For this mission, we created a moon-lander simulation game and made it run in the browser using the Processing's **JavaScript** mode and on Android devices using the **Android** mode.

In the first task, *Drawing a sprite*, we created the graphics for the game starting with a background grid to make the game look like it's drawn on a mathematics notebook. We then added a moon landscape and a landing platform. The rocket has to be able to move and rotate, so we used the `pushMatrix()` and `popMatrix()` methods to separate the translating and rotation operations we want to perform on the image form the rest of the drawing code.

In the second task, *Initiating the landing sequence*, we implemented the physics and the controls for our game. We started by adding a vector for the moon's gravity and one for the rocket's speed. For every frame, the gravity influences the speed of the ship, which in turn influences the rocket's position.

Then we implemented a `keyPressed()` method and enabled the player to rotate and accelerate the rocket. The acceleration is also added to the speed vector of the rocket.

Finally, we implemented a game loop and stopped the game when the rocket hits the moon or lands on the platform.

In the third task, *Running your sketch in the browser*, we used the Processing's **JavaScript** mode to create a JavaScript version that runs in the browser. We activated the image preloading to ensure the image for our rocket is available as soon as the game starts, and we learned how to change the HTML template where our sketch is embedded.

In the final task, *Running the game on an Android phone*, we created an Android app from our game by using the Processing's **Android** mode. We installed the Android SDK and the necessary APIs. We adapted our code a little bit to make the app run in full-screen mode and we also fixed the rotation to landscape.

To make the game playable on a device without a keyboard, we had to change the game controls to support touchscreens.

You Ready to go Gung HO? A Hotshot Challenge

We created a nice little casual game for this example, which is playable, but can be extended and completed in various ways, like for example:

- Calculate scores for the landings using the speed and the landing angle
- Create a high score list
- Use the tilt sensor of an Android device for controlling the rocket
- Limit the fuel the player has available for the landing
- Try to make the moon surface circular and calculate the position of the landing platform using polar coordinates
- Use an Android device as a game controller for the desktop version of the game

Project 7

The Neon Globe

Nearly every hero, computer hacker, or villain in an 80s movie has a spinning neon globe on one of their computer screens at their headquarters to—hmmm, well—probably emphasize their global impact. But who cares! These spinning wire frame drawings of a globe are absolutely awesome, so our current mission is to recreate these visuals and create a spinning neon globe for our mission control room.

Mission Briefing

For this mission, we are going to create a spinning neon globe starting with the mesh of a sphere. We are then going to add some lights to make our sphere smooth. We will then add a world map texture to our sphere to turn it into a spinning globe. Finally, we'll use some filters using the shader framework that has been added in Processing 2 to add a glow effect similar to the vector displays of an early arcade cabinet or the displays in an old James Bond movie.

And because we don't live in the 80s any longer, we will add the ability to switch our globe to a modern satellite image display as well.

Why Is It Awesome?

This mission gives us the opportunity to explore the awesome 3D capabilities of Processing. We start with a simple wireframe model of a sphere, and then learn how to light the scene and texture our mesh. For our final task, we will learn how to create code that runs in parallel on the graphics card without further burdening the CPU or decreasing the frame rate of our sketch.

Your Hotshot Objectives

Our current mission objectives are:

- Rotating a sphere
- Let there be light
- From sphere to globe
- From globe to neon globe

Mission Checklist

For this mission, we need no libraries, SDKs, or any additional software apart from Processing. We are going to create 3D graphics, so you do need a graphics card in your computer that is capable of accelerating 3D renderings and which supports OpenGL 2.0 or later versions. If your computer or graphics card was built after 2005, you are most certainly fine.

Rotating a sphere

The first task of our current mission is to create the mesh of a sphere and make it rotate on the screen. We will create a mesh resembling the latitude and longitude rings found on a globe. To simplify the mathematics required to create these rings, we will use polar coordinates and convert them to Cartesian XYZ coordinates when creating our sphere. Processing can make use of your graphics card's memory for storing the model data, which improves the speed of drawing the object on the screen a lot if the object itself is static. Since our sphere doesn't change while our sketch is running, we will use a `PShape` object to store the model data.

Engage Thrusters

Let's start with the creation of our sphere's mesh:

1. Open a new sketch and add the `setup()` and `draw()` methods.

```
void setup() {
}

void draw() {
}
```

2. In the `setup()` method, we define our sketch window size and set the rendering mode to `P3D`. We also create a `PShape` object named `sphere` to store the mesh data.`PShape sphere;`

```
void setup() {
   size(400,400,P3D);
}
```

3. Next, we create a new method named `makeSphere()`, which takes the radius and step size (in degrees) as parameters. The return value of our function is the new `PShape` object containing our sphere's vertices.

```
PShape makeSphere( int r, int step) {
}
```

4. Polar coordinates use two angles and a radius to define a point on a spherical surface; every point has the same distance to the origin, so our radius stays fixed, but our angles change. We will now define two nested loops that iterate over all the possible angle positions.

```
PShape makeSphere( int r, int step) {
  PShape s = createShape();

  s.noFill();
  s.stroke(255);
  s.strokeWeight(2);

  for( int i = 0; i < 180; i+=step ) {
    for( int j = 0; j <= 360; j+=step ) {

    }
  }
  return s;
}
```

5. Now we will be using the polar coordinates to generate rings on our sphere using quad strips. We need to define point pairs (like in the following figure) and use the `vertex()` method to feed the converted Cartesian coordinates to our `PShape` object:

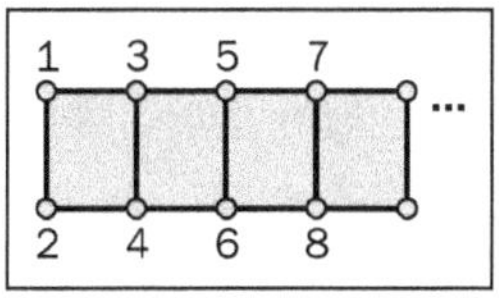

6. To convert the polar coordinates into Cartesian ones, we need to calculate the sine and cosine values of the angles. Processing expects the angles (which we use as an input for trigonometric functions or rotate statements) to be in radians, which go from 0 to 2π instead of 0 to 360 for a full circle. We will use the `radians()` method to convert the angles before feeding them to those functions.

```
PShape makeSphere( int R, int step) {
  PShape s = createShape();

  s.beginShape(QUAD_STRIP);
  s.noFill();
  s.stroke(255);
  s.strokeWeight(2);

  for( int i = 0; i < 180; i+=step ) {
    float sini = sin( radians( i ));
    float cosi = cos( radians( i ));
    float sinip = sin( radians( i + step ));
    float cosip = cos( radians( i + step ));

    for( int j = 0; j <= 360; j+=step ) {
      float sinj = sin( radians( j ));
      float cosj = cos( radians( j ));

      s.vertex( r * cosj * sini, r * -cosi, r * sinj * sini);
      s.vertex( r * cosj * sinip, r * -cosip, r * sinj * sinip);
    }
  }

  s.endShape();
  return s;
}
```

7. In our `setup()` method, we add a call to our `makeSphere()` method.

```
void setup() {
   size(400,400,P3D);
   sphere = makeSphere( 150, 5);
}
```

8. To make the sphere visible, we need to make use of our `sphere` object in the `draw()` method by using the `shape()` method.

```
void draw() {
  background(0);
  translate( width/2, height/2 );
  shape(sphere);
}
```

9. Run your sketch now. The sphere should look like this:

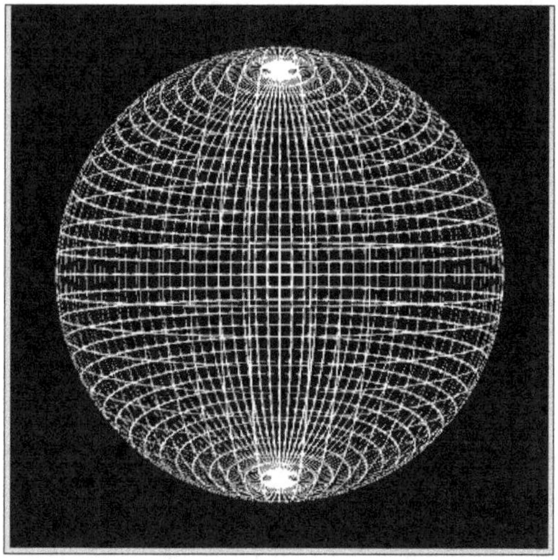

10. Now we are going to make our sphere rotate. In our `setup()` method, we fix the frame rate to `25` frames per second using the `frameRate()` method.

```
void setup() {
    size(400,400,P3D);
    frameRate(25);
    sphere = makeSphere( 150, 5);
}
```

11. Next, we define a variable for the angle of rotation and increase it with every frame in our `draw()` method. We also add a call to `rotateX()` to tilt the sphere slightly, and a call to `rotateY()` to make it rotate around the y axis.

```
float a = 0;

void draw() {
  background(0);
  translate( width/2, height/2 );
  pushMatrix();
  rotateX( radians(-30));
  rotateY( a );
  a+= 0.01;
  shape(sphere);
  popMatrix();
}
```

12. Run your sketch. We now have a rotating wireframe model of a sphere.

Objective Complete - Mini Debriefing

For our first task of this mission, we created the 3D mesh of a sphere. In steps 1 to 5, we created a method named `makeSphere()`, which uses two `for` loops to generate points on a spherical surface in polar coordinates. We then converted the points to Cartesian coordinates and generated quad strips to form our mesh. We used a `PShape` object to store our mesh data, as the mesh data won't change at runtime and Processing needs to transfer the vertex data to the graphics card's memory only once, when the mesh is created, and not in every frame.

In our `draw()` method, we used the `PShape` object; we tilted it 30 degrees on the x axis and made it rotate around the y axis by limiting the frame rate to 25 frames per second and adding a small amount to the rotation angle in every frame.

Let there be light

The second task of our current mission is to turn the mesh we created in the first task into a solid sphere with a smooth surface. We will use different light sources to illuminate our sphere and define so-called normal vectors for each vertex to make our sphere's surface look smooth without the need for a very dense mesh.

Engage Thrusters

Let's turn on some lights:

1. Open the sketch we created for the last task.
2. Our mesh is currently hollow, and we can see the front-facing lines as well as the back of the sphere. To change this, we can define a fill color for the faces.

```
PShape makeSphere( int r, int step) {
  PShape s = createShape();

  s.beginShape(QUAD_STRIP);
  s.fill(200);
  s.stroke(255);
  s.strokeWeight(2);
  for( int i = 0; i < 180; i+=step ) {
    float sini = sin( radians( i ));
    float cosi = cos( radians( i ));
    float sinip = sin( radians( i + step ));
    float cosip = cos( radians( i + step ));

    for( int j = 0; j <= 360; j+=step ) {
      float sinj = sin( radians( j ));
```

```
        float cosj = cos( radians( j ));
        s.vertex( r * cosj * sini, r * -cosi, r * sinj * sini);
        s.vertex( r * cosj * sinip, r * -cosip, r * sinj * sinip);
      }
    }
    s.endShape();
    return s;
  }
```

3. Run your sketch. The sphere should look like the one in the following screenshot:

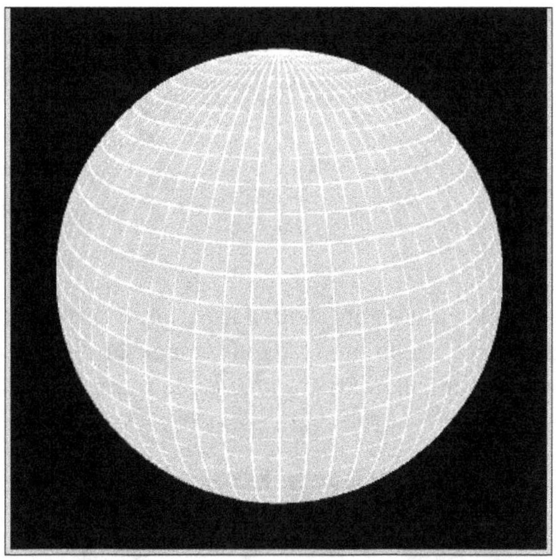

4. We will now remove the lines on our mesh by calling the `noStroke()` function.

```
PShape makeSphere( int R, int step) {
  PShape s = createShape();

  s.beginShape(QUAD_STRIP);
  s.fill(255);
  s.noStroke();
  for( int i = 0; i < 180; i+=step ) {
    float sini = sin( radians( i ));
    float cosi = cos( radians( i ));
```

5. Now our sphere has no grid lines anymore; it is rendered completely flat and looks like a white circle (because, by default, only the ambient light is allowed to remain active in Processing). To fix this, we need to add a light source. The first light source we are going to add is a point source. We need to define the color of our light source in the first three parameters, followed by the x, y, and z coordinates of its position. The point light source acts like a very small, but very bright, light bulb. Add the following line to the `draw()` method:

```
void draw() {
  background(0);
  translate( width/2, height/2 );
  pointLight(255,255,255,-250,-250,500);
  pushMatrix();
  rotateX( radians(-30));
  rotateY( a );
  a+= 0.01;
  shape(sphere);
  popMatrix();
}
```

6. Run your sketch. The sphere gets shaded now, but it doesn't look as smooth as we'd like it to be. As you can see in the following screenshot, the quad strips we define run as rings around our sphere; there are visible sharp bends where they touch each other:

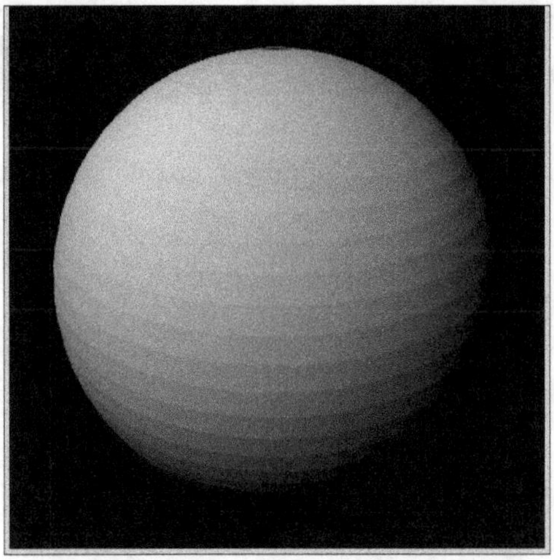

7. To fix this, we need to define normal vectors for each vertex, pointing away from the sphere's surface, as shown in this figure:

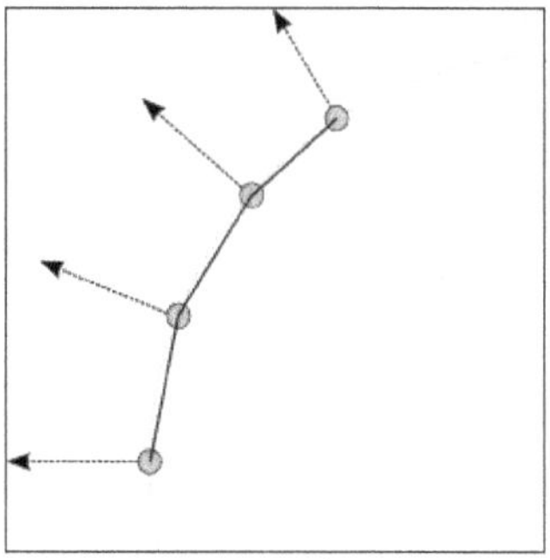

8. We have already calculated the sine and cosine values we need for the normal vectors. We will now add the normal vectors to our mesh using the `normal()` method. Each normal vector has to be defined before the `vertex()` method in our `makeSphere()` method.

```
PShape makeSphere( int r, int step) {
  PShape s = createShape();

  s.beginShape(QUAD_STRIP);
  s.fill(255);
  s.noStroke();
  for( int i = 0; i < 180; i+=step ) {
    float sini = sin( radians( i ));
    float cosi = cos( radians( i ));
    float sinip = sin( radians( i + step ));
    float cosip = cos( radians( i + step ));

    for( int j = 0; j <= 360; j+=step ) {
      float sinj = sin( radians( j ));
      float cosj = cos( radians( j ));

      s.normal( cosj * sini,  -cosi, sinj * sini);
      s.vertex( r * cosj * sini, r * -cosi, r * sinj * sini);

      s.normal( cosj * sinip,-cosip, sinj * sinip);
      s.vertex( r * cosj * sinip, r * -cosip, r * sinj * sinip);
    }
  }
  s.endShape();
  return s;
}
```

9. Run your sketch. The sphere should look smooth, like in the following screenshot:

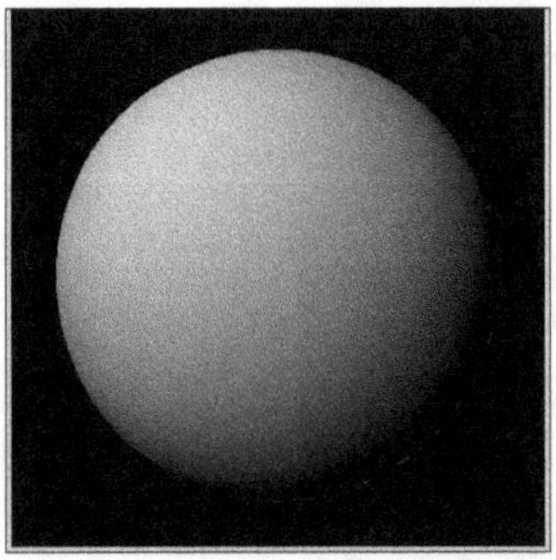

10. Currently, half of our sphere has a dark shadow, so we need a method to make the lighting more even. Fortunately, Processing has a shortcut method named `lights()`, which sets up a light source pointing from the camera to the origin. So, we will now change our `draw()` method and replace the point light source with a call to the `lights()` method.

```
void draw() {
  background(0);
  translate( width/2, height/2 );
  lights();
  pushMatrix();
  rotateX( radians(-30));
  rotateY( a );
  a+= 0.01;
  shape(sphere);

  popMatrix();
}
```

11. Run your sketch. The sphere should look like this:

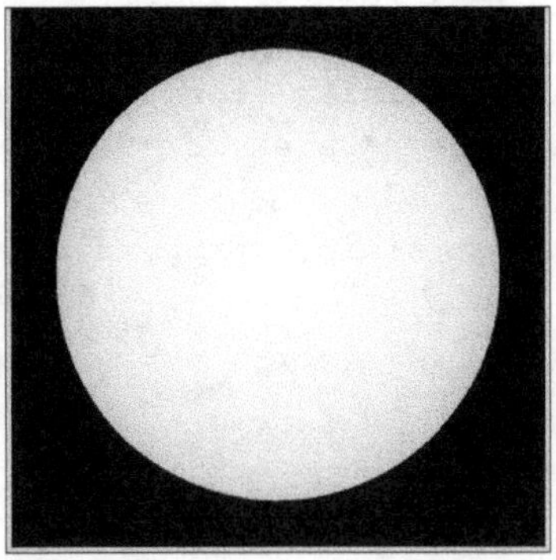

Objective Complete - Mini Debriefing

In the second task of our current mission, we turned the wireframe mesh of our sphere into a solid smooth sphere and activated some lights. In steps 1 to 5, we turned off the line strokes and activated the filling of the faces. We also activated a point light source to prevent the sphere from being rendered completely flat.

Our sphere was shaded and filled, but we had sharp bends at each of the quad strip rings that we created using our loops in the `makeShere()` method. To fix this, we added normal vectors to each vertex. These vectors stand at right angles to the surface and are needed to shade our sphere's surface smooth.

Finally, we learned how to light our sphere more evenly so that every part of it can be seen; this is because in the third task, we will turn our sphere into a globe, and we want every part of the world to be visible.

From sphere to globe

The third task of our current mission is to convert our sphere into a globe by using a texture image. We will need to define the mapping of each vertex to a part of the texture image to make it fit. We will use a black and white texture, where all the land mass is black and the sea is white. The image was created based on a vector map licensed under a Creative Commons license by STUDIO7DESIGNS, which can be found at `http://vector4free.com/vectors/id/75`. I added Antarctica and converted it to a PNG file.

After this, we will add satellite images provided by NASA's Visible Earth project (`http://visibleearth.nasa.gov/`). We will also add a callback handler for keyboard events and make the textures switchable.

Engage Thrusters

Let's start texturing our globe:

1. First we need to add an image of our globe to the sketch. Download the image from the download section at `www.packtpub.com/support`. The map looks like this:

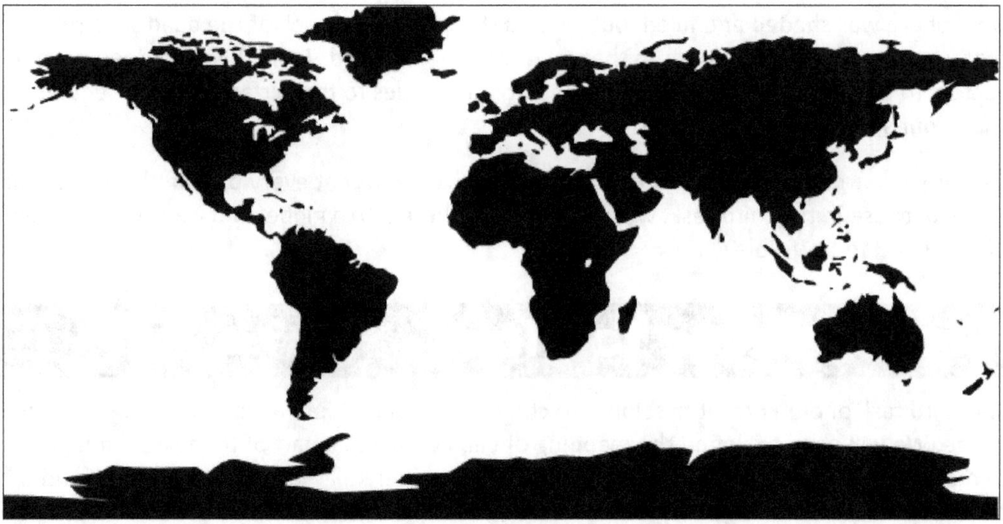

2. Drag the image to the sketch window or add it using the **Add File...** option under the **Sketch** menu.

3. Now we need to define a `PImage` variable to hold the texture image and load it in our `setup()` method.

```
PShape sphere;
PImage world;

void setup() {
   size(400,400,P3D);
   frameRate(25);
   world = loadImage( "world.png" );
   sphere = makeSphere( 150, 5);
}
```

4. We extend our `makeSphere()` method to take the texture as a parameter and adjust the call to `makeSphere()` in our `setup()` method.

```
void setup() {
   size(400,400,P3D);
   frameRate(25);
   world = loadImage( "world.png" );
```

```
    sphere = makeSphere( 150, 5, world);
}

PShape makeSphere( int r, int step, PImage tex ) {
```

5. Now let's activate the texture in our mesh.

```
PShape makeSphere( int r, int step, PImage tex) {
  PShape s = createShape();

  s.beginShape(QUAD_STRIP);
   s.texture( tex );
   s.noStroke();
```

6. If we run the sketch now, we would not be able to see anything because only a small part of the texture would be used (which is black in color). To fix this, we need to add u and v coordinates to each vertex to define which part of the texture should be used. Since we have defined our sphere mesh using two loops (which we use to iterate over the angles of our polar coordinates), we can simply map them to our u and v coordinates.

```
PShape makeSphere( int r, int step, PImage tex) {
  PShape s = createShape();

  s.beginShape(QUAD_STRIP);

  s.texture( tex );
  s.noStroke();
  for( int i = 0; i < 180; i+=step ) {
    float sini = sin( radians( i ));
    float cosi = cos( radians( i ));
    float sinip = sin( radians( i + step ));
    float cosip = cos( radians( i + step ));

    for( int j = 0; j <= 360; j+=step ) {
      float sinj = sin( radians( j ));
      float cosj = cos( radians( j ));
      float sinjp = sin( radians( j + step ));
      float cosjp = cos( radians( j + step ));

      s.normal( cosj * sini,  -cosi, sinj * sini);
      s.vertex( r * cosj * sini, r * -cosi, r * sinj * sini,
      tex.width-j * tex.width / 360, i * tex.height / 180);

      s.normal( cosj * sinip,-cosip, sinj * sinip);
      s.vertex( r * cosj * sinip, r * -cosip, r * sinj * sinip,
```

```
        tex.width-j * tex.width / 360, (i + step ) * tex.height /
180);
      }
    }
    s.endShape();
    return s;
}
```

7. Run your sketch. The sphere should look like the one in this screenshot:

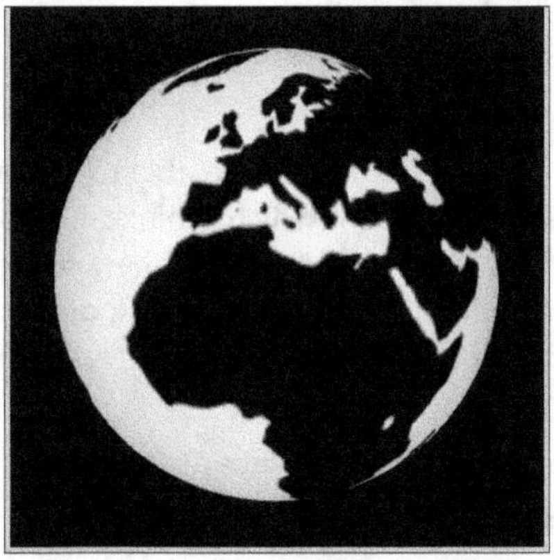

8. Now we are going to add two more textures and make them switchable. First, download the image files `bluemarble.jpg` and `night.jpg` from `www.packtpub.com/support`. These images were created using images from NASA's Landsat 2, Terra, and Aqua satellites, and are available for download at `http://visibleearth.nasa.gov/`. I have reduced the size, as the original ones were too detailed for our small globe. This is what the blue marble texture looks like:

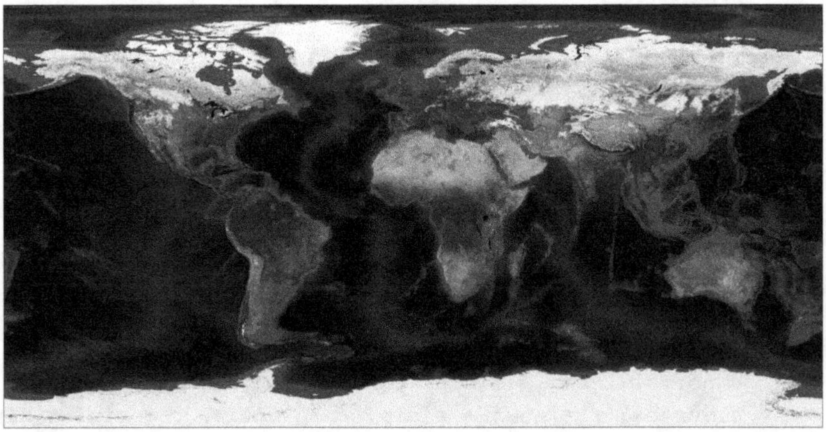

And this is the earth-by-night texture:

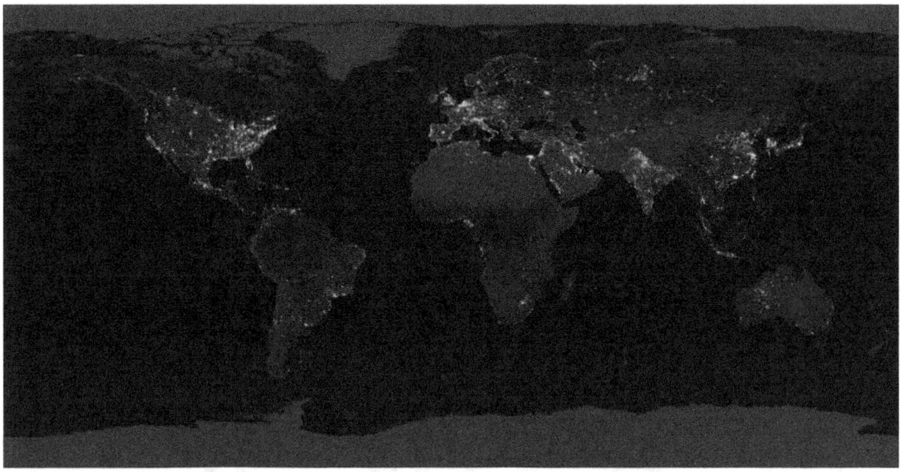

9. We add the images to our sketch by dropping them on the sketch window or by going to **Sketch** | **Add File....**
10. Now we will add two more `PImage` variables in our sketch and load the images in the `setup()` method.

```
PShape sphere;
PImage world;
PImage bluemarble;
PImage night;

void setup() {
   size(400,400,P3D);
   frameRate(25);
   world = loadImage( "world.png" );
   bluemarble = loadImage( "bluemarble.jpg" );
   night = loadImage( "night.jpg" );
   sphere = makeSphere( 150, 5, world);
}
```

11. Now we need to replace the texture of our `sphere` object in the `keyPressed()` method. We can do this by using the `setTexture()` method of the `PShape` class, which replaces the default texture. Since we only use one texture image at a time for our sphere, this works fine for us.

```
void keyPressed() {
  if( key == '1' ) {
    sphere.setTexture( world );
```

```
    } else if ( key == '2' ) {
      sphere.setTexture( bluemarble );

    } else if ( key == '3' ) {
      sphere.setTexture( night );
    }
  }
```

12. Now, run our sketch and switch the textures using the number keys. When using the blue marble texture, the globe looks like this:

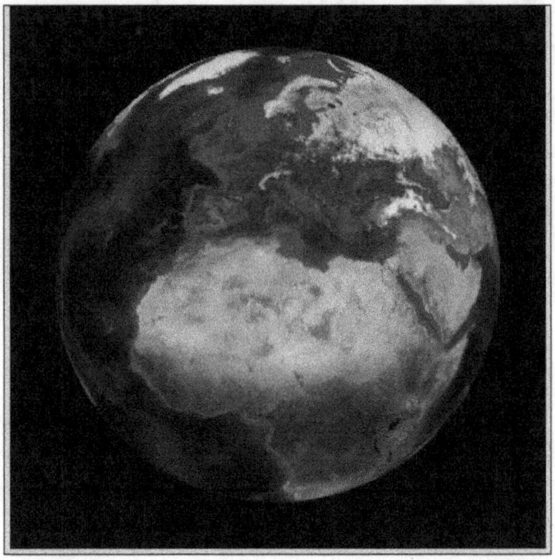

13. When the earth-by-night texture is active, the globe looks like this:

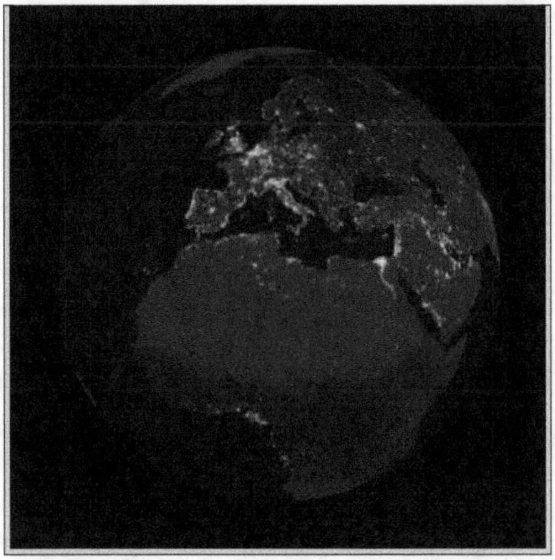

Objective Complete - Mini Debriefing

In our third task, we turned the sphere that we smoothened and lit in the second task into a globe using a texture. In step 2, we added a texture image and created a `PImage` object to store it. We extended our `makeSphere()` method to take a texture image as a parameter and then used the image as the texture for our sphere. To make sure the texture was mapped to our mesh, we needed to use an extended version of the `vertex()` method that also allowed us to specify which part of the texture we want to use for each vertex.

Since we already used two loops to iterate over the angles of the polar coordinates, we used the same coordinates as a basis for our texture coordinates. We simply needed to map them to the height and width of our texture image.

Finally, we added a callback function that handles key press events and used it to switch between the texture images. We added two satellite images from NASA's Visible Earth project. The blue marble image is a satellite image that has been processed to show no clouds on the planet, and the earth-by-night image shows the globe by night. We switched the textures of our shape using the `setTexture()` method of the `PShape` class that replaces the current texture.

From globe to neon globe

For our final task of this mission, we will be converting the globe we just created into a glowing neon globe. We will create a globe that would fit into an 80s movie like WarGames or Tron. We will create this glow effect by applying two filters to our globe. The first one is an edge detection filter, which strips away every filled area of the image and only leaves the outlines of the continents. The second filter will add a glow effect to our lines. We will implement these filters in the **OpenGL Shading Language** (**GLSL**). These GLSL filters will be executed by our graphics card; they don't need CPU resources.

We will only apply our filters if the simple texture showing the continents is active, and we will deactivate them when the satellite images from NASA's Visible Earth project are active.

Engage Thrusters

Let's create our filters:

1. First, we need to change the colors of our world map texture to make the sea appear black and the continents green. Open the sketch that we created in the third task and add the following code to our `setup()` method:

```
void setup() {
   size(400,400,P3D);
   frameRate(25);
```

```
  PGraphics g = createGraphics( 700,349);
  g.beginDraw();
  PImage tmp = loadImage( "world.png" );
  tmp.filter(INVERT);
  g.tint(100,255,0);
  g.image( tmp,0,0 );
  g.endDraw();

  world = createGraphics( 700, 349 );
  world = g.get(0,0,700,349);

  bluemarble = loadImage( "bluemarble.jpg" );
  night = loadImage( "night.jpg" );
  sphere = makeSphere( 150, 5, world);
}
```

2. We want our globe drawn with a blue grid for the ocean, so we will set the stroke color to blue and the stroke weight to `2` in our `makeSphere()` method.

```
PShape makeSphere( int r, int step, PImage tex) {
  PShape s = createShape();

  s.beginShape(QUAD_STRIP);
  s.texture( tex );
  s.stroke(0,0,255);
  s.strokeWeight( 2 );
  for( int i = 0; i < 180; i+=step ) {
    float sini = sin( radians( i ));
    float cosi = cos( radians( i ));
    float sinip = sin( radians( i + step ));
    float cosip = cos( radians( i + step ));
```

3. Run the sketch now. The globe should look like this screenshot:

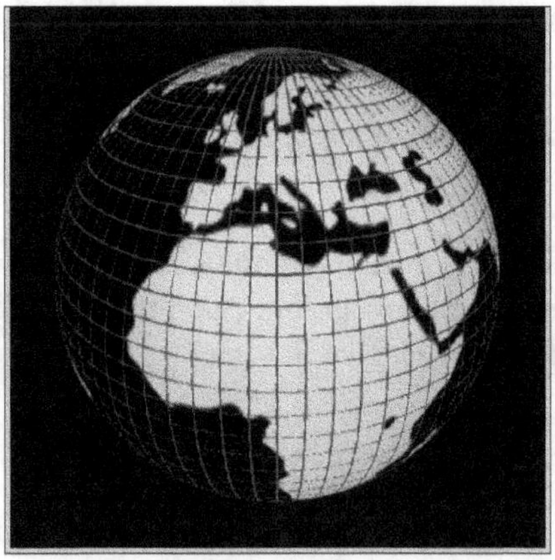

4. Now we are going to add our edge detection filter. Add a `PShape` variable to the sketch; in the `setup()` method, load a file named `edge.glsl` (which we are going to create in a minute).

```
PShape sphere;
PImage world;

PShader edge;

void setup() {
   size(400,400,P3D);
   frameRate(25);

  PGraphics g = createGraphics( 700,349);
  g.beginDraw();
  PImage tmp = loadImage( "world.png" );
  tmp.filter(INVERT);
  g.tint(100,255,0);
  g.image( tmp,0,0 );
  g.endDraw();

  world = createGraphics( 700, 349 );
  world = g.get(0,0,700,349);

  sphere = makeSphere( 150, 5, world);

  edge = loadShader("edge.glsl");
}
```

5. Now open a text editor, create a file named `edge.glsl`, and enter the following code:

```
#ifdef GL_ES
precision mediump float;
precision mediump int;
#endif

#define PROCESSING_TEXTURE_SHADER

uniform sampler2D texture;
uniform vec2 texOffset;

varying vec4 vertColor;
varying vec4 vertTexCoord;

void main(void) {
```

```
    // calculate the coordinates of the neighboring points
    vec2 tc0 = vertTexCoord.st + vec2(-texOffset.s, -texOffset.t);
    vec2 tc1 = vertTexCoord.st + vec2(  0.0, -texOffset.t);
    vec2 tc2 = vertTexCoord.st + vec2(+texOffset.s, -texOffset.t);
    vec2 tc3 = vertTexCoord.st + vec2(-texOffset.s, 0.0);
    vec2 tc4 = vertTexCoord.st + vec2( 0.0, 0.0);
    vec2 tc5 = vertTexCoord.st + vec2(+texOffset.s, 0.0);
    vec2 tc6 = vertTexCoord.st + vec2(-texOffset.s, +texOffset.t);
    vec2 tc7 = vertTexCoord.st + vec2(  0.0, +texOffset.t);
    vec2 tc8 = vertTexCoord.st + vec2(+texOffset.s, +texOffset.t);
    // get the color values from the image for each coordinate
    vec4 col0 = texture2D(texture, tc0);
    vec4 col1 = texture2D(texture, tc1);
    vec4 col2 = texture2D(texture, tc2);
    vec4 col3 = texture2D(texture, tc3);
    vec4 col4 = texture2D(texture, tc4);
    vec4 col5 = texture2D(texture, tc5);
    vec4 col6 = texture2D(texture, tc6);
    vec4 col7 = texture2D(texture, tc7);
    vec4 col8 = texture2D(texture, tc8);

    vec4 sum = 8.0 * col4 -  (col0 + col1 + col2 + col3 + col5 + col6
  + col7 + col8);
    float f = sum.r + sum.g + sum.b;
    gl_FragColor =  vec4(f,f,f,1.0)*col4;
  }
```

6. We need to add the `edge.glsl` file we just created to our sketch by dragging the file onto the sketch window or by going to **Sketch | Add File...**.
7. To use the shader we just created as a filter, we need to add a call to the `filter()` method in our `draw()` method after our globe has been drawn and add the shader variable that we initialized in our `setup()` method as a parameter.

```
void draw() {
  background(0);
  translate( width/2, height/2 );

  lights();
  pushMatrix();
  rotateX( radians(-30));
  rotateY( a );
  a+= 0.01;
  shape(sphere);
```

```
  popMatrix();

  filter(edge);
}
```

8. Now run the sketch. The globe should look like this screenshot:

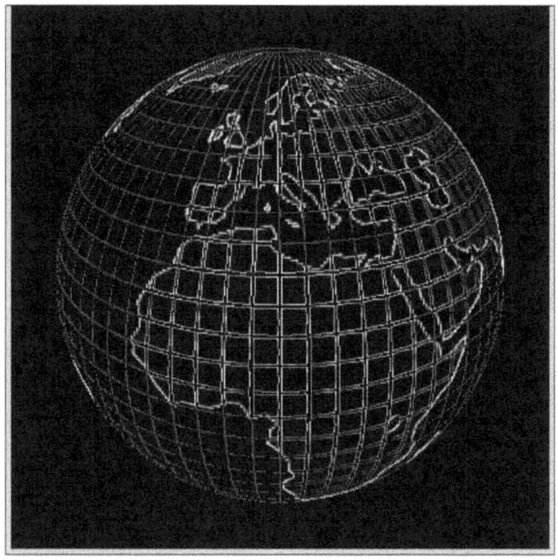

9. Our second filter will add a glow effect to the lines that our edge detection filter created to make it look like the image of an old CRT monitor. Create a file named `blur.glsl` using a text editor and insert the following code:

```
#ifdef GL_ES
precision mediump float;
precision mediump int;
#endif

#define PROCESSING_TEXTURE_SHADER

uniform sampler2D texture;
uniform vec2 texOffset;
varying vec4 vertTexCoord;

void main(void) {
  int i = 0;
  int j= 0;
  vec4 sum = vec4(0.0);

  for( i=-5;i<5;i++) {
    for( j=-5;j<5;j++) {
```

```
        sum += texture2D( texture, vertTexCoord.st +
vec2(j,i)*texOffset.st)*0.025;
      }
    }

  gl_FragColor = sum*sum+ vec4(texture2D( texture, vertTexCoord.
st).rgb, 1.0);
}
```

10. We will now add the file to our sketch by dragging it on to the sketch window or by going to **Sketch | Add File...**.
11. Now add another `PShader` variable and load the shader into our `setup()` method.

```
PShape sphere;
PImage world;

PShader blur;
PShader edge;

void setup() {
  size(400,400,P3D);
  frameRate(25);

  PGraphics g = createGraphics( 700,349);
  g.beginDraw();
  PImage tmp = loadImage( "world.png" );
  tmp.filter(INVERT);
  g.tint(100,255,0);
  g.image( tmp,0,0 );
  g.endDraw();

  world = createGraphics( 700, 349 );
  world = g.get(0,0,700,349);

  sphere = makeSphere( 150, 5, world);

  edge = loadShader("edge.glsl");
  blur = loadShader("blur.glsl");
}
```

12. In our `draw()` method, we will add a second call to `filter()` using the blur shader as a parameter.

```
void draw() {
  background(0);
```

```
    translate( width/2, height/2 );

    lights();
    pushMatrix();
    rotateX( radians(-30));
    rotateY( a );
    a+= 0.01;
    shape(sphere);

    popMatrix();

    filter(edge);
    filter(blur);
}
```

13. Now run the sketch. The globe should look like the following screenshot:

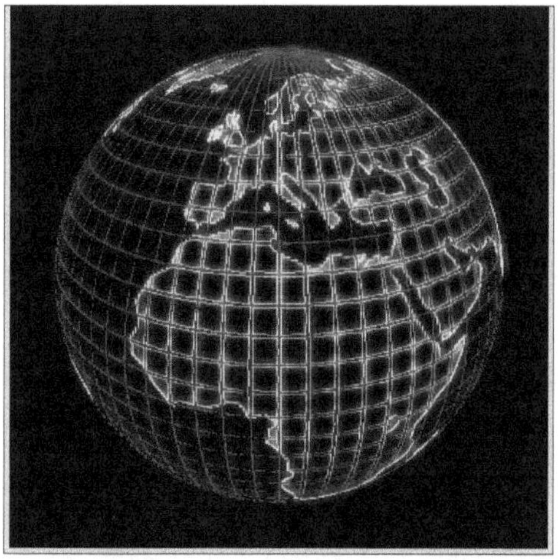

14. Currently, the filters and grid lines are active at the same time that the satellite images are active, which looks strange. So, we will now add a Boolean variable named `satelite` and set it to `true` whenever a satellite image gets selected in our `keyPressed()` method.

```
boolean satelite = false;
void keyPressed() {
  if( key == '1' ) {
    sphere.setTexture( world );
    satelite = false;

  } else if ( key == '2' ) {
```

```
    sphere.setTexture( bluemarble );
    satelite = true;

  } else if ( key == '3' ) {
    sphere.setTexture( night );
    satelite = true;
  }
}
```

15. In our `draw()` method, we will now deactivate the filters when a satellite image is selected.

```
void draw() {
  background(0);
  translate( width/2, height/2 );

  lights();
  pushMatrix();
  rotateX( radians(-30));
  rotateY( a );
  a+= 0.01;

  shape(sphere);

  popMatrix();
  if ( !satelite ) {
    filter(edge);
    filter(blur);
  }
}
```

16. The filters are deactivated now, but we still have the lines of our blue grid over the satellite images, which looks kind of weird. So, we will now set the stroke to `false` if a satellite image is active. Unfortunately, you can't reactivate the stroke lines when the neon map is activated, so we will recreate our original shape using the `makeSphere()` command.

```
void keyPressed() {
  if( key == '1' ) {
    satelite = false;
    sphere = makeSphere( 150, 5, world);

  } else if ( key == '2' ) {
    sphere.setTexture( bluemarble );
    sphere.setStroke(false);
    satelite = true;
```

```
    } else if ( key == '3' ) {
      sphere.setTexture( night );
      sphere.setStroke(false);
      satelite = true;
    }
  }
```

Objective Complete - Mini Debriefing

Our final task for this mission was to turn our globe into a neon globe, mimicking the style of the CRT monitors of the 80s. First, we inverted our texture and colored it green to make the continents appear green and the sea black. We did this on the fly while loading our texture in the `setup()` method, by creating a `PGraphics` object and filtering the image as we loaded it. In step 2, we activated the drawing of the lines on our sphere and turned them to blue.

From step 4 onwards, we created an edge detection filter using the OpenGL Shader Language. What we used for our filter is a so-called fragment shader, which means that the function we provide is called for every pixel, or as the OpenGL specification board calls them—fragments. These shaders are executed on the graphics card and are called for every pixel. The processors on the graphics card are usually capable of executing many of these functions in parallel; so not only do they free up CPU resources, depending on your graphics card, these filters are really fast. Just how fast depends on your CPU and on your graphics card; my computer, for example, runs a sketch using a blur filter with 10 frames per second on the CPU and 60 frames per second when using a GLSL filter. In steps 6 and 7, we added the shader to our sketch and activated it in our `draw()` method.

From step 9 onwards, we created a second shader that gets executed after edge detection and adds a glow effect, which looks similar to a neon sign or the afterglow of an old CRT monitor.

The filter effects look great on the simple continent map, but we wanted the satellite images from the Visible Earth project to remain unaltered. So, we added a Boolean variable from step 13 onwards, which allowed us to activate the filters only for our first texture image.

Mission Accomplished

Our mission was to build a spinning 3D globe that resembles the visual aesthetics of the world maps seen on computer displays at the headquarters of heroes and villains in movies from the 80s. We started by creating a spherical mesh in the first task. The mesh consisted of quad strips that warped around our sphere. Finally, we created the coordinates by iterating over our sphere's surface using polar coordinates and converting them to Cartesian coordinates.

In the second task, we filled the faces of our sphere and added a point light source to our world. We then added normal vectors to each vertex to smoothen the shading of our mesh. To make the lighting more even, we switched from our point light source to the default light sources in Processing.

In the third task, we turned our sphere into a globe using a world map as a texture. We extended the vertices of our mesh by the texture coordinates to make sure that the texture fits around our sphere. We also added satellite images from NASA's Visible Earth project and added a callback method that handles key press events to make the textures switchable.

In the fourth task, we finally created the visual effects we were aiming for by adding two GLSL shader-based filters to our `draw()` method. In our `setup()` method, we inverted the texture image and turned it green by adding a tint to it. We created a grid of blue lines by reactivating the stroke color in our `makeSphere()` method. Then, we added an edge detection GLSL shader that we used in our `draw()` method. To generate the glow effect, we created a second shader and used it to filter the result of our first filter.

We also added a Boolean variable that allowed us to activate the filters only when the first texture is selected and deactivate them when the satellite images are visible.

You Ready to go Gung HO? A Hotshot Challenge

In this mission, we learned how to create a globe and how to use GLSL shaders as filters in Processing. We have only scratched the surface of what is possible with shaders using a modern graphics card; there is so much more that can be done with a globe besides making it rotate and look awesome. Why don't you try one of the following ideas to extend the sketch we have just created:

- Create a "sun" that lights up the globe correctly based on the time of day, and use a GLSL filter that uses the day and night texture images and blends between the two at the day-night border.
- NASA provides satellite images for the various planets and moons of our solar system to download for free. Why not make a whole solar system?
- Create a different set of GLSL filters to recreate the hand-drawn black and white globes from the weekly newsreels in the cinemas of the 50s.

Project 8
Logfile Geo-visualizer

In the middle of the 19th century, a cholera outbreak occurred in London. A physician named John Snow drew a point on every location of a case he heard about on a map. Using this map, he could locate the source of the outbreak in a street water pump. He then removed the handle of the pump to terminate the cholera outbreak. This was one of the earliest known geographic information systems (GIS). Today, these are created using vector maps or satellite images and geocoded data.

Mission Briefing

Our current mission is to create a geographic information system that takes a web server logfile and shows where the requests of the readers came from. We will parse the logfile and then extract the IP address and the timestamp of the request. Then we will use a database of IP ranges to get a pair of geographic coordinates and display a small pin on a world map. Finally, we will replace the map with the 3D neon globe we have created in our last mission and visualize the geocoded logfile entries on its surface.

Why Is It Awesome?

For a long time, creating maps or visualizing data on a map was the realm of very expensive tools and highly paid experts. Fortunately, this has changed in recent years. More and more tools, data, maps, and satellite images are available to mere mortals for free or at very low costs. So knowing how to create visualizations that show data on a globe or map is surely a very useful tool in your toolbox.

Your Hotshot Objectives

For our current mission, we start with extracting the data we want to visualize from a web server logfile. Then, we fetch the geo-coordinates for each data record and visualize the data on our neon globe from *Project 7, The Neon Globe*. Our mission's tasks are as follows:

- Reading a logfile
- Geocoding IP addresses
- Red Dot Fever
- Interactive Red Dot Fever

Mission Checklist

For this mission, we need the neon globe we created in previous mission. If you didn't follow this recipe, you can download the examples from `www.packtpub.com/support`. We also need a database of IP addresses and their geo-coordinates, but I will guide you through the download and installation of these in the second task of this mission. If you don't have any web server logfiles to visualize, you can use the anonymized example file provided on the book's download page at `www.packtpub.com/support`.

Reading a logfile

The first task for our current mission is to take the logfile of an Apache web server and extract the interesting parts. We are going to use regular expressions to split the logfiles' lines and we are fetching the IP address and the timestamp. We will also create a new class to store the data we have extracted.

Engage Thrusters

Let's start with parsing our logfile:

1. Create a new sketch and add the `setup()` and `draw()` methods.

   ```
   void setup() {
   }

   void draw() {
   }
   ```

2. Now we add the logfile we want to visualize by dropping it on the sketch window or adding it using the **Sketch | Add File ...** menu.

3. In the `setup()` method, we read the file into an array of strings.

```
void setup() {
  size(700,350);
  String[] log = loadStrings( "access.log" );
}
```

4. Add a new tab by clicking on the little arrow icon and selecting **New Tab**. We name it `LogRow` and create a new class to store the IP address and the timestamp of each record.

```
class LogRow {
  String ip;
  String timestamp;

  public  LogRow( String ip, String timestamp ) {
    this.ip = ip;
    this.timestamp = timestamp;
  }
}
```

5. Switch back to our our main sketch and add a method named `parseLogfile()`, which takes a string array as a parameter and returns an array of the `LogRow` classes.

```
void draw() {
}

LogRow[] parseLogfile( String[] rows ) {
}
```

6. In the `parseLogfile()` method, we iterate over the strings and use the `match()` method to extract the IP address and the date part. This function uses a regular expression to filter the text and returns an array of strings. The array contains a string for each pair of brackets in the regular expression. Our regular expression extracts IP addresses in the form `xxx.xxx.xxx.xxx` followed by two dashes and a date in squared brackets. A detailed description of how to write a regular expression can be found in the Processing reference documentation.

```
LogRow[] parseLogfile( String[] rows ) {
  for( int i=0; i< rows.length; i++) {
    String[] m = match(
    rows[i], "(\\d+\\.\\d+\\.\\d+\\.\\d+) - - \\[(.*)\\]");
    if ( m != null ) {
        println( m[1] + " "+ m[2] );
    }
  }
}
```

7. Now we define an array of the `LogRow` object to store our parser's results instead of printing it on the console.

```
LogRow[] parseLogfile( String[] rows ) {
  LogRow[] res = new LogRow[ rows.length ];
  for( int i=0; i< rows.length; i++) {
    String[] m = match(
      rows[i], "(\\d+\\.\\d+\\.\\d+\\.\\d+) - - \\[(.*)\\]");
    if ( m != null ) {
        res[i] = new LogRow( m[1], m[2] );
    }
  }
  return res;
}
```

8. In our `setup()` method, we add a call to the `parseLogFile()` method and add an array of the `LogRow` object to our sketch.

```
LogRow[] data;

void setup() {
  size(700,350);
  String[] log = loadStrings( "access.log" );
  data = parseLogfile( log );
  }
```

9. Currently, the timestamps we extracted are strings, which makes them quite hard to work with for our sketch. So, let's change this by by parsing the date using a `SimpleDataFormat()` class. This Java class allows us to convert it to a Unix timestamp—the number of seconds since midnight 1970-01-01. We need to add an `import` statement at the beginning of our sketch to be able to use the `SimpleDateFormat` class.

```
import java.text.SimpleDateFormat;
```

10. Now we can add the date parsing functionality to our `parseLogfile()` method. The `parse()` method of our `SimpleDateFormat` class needs to be enclosed in a `try/catch` block because it's a Java method that can throw an exception if the parsing fails.

```
LogRow[] parseLogfile( String[] rows ) {
  SimpleDateFormat sdf =
    new SimpleDateFormat( "dd/MMM/yyyy:HH:mm:ss Z");
  LogRow[] res = new LogRow[ rows.length ];
  for( int i=0; i< rows.length; i++) {
    String[] m = match(
      rows[i], "(\\d+\\.\\d+\\.\\d+\\.\\d+) - - \\[(.*)\\]");
```

```
      if ( m != null ) {
        try {
          long time = sdf.parse( m[2] ).getTime();
          res[i] = new LogRow( m[1], time );
        } catch( Exception e ) {
          e.printStackTrace();
        }
      }
    }
    return res;
  }
```

11. We also need to change our `LogRow` class to accept the new date type.

```
class LogRow {
  String ip;
  long timestamp;

  public  LogRow( String ip, long timestamp ) {
    this.ip = ip;
    this.timestamp = timestamp;
  }
}
```

12. We will now draw a mark for each timestamp found on a timeline. Since logfiles comes ordered by the timestamp, we can take the first and the last element of our array to get the start and end time for our timeline. Switch back to our main sketch and add the following code to our `draw()` method:

```
void draw() {
  background(0);
  fill(255);
  noStroke();
  rect(0,150,width,50);
  stroke(0, 10);
  long mints = data[0].timestamp;
  long maxts = data[ data.length-1].timestamp;
  for( int i=0; i<data.length; i++) {
    float pos = map( data[i].timestamp, mints , maxts , 0, width
);
    line( pos, 150, pos,200 );
  }
}
```

13. Run our sketch. The timeline of our sketch should look similar to the following screenshot:

Objective Complete - Mini Debriefing

The first task of our current mission was to read a web server's logfile and extract the IP address and the timestamp of every log entry. We created a class that stores our log row information. We then read the logfile to an array of strings using the `loadStrings()` method. In step 6, we used a regular expression that matches and extracts the parts of our logfile we are interested in and returns them as strings.

There are an incredible number of ways a date could be represented as a string, since every corner of the world seems to be in urgent need to use a very special one. To make it easier for our sketch to work with the timestamps, we convert them to the Unix timestamp format, which stores the seconds that have elapsed since 1970-01-01.

In our `draw()` method, we take the timestamps we extracted from the logfile and visualize them on a timeline.

Geocoding IP addresses

So far we have concentrated on the timestamps of our logfile, so this part of our mission is to convert the IP addresses into a pair of coordinates that we can use for our geo-visualization. We will download and install the hostIP database—a free database that stores the geographic coordinates and the name of the city this IP address is coming from. The hostIP database is created by volunteers, so while you're there, add your own IP address and city to improve the service. The accuracy we get from this database is on city level, so you shouldn't design a pizza delivery service based on the geo-coordinates you get, but it's more than sufficient for most visualization projects.

We will keep the hostIP database in memory for geocoding our IP addresses and converting the IP addresses we extracted in the previous task.

Engage Thrusters

Let's start to convert the addresses:

1. To convert the IP addresses, we first need the hostIP database. So, open a browser and go to `http://www.hostip.info/`. Click on **Data** and then select one of the HTTP mirrors in the **Daily updates to the database?** section.

2. Download the `hip_ip4_city_lat_lng.csv` file from the `cvs` folder.
3. Now, open the sketch we created for the previous task and add the file by dragging it onto the sketch window or by using the **Sketch | Add File...** menu.
4. Create a new tab and name it `IpDB`. We add a new class to store the IP address blocks and its latitude/longitude pair.

```
public class IPdb{
  long ipblock;
  String lat;
  String lon;

  public IPdb( long ipblock, String lat, String lon ) {
    this.ipblock = ipblock;
    this.lat = lat;
    this.lon = lon;
  }
}
```

5. To load the database, we create a new method that parses the `.csv` file and stores the records in our `IpDB` class. We create a `HashMap` data structure with the IP block as an index so we can access it faster when we geocode the logfile rows. `HashMap` is a Java data structure that maps a unique key to a different object and allows us to retrieve the stored object using the key.

```
HashMap<Long,IPdb> parseIpDatabase( String filename ) {
  String[] raw = loadStrings( filename );

  HashMap<Long, IPdb> map= new HashMap<Long,IPdb>(total);
  for( int i=0; i<raw.length; i++) {
      String[] parts = raw[i].split(",");
      int ipblock = int( parts[0] );
      map.put( new Long(ipblock),  new IPdb( ipblock, parts[2],
parts[3] ));
  }
  return map;
}
```

6. In our `setup()` method, we add a call to the `parseIpDatabase()` method and `HashMap` for our database.

```
import java.text.SimpleDateFormat;

LogRow[] data;
HashMap<Long, IPdb> ipdatabase;

void setup() {
```

```
  size(700,350);

  ipdatabase = parseIpDatabase( "hip_ip4_city_lat_lng.csv" );
 String[] log = loadStrings( "access.log" );
  data = parseLogfile( log" );
}
```

7. Now we can use the table object to search the geo-coordinates for any given IP address by searching the table, but first we need to extend our `LogRow` class to store the coordinates. Switch to the **LogRow** tab of our sketch and add the following properties:

```
class LogRow {
  String ip;
  long timestamp;
  String lat;
  String lon;

  public  LogRow( String ip, long timestamp ) {
    this.ip = ip;
    this.timestamp = timestamp;
  }

  void setLatLon( String lat, String lon ) {
    this.lat = lat;
    this.lon = lon;
  }
}
```

8. Now, back in the main sketch, we add another method named `geoCode()`, which takes the array of records as a parameter.

```
void geoCode( LogRow[] data ) {
}
```

9. In our method, we iterate over all the rows and try to find the geo-coordinates for our IP address. If we are unable to find the latitude and longitude, we set them to null. The database doesn't use actual IP addresses as a key, but as a numeric representation of an IP block. To convert an IP address into this search key, we need to convert the IP address into a numeric value by splitting it at the dot and multiplying the numbers with powers of 256.

```
void geoCode( LogRow[] data ) {

  for( int i=0; i< data.length; i++) {

    String[] block = data[i].ip.split( "\\." );
```

```
      int ip = int( block[0] ) * 256 * 256 * 256 +
      int( block[1] ) * 256 * 256 + int( block[2] ) * 256;
      IPdb r = ipdatabase.get(ip);
      if ( r != null ) {
        data[i].setLatLon( r.lat, r.lon);
      }
    }
  }
```

10. Our sketch parses the logfile and geocodes the IP addresses in our `setup()` method, and depending on the size of the logfile, this can take a while. To inform our user why our startup takes so unusually long, we are now going to move the parsing into a background thread.

```
void setup() {
  size(700,350);

  Thread t = new Thread() {
      public void run() {
        ipdatabase = parseIpDatabase
          ( "hip_ip4_city_lat_lng.csv" );
        String[] log = loadStrings( "access.log" );
        data = parseLogfile( log );
        geoCode( data );
      }
  };
  t.start();
}
```

11. Now, the `setup()` method returns immediately, but there will be no rows to use in the `draw()` method until the parsing has finished. So we need to modify our `draw()` method and print a message for our users to inform them of what's going on.

```
void draw() {
  background(0);

  if ( data == null ) {
    text( "Loading ...", 35, 190 );
  } else    {
    noStroke();
    fill(255);
    rect(0, 150, 700, 50);
    stroke(0, 10);
    long mints = data[0].timestamp;
    long maxts = data[ data.length-1].timestamp;
```

```
    for ( int i=0; i<data.length; i++) {
      float pos = map( data[i].timestamp, mints, maxts, 0, 700 );
      line( pos, 150, pos, 200 );
    }
  }
}
```

12. This is much better, but our users still have no idea how long the parsing process might take, so let's add a progress bar indicating how much of the parsing or geocoding is already completed. We need to add two variables holding the total row count and the number of already processed records. We also add a state variable, which stores the parsing stage we are currently at.

```
int LOADING = 0;
int LOGFILE = 1;
int GEOCODING = 2;
int DONE = 3;

int state = LOADING;

int count = 0;
int total = 0;

HashMap<Long, IPdb> ipdatabase;
LogRow data[];

void setup() {
  size(700, 350);

  Thread t = new Thread() {
    public void run() {
      state = LOADING;
      ipdatabase = parseIpDatabase( "hip_ip4_city_lat_lng.csv" );
      state = LOGFILE;
      String[] log = loadStrings( "access.log" );
      data = parseLogfile( log );
      state = GEOCODING;
      geoCode( data );
      state = DONE;
    }
  };
  t.start();
}
```

13. In our `parseIpDatabase()` method, we set the `total` variable to the number of rows in the database and update the `count` variable in the `for` loop.

```
HashMap<Long, IPdb> parseIpDatabase( String filename ) {
  String[] raw = loadStrings( filename );
  total = raw.length;
  HashMap<Long, IPdb> map= new HashMap<Long, IPdb>(total);
  for ( int i=0; i<raw.length; i++) {
    count = i;
    String[] parts = raw[i].split(",");
    int ipblock = int( parts[0] );
    map.put( new Long(ipblock), new IPdb( ipblock, parts[2],
parts[3] ));
  }
  return map;
}
```

14. In our `parseLogfile()` method, we need to set the `total` variable to the number of rows in the logfile and also update the `count` variable in the loop.

```
LogRow[] parseLogfile( String[] rows ) {

  total = rows.length;
  SimpleDateFormat sdf = new SimpleDateFormat( "dd/MMM/
yyyy:HH:mm:ss Z");
  LogRow[] res = new LogRow[ rows.length ];
  for ( int i=0; i< rows.length; i++) {
    count = i;
    String[] m = match(
      rows[i], "(\\d+\\.\\d+\\.\\d+\\.\\d+) - - \\[(.*)\\]");
    if ( m != null ) {
      try {
        long time = sdf.parse( m[2] ).getTime();
        res[i] = new LogRow( m[1], time );
      }
      catch( Exception e ) {
        e.printStackTrace();
      }
    }
  }
  return res;
}
```

15. And finally, we need to update our `geoCode()` method to set the `total` variable to the number of parsed rows and set the `count` variable to the loop.

```
void geoCode( LogRow[] data ) {
  total = data.length;
  for ( int i=0; i< data.length; i++) {
    count = i;
    String[] block = data[i].ip.split( "\\." );
    int ip = int( block[0] ) * 256 * 256 * 256 + int( block[1] ) *
256 * 256 + int( block[2] ) * 256;
    IPdb r = ipdatabase.get(ip);
    if ( r != null ) {
      data[i].setLatLon( r.lat, r.lon);
    }
  }
}
```

16. Now we can draw the progress bar in our `draw()` method and show the name of the stage.

```
void draw() {
  background(0);

  if ( state < DONE ) {
    stroke( 0, 200 );
    strokeWeight(2);
    fill( 200, 200 );
    rect( 25, 150, 650, 50 );
    noStroke();
    fill( 255 );
    rect( 30, 155, map( count, 0, total, 0, 640 ), 40 );

    fill( 0 );
    String msg="";
    if ( state == LOADING ) {
      msg = "loading database ...";
    }
    else if ( state == LOGFILE ) {
      msg = "parsing logfile ...";
    }
    else if ( state == GEOCODING ) {
      msg = "geocoding ip adresses ...";
    }

    text( msg, 35, 190 );
```

```
    }else if (state == DONE) {
      noStroke();
      fill(255);
      rect(0, 150, 700, 50);
      stroke(0, 10);
      long mints = data[0].timestamp;
      long maxts = data[ data.length-1].timestamp;
      for ( int i=0; i<data.length; i++) {
        float pos = map( data[i].timestamp, mints, maxts, 0, 700 );
        line( pos, 150, pos, 200 );
      }
    }
  }
```

17. Now when the sketch is starting up, a progress bar as shown in the following screenshot is displayed:

Objective Complete - Mini Debriefing

This task of our current mission was to determine the geo-coordinates for each of our IP addresses and store them in our `IpDB` class. We downloaded and installed the `.csv` version of the hostIP database and added it to our sketch. We created a class to store the geo-coordinates for blocks of IP addresses and created a `parseIpDatabase()` command to create `HashMap` filled with the hostIP database. Then we wrote a new method named `geocodeIp()`, which takes an array of the `RowLine` objects and enriches them with the latitude and longitude if the IP address can be found, or null otherwise.

Since the loading and parsing in our `setup()` method slows down the startup of our sketch, we moved the logfile handing and geocoding to a separate thread and made it run in the background. We also added a progress bar in our `draw()` method to show our users how much of the database is already loaded or how much of the logfile is already processed.

Red Dot Fever

One of the first applications every GIS developer does is drawing red dots on a map. This is the "Hello World" equivalent of geo-information systems, and it's exactly what we are going to do for this task of our current mission. We will take the world map we used as a texture for our neon globe and show red dots on the map for each logfile entry.

The latitude is the coordinate that goes from the North Pole to the South Pole and ranges from `-90` degrees to `90` degrees with `0` on the equator. The longitude runs around the globe and ranges from `-180` degrees to `180` degrees. Longitude zero is on the so called "Prime Meridian", which runs through the Royal Observatory in Greenwich, London—I guess this answers the question of who invented this coordinate system.

When we think of a map, usually North and South America are on the left, Europe and Africa are in the middle, and Asia is on the right. On such a map, the origin of the geographic coordinate system we are using is at the center of the map.

Engage Thrusters

Let's draw some dots on a map:

1. First we need a map to draw on, so either use the world map we used as a texture for our last task, or download it from `www.packtpub.com/support`.
2. Now, we open our sketch and add the texture by dragging it onto the sketch window or by using the **Sketch** | **Add File...** menu.
3. Then, we add a `PImage` variable to store our map and load it in the `setup()` method.

```
PImage world;

void setup() {
  size(700,400);

  world = loadImage( "world.png" );

  Thread t = new Thread() {
      public void run() {
        state = LOADING;
        ipdatabase = parseIpDatabase( "hip_ip4_city_lat_lng.csv" );
        state = LOGFILE;
        String[] log = loadStrings( "access.log" );
        data = parseLogfile( log );
        state = GEOCODING;
        geoCode( data );
        state = DONE;
      }
  };
  t.start();
}
```

4. In our `draw()` method, we move the timeline to the bottom of the window and show the map above it.

```
void draw() {
  background(255);
  image( world, 0, 0, width, 350 );

  if ( state < DONE ) {
    stroke( 0, 200 );
    strokeWeight(2);
    fill( 200, 200 );
    rect( 25, 150, 650, 50 );
    noStroke();
    fill( 255 );
    rect( 30, 155, map( count, 0, total, 0, 640 ), 40 );

    fill( 0 );
    String msg="";
    if ( state == LOADING ) {
      msg = "loading database ...";
    } else if ( state == LOGFILE ) {
      msg = "parsing logfile ...";
    } else if ( state == GEOCODING ) {
      msg = "geocoding ip adresses ...";
    }

    text( msg, 35, 190 );
  } else if (state == DONE) {
    noStroke();
    fill(255);
    rect(0,350,700,50);
    stroke(0, 10);
    long mints = data[0].timestamp;
    long maxts = data[ data.length-1].timestamp;
    for( int i=0; i<data.length; i++) {
      float pos = map( data[i].timestamp, mints , maxts , 0, 700
);
      line( pos, 350, pos,400 );
    }
  }
}
```

5. Run the sketch. Our map should look as shown in the following screenshot:

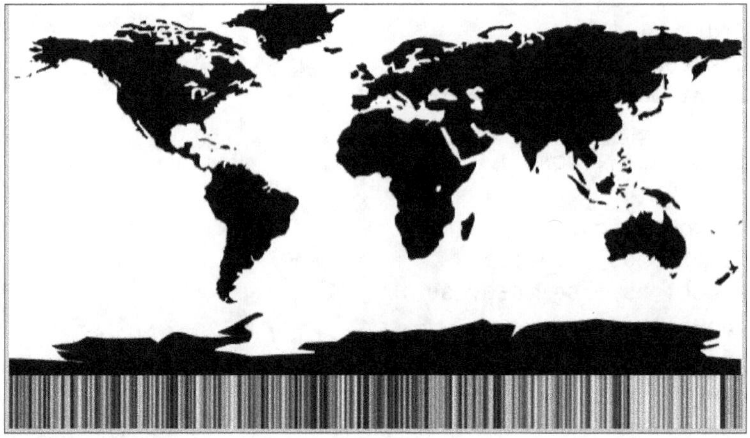

6. When our loading thread has set the state to `DONE`, we will iterate over the logfile rows and draw a red dot for each pair of geo-coordinates on our map.

```
void draw() {
  background(255);
  image( world, 0, 0, width, 350 );

  if ( state < DONE ) {
    stroke( 0, 200 );
    strokeWeight(2);
    fill( 200, 200 );
    rect( 25, 150, 650, 50 );
    noStroke();
    fill( 255 );
    rect( 30, 155, map( count, 0, total, 0, 640 ), 40 );

    fill( 0 );
    String msg="";
    if ( state == LOADING ) {
      msg = "loading database ...";
    }
    else if ( state == LOGFILE ) {
      msg = "parsing logfile ...";
    }
    else if ( state == GEOCODING ) {
      msg = "geocoding ip adresses ...";
    }
```

```
    text( msg, 35, 190 );
  } else if (state == DONE) {
    noStroke();
    fill(255);
    rect(0, 350, 700, 50);
    stroke(0, 10);
    long mints = data[0].timestamp;
    long maxts = data[ data.length-1].timestamp;
    for ( int i=0; i<data.length; i++) {
      float pos = map( data[i].timestamp, mints, maxts, 0, 700 );
      line( pos, 350, pos, 400 );
    }

    stroke(255, 0, 0);
    for ( int i=0; i < data.length; i++) {
      if ( data[i].lat != null && data[i].lon != null ) {
        float x = map( float( data[i].lon), -180, 180, 0, width );
        float y = map( float( data[i].lat), 90, -90, 0, height -50
);
        point(x, y);
      }
    }
  }
}
```

7. Run the sketch. Our map should now be sprinkled with red dots, as shown in the following screenshot:

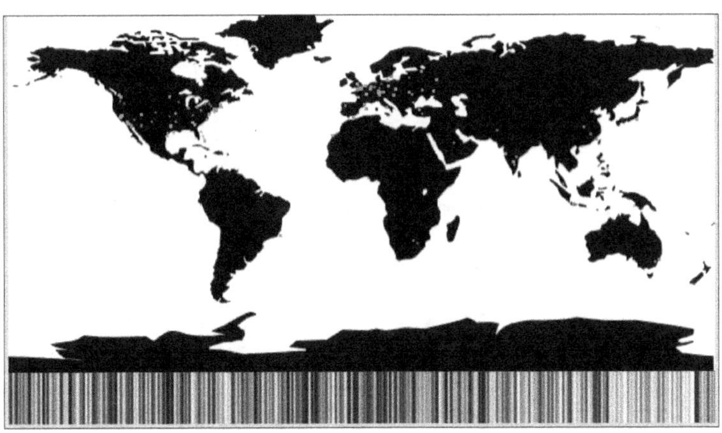

8. To make our map look even more fancy, we are now going to replace the red dots by a vector graphic of a small pin. Download the `pin.svg` file from `www.packtpub.com/support`.
9. Add the `.svg` file to our sketch by dragging it on the sketch window or by using the **Sketch | Add File...** menu.
10. Now, we need to define a `PShape` variable for our pin and load the shape in our `setup()` method.

```
import java.text.SimpleDateFormat;

PImage world;
PShape pin;

void setup() {
  size(700, 400);
  pin = loadShape( "pin.svg" );
  world = loadImage( "world.png" );

  Thread t = new Thread() {
    public void run() {
      state = LOADING;
      ipdatabase = parseIpDatabase( "hip_ip4_city_lat_lng.csv" );
      state = LOGFILE;
       String[] log = loadStrings( "access.log" );
      data = parseLogfile( log );
      state = GEOCODING;
      geoCode( data );
      state = DONE;
    }
  };
  t.start();
}
```

11. In our `draw()` method, we replace `point()` with a call to `shape()`.

```
void draw() {
   ...

    stroke(255, 0, 0);

    for ( int i=0; i < data.length; i++) {
      if ( data[i].lat != null && data[i].lon != null ) {
        float x = map( float( data[i].lon), -180, 180, 0, width );
```

```
            float y = map( float( data[i].lat), 90, -90, 0, height -50
);
            shape( pin, int(x)-5,int(y)-15);
        }
      }
    }
}
```

12. Run the sketch, and after loading the database and encoding all the IP addresses, our map now looks as shown in the following screenshot:

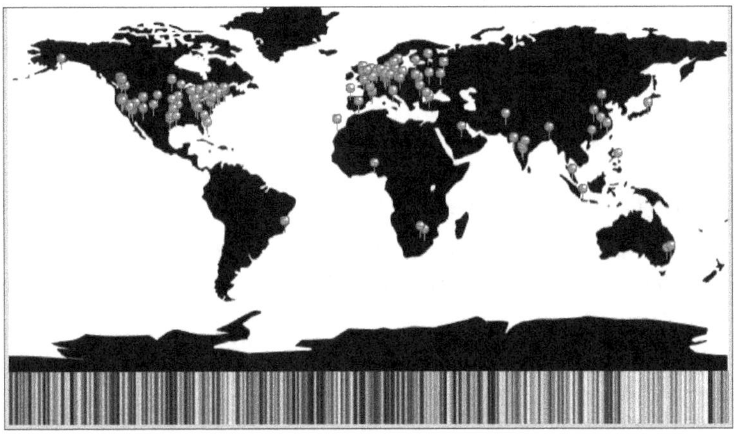

Objective Complete - Mini Debriefing

This task of our current mission was to create a Red Dot Fever using the geocoded logfile rows we created in the previous task. We added a schematic representation of the world where the continents are drawn black and the sea is white to our sketch. This map was used as a texture for the globe we created in the last project.

Then we added a loop to our `draw()` method that iterates over `LogRow`. For each row, we check whether we have found some geo-coordinates in our database and draw a red dot if we did.

To make our map look even more fancy and, to leave the Red Dot Fever stage of map creation behind us—at least a little bit—we replaced the red dots with a vector graphic of a small red pin. We added a `PShape` variable for it and loaded a SVG graphic in our `setup()` method. The pin is then drawn in the `draw()` method using the `shape()` command.

Interactive Red Dot Fever

For this final task of our current project, we will use the rotating neon globe we created for our last project. We will replace our red pins with yellow lines that stick out of our globe. These yellow pins also work very well with our shader-based filter that creates a neon representation.

Engage Thrusters

Let's add our pins to a globe:

1. Open the sketch we created in the previous task of this mission and the final sketch from our last mission. If you didn't follow the last mission, you can also download the sketch from `www.packtpub.com/support`.
2. In the neon globe sketch, select the **Sketch** | **Add File...** menu and open the `data` folder.
3. Add the two GLSL files and the images to our Red Dot Fever sketch.
4. Now add a `PImage` variable for the mission textures, a `PShape` variable for our globe, and the two `PShader` variables for the blur and the edge detection filter.

   ```
   PImage world;
   PImage bluemarble;
   PImage night;
   PShape pin;
   PShape sphere;
   PShader blur;
   PShader edge;
   LogRow[] data;

   int LOADING = 0;
   int LOGFILE = 1;
   int GEOCODING = 2;
   int DONE = 3;
   int state = LOADING;

   int count = 0;
   int total = 0;
   float a =0;
   ```

5. We now create a new method named `initGlobe()` and call it from our `setup()` method. We also change the size of our sketch to `400` by `450` pixels and enable the `P3D` rendering mode.

   ```
   void setup() {
     size(400, 450, P3D);
   ```

```
  pin = loadShape( "pin.svg" );
  world = loadImage( "world.png" );

  frameRate(25);
  initGlobe();

  Thread t = new Thread() {
    public void run() {
      state = LOADING;
      ipdatabase = parseIpDatabase( "hip_ip4_city_lat_lng.csv" );
      state = LOGFILE;
     String[] log = loadStrings( "access.log" );
      data = parseLogfile( log );
      state = GEOCODING;
      geoCode( data );
      state = DONE;
    }
  };
  t.start();
}

void initGlobe() {
}
```

6. Copy the initialization code from the `setup()` method of the neon globe sketch to the new `initGlobe()` method.

```
void initGlobe() {
  PGraphics g = createGraphics( 700, 349);
  g.beginDraw();
  PImage tmp = loadImage( "world.png" );
  tmp.filter(INVERT);
  g.tint(100, 255, 0);
  g.image( tmp, 0, 0 );
  g.endDraw();

  world = createGraphics( 700, 349 );
  world = g.get(0, 0, 700, 349);

  bluemarble = loadImage( "bluemarble.jpg" );
  night = loadImage( "night.jpg" );

  sphere = makeSphere( 150, 5, world);

  edge = loadShader("edges.glsl");
  blur = loadShader("blur.glsl");
}
```

7. Now we need to copy the `makeSphere()` and `keyPressed()` methods to our new sketch.

```
PShape makeSphere( int R, int step, PImage tex) {
  PShape s = createShape();

  s.beginShape(QUAD_STRIP);
  s.texture( tex );
  s.stroke(0, 0, 255);
  s.strokeWeight( 2 );
  for ( int i = 0; i < 180; i+=step ) {
    float sini = sin( radians( i ));
    float cosi = cos( radians( i ));
    float sinip = sin( radians( i + step ));
    float cosip = cos( radians( i + step ));

    for ( int j = 0; j <= 360; j+=step ) {
      float sinj = sin( radians( j ));
      float cosj = cos( radians( j ));
      float sinjp = sin( radians( j + step ));
      float cosjp = cos( radians( j + step ));

      s.normal( cosj * sini, -cosi, sinj * sini);
      s.vertex( R * cosj * sini, R * -cosi, R * sinj * sini,
      tex.width-j * tex.width / 360, i * tex.height / 180);

      s.normal( cosj * sinip, -cosip, sinj * sinip);
      s.vertex( R * cosj * sinip, R * -cosip, R * sinj * sinip,
      tex.width-j * tex.width / 360, (i + step ) * tex.height /
180);
    }
  }

  s.endShape();
  return s;
}
boolean satelite = false;
void keyPressed() {
  if ( key == '1' ) {

    satelite = false;
    sphere = makeSphere( 150, 5, world);
  }
  else if ( key == '2' ) {
```

```
      sphere.setTexture( bluemarble );
      sphere.setStroke(false);
      satelite = true;
    }
    else if ( key == '3' ) {
      sphere.setTexture( night );
      sphere.setStroke(false);
      satelite = true;
    }
  }
```

8. In our `draw()` method, we need to switch between 2D and 3D drawing, because we want our progress bar and our timeline to be drawn on top of the rotating globe. To make this work, we need to disable the 3D depth sorting before our globe gets drawn and disable it afterward.

```
void draw() {
  background(0);
  hint(ENABLE_DEPTH_TEST);
  drawGlobe();
  hint(DISABLE_DEPTH_TEST);
  noLights();
  if ( state < DONE ) {
    stroke( 0, 200 );
    strokeWeight(2);
    fill( 200, 200 );
    rect( 25, 150, 350, 50 );
    noStroke();
    fill( 255 );
    rect( 30, 155, map( count, 0, total, 0, 340 ), 40 );

    fill( 0 );
    String msg="";
    if ( state == LOADING ) {
      msg = "loading database ...";
    }
    else if ( state == LOGFILE ) {
      msg = "parsing logfile ...";
    }
    else if ( state == GEOCODING ) {
      msg = "geocoding ip adresses ...";
    }

    text( msg, 35, 190 );
  }
```

```
    fill(255, 0, 0);

    if (state == DONE) {
      noStroke();
      fill(0);
      rect(0, 400, width, 50);
      stroke(255, 255, 0, 5);
      long mints = data[0].timestamp;
      long maxts = data[ data.length-1].timestamp;
      for ( int i=0; i<data.length; i++) {
        float pos = map( data[i].timestamp, mints, maxts, 0, width );
        line( pos, 400, pos, 450 );
      }
    }
```

9. Now add a new method named `drawGlobe()` and add the code that rotates and draws our globe.

```
void drawGlobe() {
  pushMatrix();
  translate( width/2, (height-50)/2);

  lights();
  pushMatrix();
  rotateX( radians(-30));
  rotateY( a );
  a+= 0.01;

  shape(sphere);

  popMatrix();
  popMatrix();
  if ( !satelite ) {
    filter(edge);
    filter(blur);
  }
}
```

10. So far, our globe and the progress bar have been drawn, but we still need to add our geocoded data. We will create short yellow neon pins for our globe. Add a `drawPin()` method and call it from our `drawGlobe()` method.

```
void drawGlobe() {
  pushMatrix();
```

```
  translate( width/2, (height-50)/2);

  lights();
  pushMatrix();
  rotateX( radians(-30));
  rotateY( a );
  a+= 0.01;

  drawPins();
  shape(sphere);

  popMatrix();
  popMatrix();
  if ( !satelite ) {
    filter(edge);
    filter(blur);
  }
}

void drawPins() {
}
```

11. In our `drawPin()` method, we need to convert the latitude and longitude coordinates to match the angles we used to create our sphere. Then we draw a line from the origin of our sphere to a point slightly above the surface.

```
void drawPins() {
  float R = 160;
  if (state == DONE ) {
    strokeWeight(2);
    stroke(255, 250, 0);

    for ( int i=0; i<data.length; i++) {
      beginShape(LINES);

      if ( data[i].lat != null && data[i].lon != null ) {
        float la = map(float(data[i].lat), 90, -90, 0, 180);
        float lo = map(float(data[i].lon), 180, -180, 0, 360);

        float sini = sin( radians( la ));
        float cosi = cos( radians( la ));
        float sinj = sin( radians( lo ));
        float cosj = cos( radians( lo ));
        vertex(0, 0, 0);
```

```
                vertex( R * cosj * sini, R * -cosi, R * sinj * sini );
            }
            endShape();
        }
    }
}
```

12. Run the sketch, and after loading the database and encoding all the IP addresses, our map looks like the following screenshot:

Objective Complete - Mini Debriefing

For this final task of our current mission, we have combined our Red Dot Fever and our neon globe from *Project 7, The Neon Globe*. We added the textures and the code of our GLSL filters to our sketch and copied the `setup` code of our globe to a method named `initGlobe()`.

Then we added the `makeSphere()` and `keyPressed()` methods to our sketch. In the `draw()` method, we had to enable the depth sorting before drawing our globe, and deactivate it before drawing our loading progress bar and the timeline. We moved the code for drawing and rotating the globe to a separate method named `drawGlobe()`.

Finally, we added a method named `drawPins()` that converts the geo-coordinates of our log lines to the polar coordinates we used to create our sphere and then draws a line for each of them starting at the origin of our sphere and ending shortly above the surface of our globe.

Mission Accomplished

Our current mission was to use the neon globe we created in the previous project and turn it into a geographic information system showing where the requests for a website are coming from. We started by parsing the logfile using regular expressions and extracting the IP address and the timestamp from each line. To make the timestamps easier to work with, we used `SimpleDateFormater` to convert the `string` representation to a `long`. In the `draw()` method, we created a timeline showing the timestamps of a logfile.

In the second task, we added the database from the hostIP project, which allows us to map blocks of IP addresses to geo-coordinates on city level. To speed up the geocoding, we created `HashMap` using the IP address block as a key. Since the loading of the hostIP database takes some time, we moved the initialization code to a separate thread and added a progress bar to our `draw()` method.

In the third task, we used the geocoded data to draw a small red dot for each request on a map. The map we used is the texture image we used for our neon globe in the last project. To make our map look fancier, we replaced the red dots with a vector graphic of a pin.

Our final task for this mission was to use the globe we created in the previous project and to add our visualization to it. We moved the code for initialization of the globe to our new sketch. Then we adapted our `draw()` method to make sure the two-dimensional elements like the progress bar get drawn on top of the globe. Instead of the red dots, we used yellow lines that stick out of the globe's surface. These lines are also drawn as neon lines if our GLSL filters are active.

You Ready to go Gung HO? A Hotshot Challenge

In this mission, we created geographic visualizations on a 2D map and a 3D globe, but geographic information systems are a very wide and interesting field, and we certainly have only scratched the surface. Why don't you try to reach the next level and try one of the following ideas:

- Allow the user to rotate the globe using the mouse
- Use different colored pins for the requested file types
- Parse your logfile in real time using a server process and send live updates to your globe
- Visualize where your spam mails are coming from
- Use the zoomable vector maps for your visualizations

Project 9

From Virtual to Real

A few years ago, if you had an idea for a vase or a pen holder, and you wanted it to be turned into a physical object that you could put on your desk, you would have started drawing blueprints. Depending on the material, you would have started carving wood, created a mould, made articles of clay, or paid someone to do it for you. But at the wake of this century, another opportunity presented itself—designing the object you like on your computer and feeding it to a 3D printer.

Mission Briefing

Our mission is to generate a small vase from a mathematical expression. We will start with a simple formula and create 2D shapes; we will make the shape changeable using a GUI. Then, we will extend our 2D shape to the third dimension and add some more changeable parameters. We will add a camera control to our sketch, which will allow us to inspect our object from every angle before we decide whether that is what we want on our desk, window board, or cupboard.

Then, we will add an export function that will allow us to either create an STL file that can be used as an input for a 3D desktop printer or order the vase from an online 3D printing service.

Why Is It Awesome?

When I was a kid, I loved playing with Lego sets. And whenever I made a big building, I was always missing ONE special block that was required to finish my masterpiece. One roof stone, one window, one door (a green one), and so on. Later when I started watching Star Trek and saw a replicator for the first time, I knew that this was the solution to all my Lego problems. You need a Lego piece? One more horse to rescue a princess from a huge dragon? One more spaceship to fend off the evil aliens? Just tell your replicator.

Desktop 3D printing is still far from being as easy-to-use or as versatile as a replicator from Star Trek, but I think it's a very promising step in the right direction.

Your Hotshot Objectives

To complete our current mission, we need to undertake the following tasks:

- Beautiful functions
- Generating an object
- Exporting the object
- Making it real

Mission Checklist

Our current mission is to create and export a 3D object in a format that can be printed on a 3D printer. All the examples run without any additional requirements, but if you want to follow the last task, you need access to a 3D printer or an online 3D printing service.

Beautiful functions

The first task for our current mission is to create a 2D shape that can be used as a cross section for a vase. We will use polar coordinates to create a circular shape and a function that alters the radius based on the rotational angle to make it look more interesting.

We will also add a GUI using the controlP5 library by Andreas Schlegel to enable the users of our sketch to modify the curve.

Engage Thrusters

Let's start drawing curves:

1. Start a new Processing sketch and add the `setup()` and `draw()` methods.

   ```
   void setup() {
   }

   void draw() {
   }
   ```

2. Now add two float arrays that will hold the vertex coordinates of our shape. Also add the initialization code to your `setup()` method. We will use a vertex every 5 degrees, so we need 72 vertices for our shape.

   ```
   float vertx[];
   float verty[];
   ```

```
void setup() {
  size(400,400);
  vertx = new float[72];
  verty = new float[72];
}
```

3. To create the values for our coordinates, we add two methods; one that calculates the radius of our polar coordinates for a given angle, and a second one that uses this radius to calculate the Cartesian coordinates of our vertices and then stores them in our arrays.

```
float getR( float a ) {
  return 100;
}

void initPoints() {
  for( int a = 0; a < 72; a++) {
    vertx[a] = cos( radians( a * 5.0 )) * getR( a * 5.0 );
    verty[a] = sin( radians( a * 5.0 )) * getR( a * 5.0 );
  }
}
```

4. In our `draw()` method, we need to add a call to the `initPoints()` method. Then we can iterate over our arrays and create a shape.

```
void draw() {
  pushMatrix();
  background(255);
  translate( width/2, height/2 );
  noFill();
  initPoints();
  beginShape();
  for( int a = 0; a < 72; a++) {
     vertex( vertx[a], verty[a] );
  }
  vertex( vertx[0], verty[0] );
  endShape();
  popMatrix();
}
```

5. Currently, our `getR()` function returns the same radius for every angle, which is fine if we want to draw a circle. But because we want to create a more interesting shape, we add the following code to our `getR()` function:

```
float getR( float a ) {
  return sin( radians(a)*6) * 20 + 100;
}
```

6. Run your sketch. The shape we created should look like the one in this screenshot:

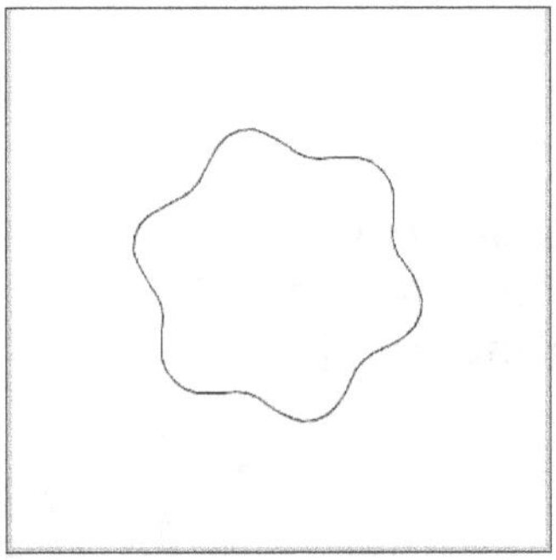

7. Now we need a simple way for our user to change the parameters of the function we just created. We will use the controlP5 library to create our GUI, so let's install it using the Library Manager. Go to **Sketch** | **Import Library...** | **Add Library...** to open the Library Manager, and then type in `controlP5` in the search field.
8. Click on the **Install** button in the dialog you see in this screenshot:

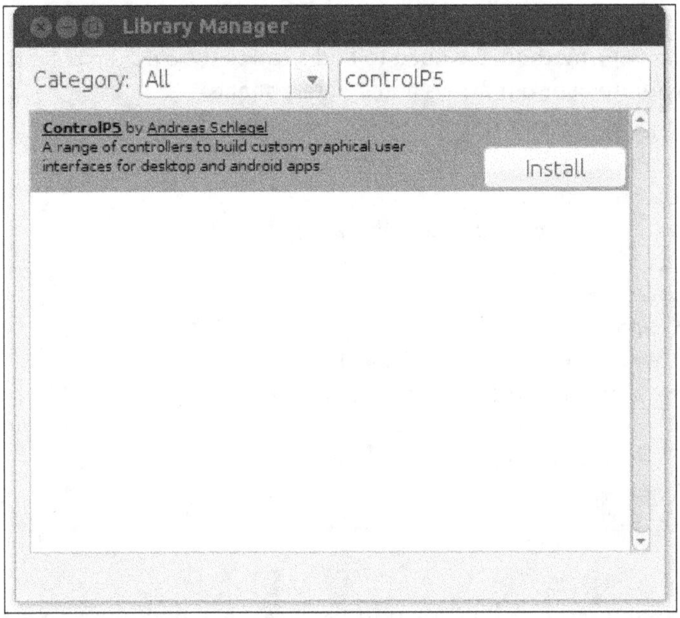

9. Now let's import the library to our sketch by selecting **ControlP5** when we go to **Sketch** | **Import Library...**.

10. We will now add a group box that will act as our control panel and a button that will allow the user to toggle the visibility of our menu.

```
import controlP5.*;

ControlGroup box;
ControlP5 cp5;
Button toggleButton;

float vertx[];
float verty[];
```

11. To separate the GUI setup code from the initialization of our shape, we add a method named `setupGUI()` and call it from our `setup()` method.

```
void setup() {
  size(400,400);
  setupGUI();
  vertx = new float[72];
  verty = new float[72];
}

void setupGUI() {
}
```

12. In our `setupGUI()` method, we create the toggle button and our menu box.

```
void setupGUI() {
  cp5 = new ControlP5(this);
  toggleButton = cp5.addButton("toggleBox", 1, 00, 00, 100, 20);
  toggleButton.setLabel("Hide Menu");

  box = cp5.addGroup( "box", 0, 0, 150);
  box.setBackgroundHeight(120);
  box.setBackgroundColor(color(0, 100));
}
```

13. ControlP5 uses callback functions for each GUI element. The function name is the first parameter to the `addButton()` method that we used in our `setupGUI()` function. So the callback method that gets notified when someone clicks on our button has to be named `toggleBox()`.

```
void toggleBox(int theValue) {
  if (box.isVisible()) {
    toggleButton.setLabel("Show Menu");
    box.hide();
  } else {
```

```
    toggleButton.setLabel("Hide Menu");
    box.show();
  }
}
```

14. Currently, our menu box is completely empty. Let's change this by adding two sliders, one for controlling the number of oscillations that our curve has, and one for their size. We will limit the number of oscillations to whole numbers as we don't want any ugly jumps in our function.

```
void setupGUI() {
  cp5 = new ControlP5(this);
  toggleButton = cp5.addButton("toggleBox", 1, 00, 00, 100, 20);
  toggleButton.setLabel("Hide Menu");

  box = cp5.addGroup( "box", 0, 0, 150);
  box.setBackgroundHeight(120);
  box.setBackgroundColor(color(0, 100));

  Slider slider =  cp5.addSlider("slider");
  slider.setPosition(10, 50);
  slider.setSize(80, 10);
  slider.setRange(1, 8);
  slider.setValue(6);
  slider.setNumberOfTickMarks(8);
  slider.setLabel( "count" );
  slider.moveTo( box );

  Slider slider2 =  cp5.addSlider("slider2");
  slider2.setPosition(10, 80);
  slider2.setSize(80, 10);
  slider2.setRange(-20, 20);
  slider2.setValue(10);
  slider2.setLabel( "radius" );
  slider2.moveTo( box );
}
```

15. Now we need to add two float variables that store our parameters and two callback functions that get called when our users move the sliders.

```
float v1 = 0;
float v2 = 0;

void slider( float val ) {  v1 = val; }
void slider2( float val ) {  v2 = val; }
```

16. We will then use the two float variables to influence the radius in our `getR()` method.

```
float getR( float a ) {
  return sin( radians(a)*v1) * v2 + 100;
}
```

17. Run your sketch now and change the slider values. In the following screenshot, you can see how the GUI looks after editing the shapes:

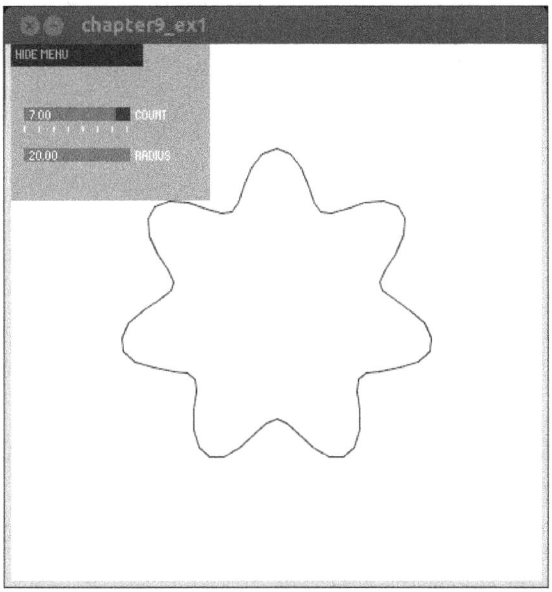

Objective Complete - Mini Debriefing

In the first task of our current mission, we created a 2D, closed shape that we can use as a cross section for our vase. We used polar coordinates to create the vertices of our shape by changing the radius depending upon the angle.

To enable our users to change the parameters of our curve without having to change the source code, we added a GUI. From step 6 onwards, we installed the controlP5 library and added a button and a menu box. The button toggles the visibility of our menu box by calling the `show()` and `hide()` methods in our callback function.

From step 14 onwards, we added two sliders to our menu box that allow us to control the number and size of the oscillations on our curve.

Generating an object

The second task of our current mission is to generate a 3D object that can be used as a small pen holder or vase. We will use the 2D shape we created in task 1 as a cross section of our object by extruding it along the z axis. We will extend our `getR()` method and add a bunch of additional control variables that will allow us to change the circular shape depending on the object's height.

To make it easier for our users to look at the object, we will add the `mousePressed()` and `mouseDragged()` functions, which rotate the object in any direction. We will use a mathematical construct named *quaternion* to implement these rotations.

Engage Thrusters

Let's bring our shape to the third dimension:

1. To turn our shape into a 3D object, we need to extend our `vertx` and `verty` arrays.

```
import controlP5.*;

ControlGroup box;
ControlP5 cp5;
Button toggleButton;
float[][] vertx;
float[][] verty;
```

2. In our `setup()` method, we change the display mode to `P3D` and define our array initialization. Our shape will consist of 20 triangle strips, each containing 72 vertices.

```
void setup() {
  size(400, 400, P3D);
  setupGUI();

  vertx = new float[20][72];
  verty = new float[20][72];
}
```

3. Because we changed our vertex arrays, we also need to change our `initPoints()` method. We will now add a second `for` loop that iterates over the height.

```
void initPoints() {
  for ( int h = 0; h < 20; h++) {
    for ( int a = 0; a<72; a++) {
      float r = getR( a*5.0 );
      vertx[h][a] = cos( radians( a*5.0 )) * r;
```

```
      verty[h][a] = sin( radians( a*5.0 )) * r;
    }
  }
}
```

4. Now we can replace our shape with a stack of triangle strips in our `draw()` method. We need to enable the depth test before we start drawing our shape and disable it afterwards to make sure that the GUI elements are drawn correctly. We will also enable some light sources to prevent our object from being shaded completely flat.

```
void draw() {
  hint( ENABLE_DEPTH_TEST );
  pushMatrix();
  background(255);
  fill(200);
  noStroke();

  translate( width/2, height/2);
  scale( 1.5 );
  ambientLight( 50, 50, 50);
  directionalLight( 100, 95, 55, 0, 0, -10 );
  pointLight( 150, 150, 200, 100, -100, 200 );

  translate(0, -50, 0);
  initPoints();

  beginShape(TRIANGLE_STRIP );
  for ( int h = 1; h < 20; h++) {
    for ( int a = 0; a<73; a++ ) {
      int aa = a % 72;
      normal( vertx[h][aa], 0, verty[h][aa]);
      vertex( vertx[h][aa], h*5.0, verty[h][aa] );
      normal( vertx[h-1][aa], 0, verty[h-1][aa]);
      vertex( vertx[h-1][aa], (h-1)*5.0, verty[h-1][aa] );
    }
  }
  endShape();

  popMatrix();
  hint(DISABLE_DEPTH_TEST);
}
```

5. Currently, our object is only visible from the side and can't be turned. To fix this, we need to calculate an axis of rotation and a rotational angle. To simplify these calculations, we need to add a class named `Quaternion`. Quaternions are mathematical constructs similar to complex numbers, only they are four-dimensional. Click on the **New Tab** menu to the right and enter the name as `Quaternion`. Then, add the following code:

```
class Quaternion {
  float w = 1.0;
  float x = 0.0;
  float y = 0.0;
  float z = 0.0;

  void mult( Quaternion b ) {
    Quaternion res = new Quaternion();
    res.w = this.w * b.w - this.x * b.x - this.y * b.y - this.z *
    b.z;
    res.x = this.w * b.x + this.x * b.w + this.y * b.z - this.z *
    b.y;
    res.y = this.w * b.y - this.x * b.z + this.y * b.w + this.z *
    b.x;
    res.z = this.w * b.z + this.x * b.y - this.y * b.x + this.z *
    b.w;
    set( res );
  }

  void set( PVector cross, float dot ) {
    this.x = cross.x;
    this.y = cross.y;
    this.z = cross.z;
    this.w = dot;
  }

  void set( Quaternion in ) {
    this.w = in.w;
    this.x = in.x;
    this.y = in.y;
    this.z = in.z;

  }

  float[] matrix() {
    float[] res = new float[4];
    float sa = (float) Math.sqrt(1.0f - w * w);
```

```
      if (sa < EPSILON){ sa = 1.0f; }

      res[0] = (float) Math.acos(w) * 2.0f;
      res[1] = x / sa;
      res[2] = y / sa;
      res[3] = z / sa;

      return res;
    }
  }
```

6. We need to define three `Quaternion` objects in our main tab, which we will use to calculate the current rotation matrix when the user is dragging the mouse. We also need a `radius` variable and two `PVector` objects to track the current mouse position and state.

```
import controlP5.*;

ControlGroup box;
ControlP5 cp5;
Button toggleButton;

Quaternion qdown = new Quaternion();
Quaternion qnow = new Quaternion();
Quaternion qdrag = new Quaternion();

float radius = 200;
PVector down = new PVector();
PVector drag = new PVector();

float[][] vertx;
float[][] verty;
```

7. Now we need to add the `mousePressed()` and `mouseDragged()` methods, which change our variables when the mouse moves. We also add a helper function named `mouseToSphere()`, which is used to convert the coordinates of our mouse pointer to a point on a virtual sphere around our object, to calculate our quaternions.

```
PVector mouseToSphere(float x, float y) {
  PVector v = new PVector();
  v.x = (x - width/2) / radius;;
  v.y = (y - height/2) / radius;

  float mag = v.x * v.x + v.y * v.y;
  if (mag > 1.0f) {
```

```
    v.normalize();
  } else {
    v.z = sqrt(1.0f - mag);
  }
  return v;
}

void mousePressed() {
  if (!box.isVisible() || ( mouseX > box.getWidth()
      || mouseY > box.getBackgroundHeight())) {
    down = mouseToSphere( mouseX, mouseY );
    qdown.set( qnow );
    qdrag = new Quaternion();
  }
}

void mouseDragged() {
  if (!box.isVisible() || ( mouseX > box.getWidth()
      || mouseY > box.getBackgroundHeight())) {
    drag= mouseToSphere( mouseX, mouseY );
    qdrag.set( down.cross( drag), down.dot( drag ));
  }
}
```

8. To make use of our rotation matrix, we need to add the following code to our `draw()` method:

```
void draw() {
  hint( ENABLE_DEPTH_TEST );
  pushMatrix();
  background(255);
  fill(200);
  noStroke();

  translate( width/2, height/2);
  scale( 1.5 );
  ambientLight( 50, 50, 50);
  directionalLight( 100, 95, 55, 0, 0, -10 );
  pointLight( 150, 150, 200, 100, -100, 200 );

  qnow.set( qdrag );
  qnow.mult( qdown );

  float[] matrix = qnow.matrix();
```

```
  rotate( matrix[0], matrix[1], matrix[2], matrix[3] );

  translate(0, -50, 0);

  initPoints();
```

9. Now we can rotate our object by dragging the mouse, but it's hard to distinguish between the top and bottom of our object after a few rotations. So we're going to close the bottom by adding a triangular fan to our `draw()` method.

```
void draw() {

  beginShape(TRIANGLE_STRIP );
  for ( int h = 1; h < 20; h++) {
    for ( int a = 0; a<73; a++ ) {
      int aa = a % 72;
      normal( vertx[h][aa], 0, verty[h][aa]);
      vertex( vertx[h][aa], h*5.0, verty[h][aa] );
      normal( vertx[h-1][aa], 0, verty[h-1][aa]);
      vertex( vertx[h-1][aa], (h-1)*5.0, verty[h-1][aa] );
    }
  }
  endShape();

  beginShape(TRIANGLE_FAN);
  int h = 19;
  vertex( 0, h*5, 0 );
  for ( int a = 0; a<73; a++ ) {
    int aa = a % 72;
    vertex( vertx[h][aa], h*5, verty[h][aa] );
  }
  endShape();


  popMatrix();
  hint(DISABLE_DEPTH_TEST);
}
```

10. So far, our object is a cylindrical extrusion of our shape from the first task. Currently, we're only using the angle as an input parameter for our `getR()` function. Now let's add the height as an additional input and create some new control variables.

```
float getR( float a, float h ) {
  float r = v2 * sin( radians(a) * v1 +( h/15 )*v3) +
sin(radians(3.6*h) * v4 + v5)*v6 + 40;
```

```
    return r;
  }

  void initPoints() {
    for ( int h = 0; h < 20; h++) {
      for ( int a = 0; a<72; a++) {
        float r = getR( a*5.0, h*5.0 );
        vertx[h][a] = cos( radians( a*5.0 )) * r;
        verty[h][a] = sin( radians( a*5.0 )) * r;
      }
    }
  }
```

11. In our `setupGUI()` method, we need to add four more sliders to enter the new control values. To simplify the creation of the sliders, we will add a method named `addSlider()`.

```
float v1;
float v2;
float v3;
float v4;
float v5;
float v6;

void setupGUI() {
  cp5 = new ControlP5(this);
  toggleButton = cp5.addButton("toggleBox", 1, 00, 00, 100, 20);
  toggleButton.setLabel("Hide Menu");

  box = cp5.addGroup( "box", 0, 0, 150);
  box.setBackgroundHeight(170);
  box.setBackgroundColor(color(0, 100));

  Slider slider =  addSlider( "slider", 40, 1, 8, 5, "count" );
  slider.setNumberOfTickMarks(8);
  Slider slider2 =  addSlider( "slider2", 60, -10, 10, 5, "radius"
);
  Slider slider3 =  addSlider( "slider3", 80, -2, 2, 2, "twist" );
  Slider slider4 =  addSlider( "slider4", 100, 0, 2, 1.5, "hcount"
);
  Slider slider5 =  addSlider( "slider5", 120, -2, 2, 2, "phase"
);
  Slider slider6 =  addSlider( "slider6", 140, 0, 5, 5, "hradius"
);
}
```

```
Slider addSlider( String callback, int pos, float start, float
end, float value, String label ) {
  Slider slider =  cp5.addSlider(callback);
  slider.setPosition(10, pos);
  slider.setSize(80, 10);
  slider.setRange(start, end);
  slider.setValue(value);
  slider.setLabel( label );
  slider.moveTo( box );
  return slider;
}
```

12. We also need a new callback variable for each one of our sliders.

```
void slider( float val ) {  v1 = val;}
void slider2( float val ) {  v2 = val;}
void slider3( float val ) {  v3 = val;}
void slider4( float val ) {  v4 = val;}
void slider5( float val ) {  v5 = val;}
void slider6( float val ) {  v6 = val;}
```

13. Run your sketch now and change the sliders to create shapes like the one in this screenshot:

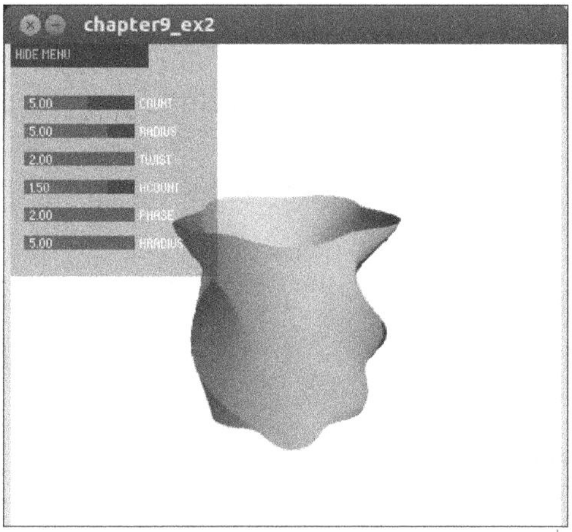

Objective Complete - Mini Debriefing

For this task of our current mission, we extruded the 2D shape from the first task and created a cylindrical form from it. We added a `Quaternion` class and two callback functions that receive mouse press and mouse drag events, and calculated a rotation matrix that allows the user of our sketch to view the object from all sides.

To make our object more interesting, we added four additional control parameters to our GUI and extended the `getR()` function to take the height of the cylinder into account for calculating the radius.

Exporting the object

We have created a 3D object in our previous task that can be changed using some sliders, but to print the object on a 3D printer, we have to save the object in a format that a 3D printer understands. Our current task is to add an export function that saves the object to an **STL (STereo Lithography)** file. This file format was originally invented to serve as an input format for Stereo Lithograph machines (hence the name), but nearly every currently available 3D software can import these files. The file stores the coordinates of triangles and a normal vector for each of these triangles. This is why the format has the nickname **Triangle Soup**.

An STL file has an 80-byte header that is ignored by every known 3D program, so we set it to `0`. Then, we need to write the count of the triangles as a four-byte unsigned long. This is followed by 12 float values for each triangle, which contain the normal vector and the coordinates of the vertices. Each triangle ends with a two-byte zero.

Engage Thrusters

Let's export some triangles:

1. First, we add a class where we can store the triangles that our mesh is made of. Add a new tab by clicking on the icon on the right and select the **New Tab ...** menu. Name it `Triangle` and add the following code:

```
public class Triangle {
  PVector a;
  PVector b;
  PVector c;
  PVector n;

  public Triangle( PVector a, PVector b, PVector c, PVector n ) {
    this.a = a;
    this.b = b;
    this.c = c;
    this.n = n;
  }
}
```

2. Now we add another tab and create a class named `TriangleSoup`. This class stores the triangles and writes them to the file in the STL format.

```
import java.io.FileOutputStream;
import java.nio.ByteBuffer;
import java.nio.ByteOrder;
import java.util.Arrays;
import java.io.FileOutputStream;
import java.io.IOException;
import java.util.List;

public class TriangleSoup {

  List<Triangle> triangles = new ArrayList<Triangle>();
  float scale = 1;

  void scale( float scale ) {
    this.scale = scale;
  }

  void add( PVector a, PVector b, PVector c, PVector n ) {
    triangles.add( new Triangle( a, b, c, n ));
  }
}
```

3. When all the triangle objects of our mesh have been added to our Triangle Soup, we need to save it to an STL file. Add the following method to our class:

```
  void save( String filename ) {
    try {
    byte[] header = new byte[80];
    byte[] count = new byte[4];
    byte[] tri = new byte[50];

    FileOutputStream out = new FileOutputStream( filename );
    ByteBuffer buffer = ByteBuffer.allocate( 80 );
    buffer.order( ByteOrder.LITTLE_ENDIAN );

    Arrays.fill(header,0, 80, (byte)0);
    out.write( header, 0, 80 );
    buffer.putInt( triangles.size());
    buffer.rewind();
    buffer.get( count, 0, 4 );
    out.write( count, 0, 4 );
```

```
    for( int i=0; i<triangles.size(); i++) {
      buffer.rewind();
      buffer.putFloat( triangles.get(i).n.x * scale);
      buffer.putFloat( triangles.get(i).n.z * scale);
      buffer.putFloat( triangles.get(i).n.y * scale);

      buffer.putFloat( triangles.get(i).a.x * scale);
      buffer.putFloat( triangles.get(i).a.z * scale);
      buffer.putFloat( triangles.get(i).a.y * scale);

      buffer.putFloat( triangles.get(i).b.x * scale);
      buffer.putFloat( triangles.get(i).b.z * scale);
      buffer.putFloat( triangles.get(i).b.y * scale);

      buffer.putFloat( triangles.get(i).c.x * scale);
      buffer.putFloat( triangles.get(i).c.z * scale);
      buffer.putFloat( triangles.get(i).c.y * scale);

      buffer.putShort( (short)0 );
      buffer.rewind();
      buffer.get( tri, 0, 50 );
      out.write( tri, 0, 50 );
    }

    out.flush();
    out.close();

    } catch ( IOException ioe ) {
      ioe.printStackTrace();
    }
  }
```

4. Back on our main tab, we need to add a new button to our menu that opens a file selection box and lets the user enter the filename for the export file. So, we will now add a new button definition to our `setupGUI()` method.

```
void setupGUI() {

  Button exportButton = cp5.addButton( "export", 1, 10, 165, 120,
15 );
  exportButton.setLabel( "export" );
  exportButton.moveTo( box );
}
```

5. Now add a callback function for the export button and create a file dialog using the `selectOutput()` method. The first parameter is the title of the dialog box, and the second parameter is the name of a callback method that gets activated when the user selects a filename and clicks on OK.

```
void export() {
  selectOutput( "Export to STL", "exportCallback" );
}
```

6. The callback method for the dialog box gets the filename that the user selects, as a string parameter. If the user cancels the dialog, the filename string is set to null. If we get a valid filename, we convert it to an absolute path and create a `TriangleSoup` object. To make our object printable, we need to make sure that it is a closed volume and not a single wall. We add the `exportOuter()` and `exportInner()` methods, which create the walls, and the `exportBottom()` and `exportTop()` methods, which close our object.

```
void exportCallback(File exportFile) {
  if ( exportFile != null ) {
    String filename = exportFile.getAbsolutePath();
    TriangleSoup export = new TriangleSoup();
    export.scale( .5 );

    exportOuter( export );
    exportInner( export );
    exportBottom( export );
    exportTop( export );
    export.save(filename);
  }
}
```

7. Now we need to add the export functions for each of the meshes. The `exportOuter()` method creates triangles for the outer walls and then calculates the normal vectors for the triangles.

```
void exportOuter( TriangleSoup export ) {
  for ( int h = 1; h < 20; h++) {
    for ( int a = 0; a<72; a++ ) {
      int ab = (a+1) % 72;
      PVector p1 = new PVector( vertx[h][a], 95-h*5.0, verty[h][a]
);
      PVector p2 = new PVector( vertx[h-1][a], 95-(h-1)*5.0,
verty[h-1][a] );
      PVector p3 = new PVector( vertx[h][ab], 95-h*5.0, verty[h]
[ab] );
      PVector p4 = new PVector( vertx[h-1][ab], 95-(h-1)*5.0,
verty[h-1][ab] );
```

```
      PVector n1 = new PVector( -(p1.x+p2.x+p3.x)/3, 0, -(p1.y+p2.
y+p3.y)/3);
      n1.normalize();
      PVector n2 = new PVector( -(p2.x+p3.x+p4.x)/3, 0, -(p2.y+p3.
y+p4.y)/3);
      n2.normalize();
      export.add( p1, p2, p3, n1 );
      export.add( p3, p2, p4, n2 );
    }
  }
}
```

8. Our `exportInner()` method is similar to the `exportOuter()` method, but the normals point in the opposite directions compared to the ones used in the `exportOuter()` method and the radius is reduced by `0.8`.

```
void exportInner( TriangleSoup export ) {
  for ( int h = 1; h < 19; h++) {
    for ( int a = 0; a<72; a++ ) {
      int ab = (a+1) % 72;
      PVector p1 = new PVector( vertx[h][a] * 0.8, 95-h*5.0,
verty[h][a]* 0.8 );
      PVector p2 = new PVector( vertx[h-1][a]* 0.8, 95-(h-1)*5.0,
verty[h-1][a] * 0.8);
      PVector p3 = new PVector( vertx[h][ab]* 0.8, 95-h*5.0,
verty[h][ab]* 0.8 );
      PVector p4 = new PVector( vertx[h-1][ab]* 0.8, 95-(h-1)*5.0,
verty[h-1][ab]* 0.8 );
      PVector n1 = new PVector( -(p1.x+p2.x+p3.x)/3, 0, -(p1.y+p2.
y+p3.y)/3);
      n1.normalize();
      PVector n2 = new PVector( -(p2.x+p3.x+p4.x)/3, 0, -(p2.y+p3.
y+p4.y)/3);
      n2.normalize();
      export.add( p1, p2, p3, n1 );
      export.add( p3, p2, p4, n2 );
    }
  }
}
```

9. The `exportBottom()` method creates two triangle fans to close the bottom of our mesh. We need one bottom mesh for the outer wall and one that's slightly smaller and above it for the inner wall.

```
void exportBottom(TriangleSoup export) {
  PVector n = new PVector( 0, -1, 0);
  PVector p1 = new PVector( 0, 5, 0 );
  for ( int a = 0; a < 72; a++) {
    int ab = (a+1) % 72;
    PVector p2 = new PVector( vertx[18][a]*0.8, 5, verty[18]
[a]*0.8 );
    PVector p3 = new PVector(vertx[18][ab]*0.8, 5, verty[18]
[ab]*0.8 );
    export.add( p1, p2, p3, n );
  }

  n = new PVector( 0, 1, 0);
  p1 = new PVector( 0, 0, 0 );
  for ( int a = 0; a < 72; a++) {
    int ab = (a+1) % 72;
    PVector p2 = new PVector( vertx[19][a], 0, verty[19][a] );
    PVector p3 = new PVector( vertx[19][ab], 0, verty[19][ab] );
    export.add( p1, p2, p3, n );
  }
}
```

10. Finally, we need an `exportTop()` method that creates the top ring that connects the inner and the outer mesh.

```
void exportTop(TriangleSoup export) {
  PVector n = new PVector( 0, 1, 0);
  for ( int a = 0; a < 72; a++) {
    int ab = (a+1) % 72;
    PVector p1 = new PVector( vertx[0][a], 95, verty[0][a] );
    PVector p2 = new PVector( vertx[0][a]*0.8, 95, verty[0][a]*0.8
);
    PVector p3 = new PVector( vertx[0][ab], 95, verty[0][ab] );
    PVector p4 = new PVector( vertx[0][ab]*0.8, 95, verty[0]
[ab]*0.8 );

    export.add( p1, p2, p3, n );
    export.add( p3, p2, p4, n );
  }
}
```

11. Run the sketch now and adjust the parameters until you have created a vase that pleases you. Export the mesh as an STL file. One of the meshes I created looks like this:

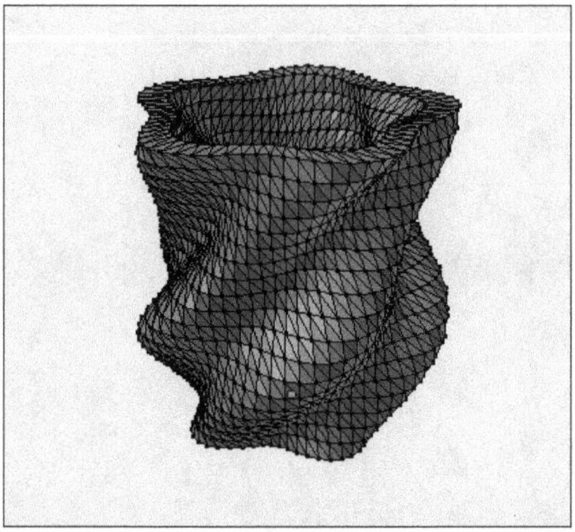

Objective Complete - Mini Debriefing

Our third task for this mission was to export the mesh of our vase to an STL file. We added a `Triangle` class and a `TriangleSoup` class, which allowed us to store the triangles of our mesh in a list and then export the list. The `TriangleSoup` class takes care of creating the header and vertex data in the correct binary format.

We added a button to our GUI, which opens a file selection box and a callback function that gets called when the user selects a filename. We added a `TriangleSoup` object to our sketch and created export methods that create our inner and outer walls, the bottom triangle fans, and the top ring that connects the inner and outer wall.

After all the triangles are created and added to our `List`, the `save()` method is called and an STL file with the selected filename is created.

Making it real

The final task of our current mission is to take the file we exported in the third task and turn it into a physical object. I will show you how to print these STL files on a desktop 3D printer, and how to order them from an online 3D printing service. The 3D printer I used for these examples is the Makerbot CupCake CNC (2009). Other printers use different control software, but the steps required to convert an STL file to a physical object are very similar on each of them.

If you don't have a 3D printer at home, you can try to find a hackerspace or fab lab near you. These are groups of makers and hackers who meet on a regular basis to share their projects and provide the tools and information to get them done. Many of them have 3D printers these days.

From step 9 onwards, I also show you how to use an online 3D printing service to order your object. I used `http://www.shapeways.com` for this example because they offer a wide range of materials to choose from and deliver to most countries.

Engage Thrusters

Let's print our object:

1. The software that's needed to control the Makerbot Cupcake is called ReplicatorG and can be downloaded from `http://replicat.org`. For this example, I used Version 0037 because the newest version doesn't support my printer. Download ReplicatorG for your platform.
2. Open the file you downloaded in the previous step and start ReplicatorG.
3. To generate the correct control commands, you have to select the type of printer you want to use by going to **Machine** | **Machine Type (Driver)**.
4. Now we can open the STL file that we exported from our sketch in the last task. The mesh gets rendered as a preview and should look like the one in this screenshot:

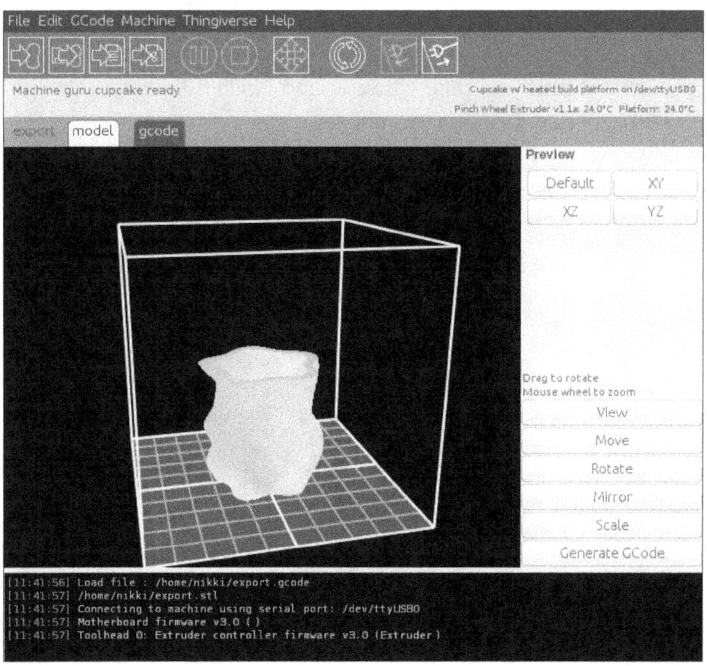

5. Make sure the object you want to print fits the build platform. Move and scale it (if necessary) using the menu on the right-hand side of the preview image.
6. When the size and placement of the object are correct, we need to generate the GCode for your machine. This step slices the object into printable layers and generates the control commands that are interpreted by the printer to position the printing head and control the extrusion. Click on the **Generate GCode** button and select the printing profile you would like to use.
7. When the GCode generation is finished, you can start your build by going to **GCode** | **Build**. The following image shows my vase while it's being printed:

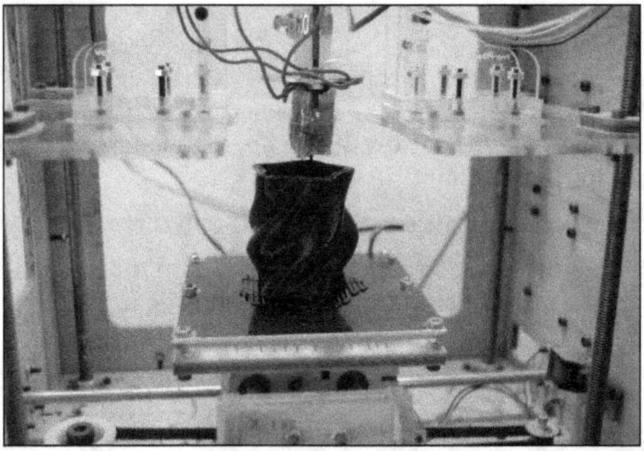

8. When the print is finished, take a flower and place it in what was not too long ago just a few lines of code on your computer.

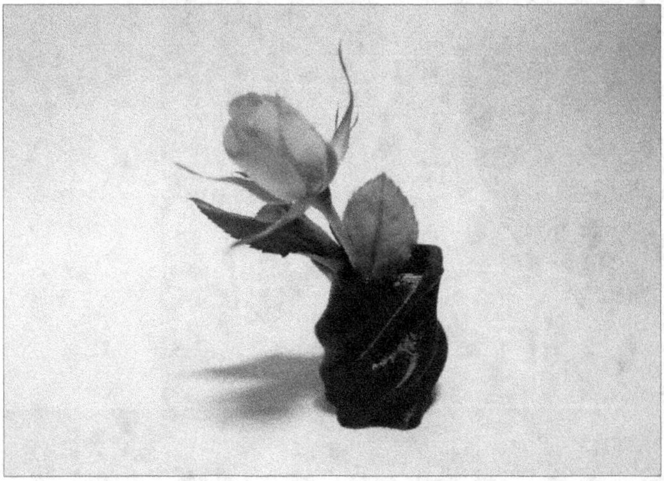

9. If you don't have access to a desktop 3D printer, you can use an online printing service, like the one from `http://www.shapeways.com`.
10. Register for a user account and start the ordering process by clicking on **Create** and then on **New Product**.
11. Then, click on **Select 3D file** and upload the STL file that we exported from our sketch in the third task.
12. Now select the material for your object. Shapeways offers a whole range of materials, from plastic to ceramic or even stainless steel.
13. Once you are satisfied with the material, add it to the cart and order it.
14. This is how the vase (which I created using the sketch) looks when the **White Strong & Flexible** material is used.

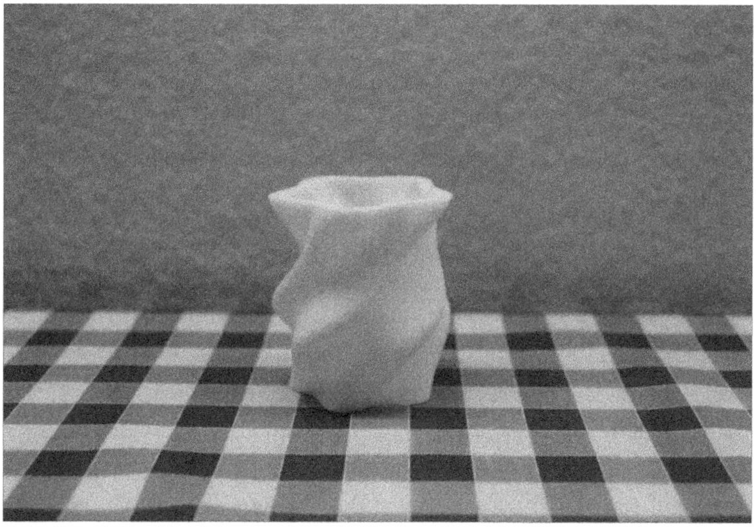

Objective Complete - Mini Debriefing

For the final task of our current mission, we turned our virtual 3D object into a real one. We used ReplicatorG to slice our model and turn it into GCode instructions. These codes are then interpreted by the printer and used to position the printer head and control the extrusion of the plastic filaments.

From step 9 onwards, we learned how to use an online printing service to order the object we created. I chose Shapeways for this example because they use a different kind of 3D printer that supports a very wide range of materials, from plastics to ceramics or even metal. Depending on what you need your object for, this makes online services an interesting option, even when you have access to a desktop 3D printer.

Mission Accomplished

For this mission, we created a virtual 3D object using a mathematical function that generates our vertices in a cylindrical coordinate system and then turns it into a physical object using a desktop 3D printer or an online printing service.

In the first task, we created a closed, circular 2D shape using a function that takes an angle as input and calculates a radius for that angle. We converted this point from the polar to the Cartesian coordinate system and used it as a vertex for our shape. We then added a GUI using the controlP5 framework to enable the users of our sketch to change the parameters of our function.

In the second task, we extruded the shape that we created along the z axis and created a three-dimensional cylindrical form. We changed to the so-called cylindrical coordinate system, which uses an angle, a radius, and a height to define its points. We extended our function to take the height as a second parameter and added four more sliders to our GUI to influence the created shape. We also implemented support for rotating the object using the mouse by adding two callback functions for mouse events. We calculated the rotational axis and angle using quaternions. This is a mathematical construct similar to complex numbers.

In the third task, we added support for exporting our mesh as an STL file. This file format stores 3D meshes and can be used as an input for most 3D printers or 3D modelling tools. We added a `Triangle` class and a `TriangleSoup` class, which handle file creation. To make our object printable, we had to make sure that the object encloses a printable volume, so we added a second inner wall that's slightly smaller and closed the mesh by adding two triangle fans at the bottom and one mesh that connected the outer and the inner wall at the top.

We finished off by using the exported STL file as an input for a desktop 3D printer. The control software uses this file to create the GCode instructions for a 3D printer that positions the printing head and controls the extrusion of the plastic filament. We also used the STL file to order our object from an online 3D printing service.

You Ready to go Gung HO? A Hotshot Challenge

We learned how to create a physical object that started life as a mathematical function and a few lines of code, but of course, this is not limited to creating small vases for your favorite flowers. Why don't you try one of the following ideas:

- Generate 3D printed jewelry.
- Create objects from various parts, which can be combined to form bigger objects.
- Use an additional input source for your function, such as stack exchange rates or even an audio file!
- Use a Kinect to scan an object and create a printable shape from it.

Index

Symbols

A

B

C

D

E

F

G

H

I

J

K

L

M

N

O

P

R

S

T

U

V

X

Thank you for buying
Processing 2: Creative Coding Hotshot

About Packt Publishing

Packt, pronounced 'packed', published its first book "*Mastering phpMyAdmin for Effective MySQL Management*" in April 2004 and subsequently continued to specialize in publishing highly focused books on specific technologies and solutions.

Our books and publications share the experiences of your fellow IT professionals in adapting and customizing today's systems, applications, and frameworks. Our solution based books give you the knowledge and power to customize the software and technologies you're using to get the job done. Packt books are more specific and less general than the IT books you have seen in the past. Our unique business model allows us to bring you more focused information, giving you more of what you need to know, and less of what you don't.

Packt is a modern, yet unique publishing company, which focuses on producing quality, cutting-edge books for communities of developers, administrators, and newbies alike. For more information, please visit our website: `www.packtpub.com`.

About Packt Open Source

In 2010, Packt launched two new brands, Packt Open Source and Packt Enterprise, in order to continue its focus on specialization. This book is part of the Packt Open Source brand, home to books published on software built around Open Source licences, and offering information to anybody from advanced developers to budding web designers. The Open Source brand also runs Packt's Open Source Royalty Scheme, by which Packt gives a royalty to each Open Source project about whose software a book is sold.

Writing for Packt

We welcome all inquiries from people who are interested in authoring. Book proposals should be sent to author@packtpub.com. If your book idea is still at an early stage and you would like to discuss it first before writing a formal book proposal, contact us; one of our commissioning editors will get in touch with you.

We're not just looking for published authors; if you have strong technical skills but no writing experience, our experienced editors can help you develop a writing career, or simply get some additional reward for your expertise.

[PACKT] open source
community experience distilled
PUBLISHING

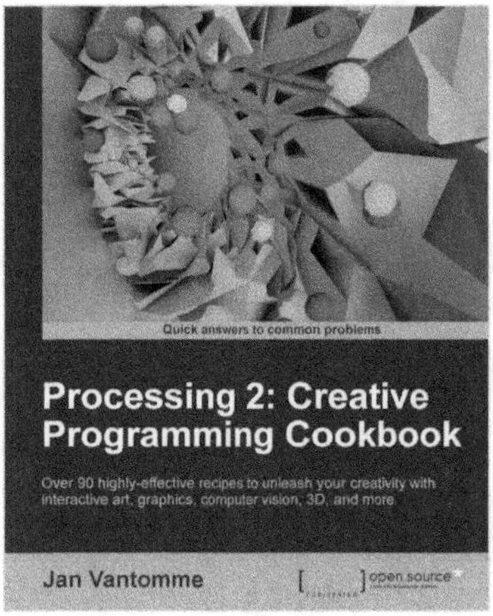

Processing 2: Creative Programming Cookbook

ISBN: 978-1-84951-794-2 Paperback: 306 pages

Over 90 highly-effective recipes to unleash your creativity with interactive art, graphics, computer vision, 3D, and more

1. Explore the Processing language with a broad range of practical recipes for computational art and graphics
2. Wide coverage of topics including interactive art, computer vision, visualization, drawing in 3D, and much more with Processing
3. Create interactive art installations and learn to export your artwork for print, screen, Internet, and mobile devices

---

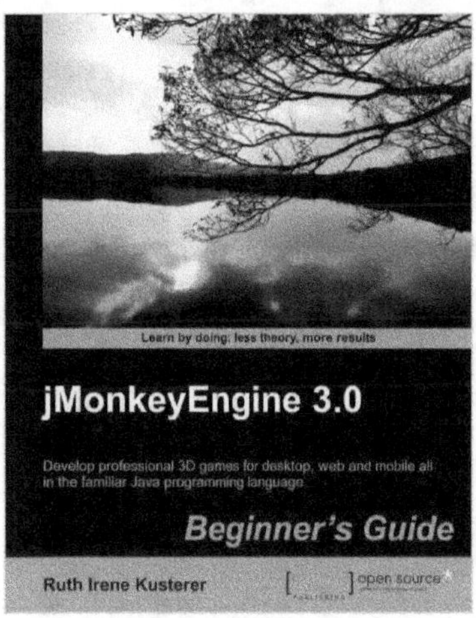

jMonkeyEngine 3.0 Beginner's Guide

ISBN: 978-1-84951-646-4 Paperback: 314 pages

Develop professional 3D games for desktop, web and mobile all in the familiar Java programming language

1. Create 3D games that run on Android devices, Windows, Mac OS, Linux desktop PCs and in web browsers – for commercial, hobbyists, or educational purposes.
2. Follow end-to-end examples that teach essential concepts and processes of game development, from the basic layout of a scene to interactive game characters.
3. Make your artwork come alive and publish your game to multiple platforms, all from one unified development environment.

Please check **www.PacktPub.com** for information on our titles

[PACKT] open source
community experience distilled
PUBLISHING

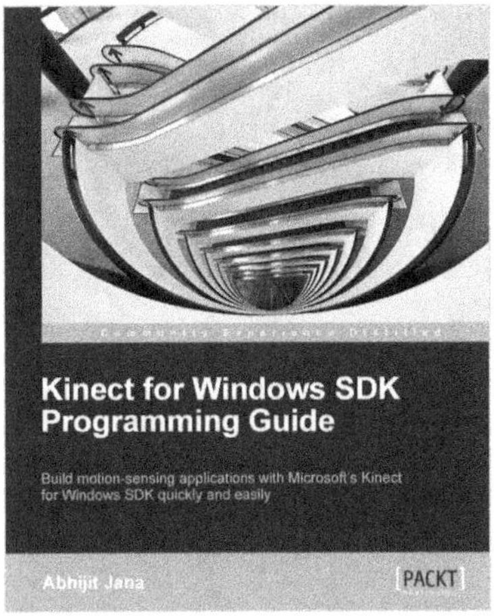

Kinect for Windows SDK Programming Guide

ISBN: 978-1-84969-238-0 Paperback: 392 pages

Build motion-sensing applications with Microsoft's Kinect for Windows SDK quickly and easily

1. Building application using Kinect for Windows SDK.
2. Covers the Kinect for Windows SDK v1.6
3. A practical step-by-step tutorial to make learning easy for a beginner.
4. A detailed discussion of all the APIs involved and the explanations of their usage in detail

---

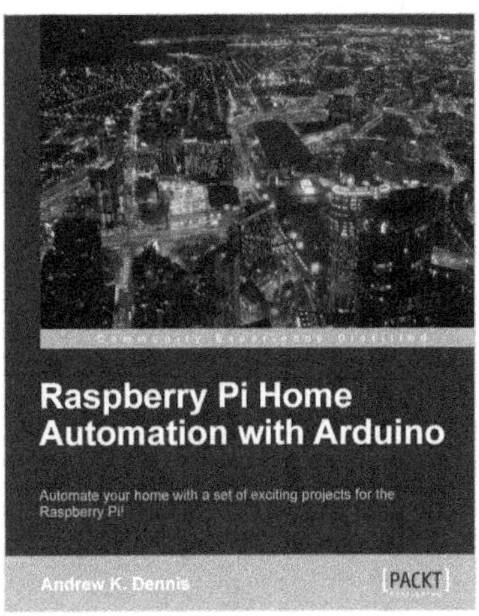

Raspberry Pi Home Automation with Arduino

ISBN: 978-1-84969-586-2 Paperback: 176 pages

Automate your home with a set of exciting projects for the Raspberry Pi!

1. Learn how to dynamically adjust your living environment with detailed step-by-step examples
2. Discover how you can utilize the combined power of the Raspberry Pi and Arduino for your own projects
3. Revolutionize the way you interact with your home on a daily basis

Please check **www.PacktPub.com** for information on our titles

www.ingramcontent.com/pod-product-compliance
Lightning Source LLC
LaVergne TN
LVHW080040210926
848481LV00011B/3247